INTERMEDIATE VOCABULARY WORKBOOK

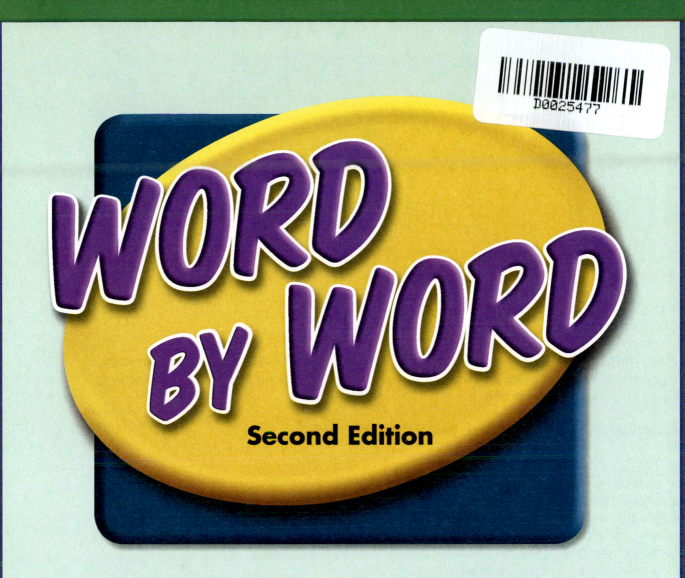

WORD BY WORD

Second Edition

Steven J. Molinsky • Bill Bliss

Contributing Authors
Robert Doherty
Joan Kimball
Elizabeth Kyle

Illustrated by
Richard E. Hill

PEARSON
Longman

Dedicated to Janet Johnston in honor of her wonderful contribution
to the development of our textbooks over three decades.

Steven J. Molinsky
Bill Bliss

Word by Word Intermediate Vocabulary Workbook, second edition

Pearson Education, 10 Bank Street, White Plains, NY 10606

Editorial director: Pam Fishman
Vice president, director of design and production: Rhea Banker
Director of electronic production: Aliza Greenblatt
Director of manufacturing: Patrice Fraccio
Senior manufacturing manager: Edith Pullman
Marketing manager: Oliva Fernandez, Carol Brown, Kyoko Oinama
Production editor: Diane Cipollone
Associate paging manager: Paula Williams
Text design: Wendy Wolf
Cover design: Tracey Munz Cataldo, Warren Fischbach
Realia creation: Warren Fischbach, Paula Williams
Illustrations: Richard E. Hill
Contributing artist: Charles Cawley

ISBN 0-13-189230-4
Longman on the Web
Longman.com offers online resources for teachers and students. Access our Companion Websites, our online
catalog, and our local offices around the world.

Visit us at longman.com.

Printed in the United States of America
1 2 3 4 5 6 7 8 9 10 – QWD – 11 10 09 08 07

CONTENTS

A WHAT'S THE QUESTION?

1. _____What's your name?_____
Susan Ann Wilson.

2. _____
Susan.

3. _____
A.

4. _____
Wilson.

5. _____
1232 Cedar Street, Chicago, Illinois.

6. _____
susanw@sbs.com.

7. _____
023–41–9782.

8. _____
May 23, 1981.

B WHAT INFORMATION DO YOU NEED?

What personal information do you need to . . .

1. send a letter to a friend? _____*name, address*_____

2. call someone in another state? _____

3. visit a classmate at home? _____

4. call someone on his or her birthday? _____

5. introduce two people to each other? _____

6. fill out a registration form? _____

C LISTENING

Listen and choose the correct answer.

1. first name
a. Richard
b. Roger
c. Robert

2. last name
a. Peterson
b. Patterson
c. Addison

3. middle initial
a. V
b. B
c. P

4. telephone number
a. 295–3609
b. 259–3690
c. 259–3960

5. area code
a. 718
b. 781
c. 817

6. cell phone number
a. 767–340–6583
b. 676–340–6583
c. 767–304–5638

7. address
a. 14 Harrison Road in Easton
b. 40 Harrison Road in Weston
c. 14 Harrison Road in Weston

8. zip code
a. 22940
b. 24920
c. 22490

9. e-mail address
a. rvp@worldlike.com
b. rpv@worldlink.com
c. rvp@worldlink.com

1

A   WHO ARE THEY?

Replace the underlined words with a single word.

Here are some pictures from my family reunion.
Here's my <u>father's mother</u>[1]. And here's my <u>mother's brother</u>[2]
and <u>his wife</u>[3]. My father's sister and <u>her children</u>[4]
are in this picture. And with them is my brother,
<u>his wife</u>[5], and <u>their baby daughter</u>[6]. Here are my <u>brother's sons</u>[7].
And in this last picture is my <u>wife's father</u>[8] and <u>his son</u>[9].

1. my _____grandmother_____
2. my _____
3. my _____

4. my _____
5. my _____
6. my _____

7. my _____
8. my _____
9. my _____

B   TRUE OR FALSE?

Look at page 3 of the Picture Dictionary and answer the following questions.

1. Nancy is Frank's sister.   (True)   False
2. Helen is Nancy's mother-in-law.   True   False
3. Timmy is Frank's son-in-law.   True   False

4. Alan is Jack's nephew.   True   False
5. Jack is Linda's cousin.   True   False
6. Linda is Jennifer's aunt. True   False

C   WHAT'S THE RELATIONSHIP?

Look at the family tree below. What are the relationships between the following people?

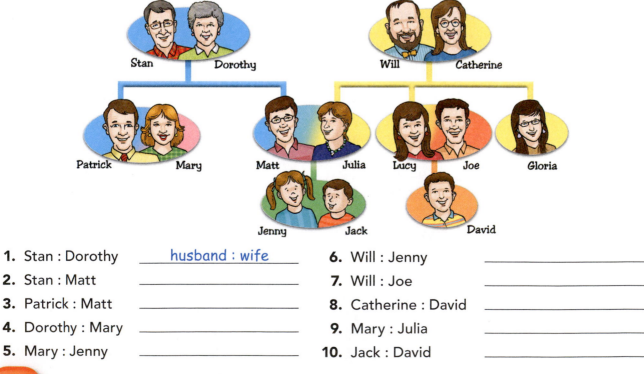

1. Stan : Dorothy   _____husband : wife_____
2. Stan : Matt   _____
3. Patrick : Matt   _____
4. Dorothy : Mary   _____
5. Mary : Jenny   _____

6. Will : Jenny   _____
7. Will : Joe   _____
8. Catherine : David _____
9. Mary : Julia   _____
10. Jack : David   _____

A FINISH THE SENTENCE

___c___ **1.** I have a question. I think I'll ask the _____.

_____ **2.** All right, class. Please open your _____.

_____ **3.** To figure out this problem, you'll definitely need a _____.

_____ **4.** Did you hear that announcement on the _____?

_____ **5.** Put this on the bulletin board with a _____.

_____ **6.** I'll write the answers on the _____.

_____ **7.** Can I write on the whiteboard with this _____?

a. marker
b. chalkboard
c. teacher's aide
d. thumbtack
e. textbooks
f. loudspeaker
g. calculator

B 20 QUESTIONS: *What's the Object?*

1. We use it to write something in ink. _____pen_____
2. It tells the time. _____
3. We use it to write on a whiteboard. _____
4. It's square and flat, and we watch movies on it. _____
5. We find countries, continents, oceans, and seas on it. _____
6. When we use it to write, we get dust on our hands. _____
7. It makes a sharp point on the end of a pencil. _____
8. You look at it when you work at a computer. _____
9. We use it to measure feet and inches. _____
10. It has small squares on it. We use it to make charts. _____
11. Students take notes and write homework assignments in it. _____
12. We practice and do exercises in this kind of book. _____
13. Students and teachers use it when they aren't standing. _____
14. It's rectangular and gray, and it makes words on a board disappear. _____
15. It fits in our hands, and it adds, subtracts, multiplies, and divides. _____
16. Everybody sits at one, but the teacher's is bigger. _____
17. It makes words on paper disappear. _____
18. It's a place for dictionaries and other books when we aren't using them. _____
19. It's sharp, pointed, and very small and can hold things up on the wall. _____
20. You type on this when you use a computer. _____

A OPPOSITES

Find the words in the second column that mean the opposite of the ones in the first column.

_b_	**1.** write	**a.** stand up	
____	**2.** alone	**b.** erase	
____	**3.** turn on	**c.** open	
____	**4.** sit down	**d.** in a group	
____	**5.** collect	**e.** turn off	
____	**6.** close	**f.** ask	
____	**7.** answer	**g.** pass out	

B MATCH THE ACTIONS

Find the words in the second column that mean something similar to the ones in the first column.

_c_ **1.** Work together.   **a.** Print your name.

____ **2.** Go over the answers.   **b.** Circle the answer.

____ **3.** Write your name.   **c.** Work in a group.

____ **4.** Choose the answer.   **d.** Put the letters in order.

____ **5.** Unscramble the word.   **e.** Mark the answer sheet.

____ **6.** Bubble the answer.   **f.** Check your answers.

C WHAT'S THE ACTION?

Fill in the blank with an appropriate action.

1. • Raise your hand.

   • Ask a question.

   • _Listen_ _to_ the answer.

2. • Work together.

   • _____ the question.

   • Share with the class.

3. • _____ _____ a word in the dictionary.

   • Read the definition.

   • Copy the word.

4. • Take out a piece of paper.

   • _____ _____ the screen.

   • Take notes.

5. • _____ _____ the board.

   • Write the answer on the board.

   • Take your seat.

6. • Work with a partner.

   • Check your answers.

   • _____ your mistakes.

D LISTENING

Listen and write the number of the sentence that has the same meaning.

[ ]	Please sit down.	[ ] Please give the assignment to the teacher.
[1]	Please give students the exams.	[ ] Please write on a separate piece of paper.
[ ]	Please check the errors.	[ ] Do your own work.

A OPPOSITES

1. The dictionary isn't ____under____ the desk. It's on it.

2. The clock isn't below the chalkboard. It's _____ it.

3. You can find the globe to the right of the computer, not to the _____ of it.

4. There's a chair behind the desk, not _____ it.

5. Is the pencil next to the book? No, it's _____ the eraser and the ruler.

B WHERE IS IT?

Look at the picture of the classroom on page 4 of the Picture Dictionary and answer the questions.

1. Where's the calculator?

   It's _on_ the desk.

2. Where's the clock?

   It's _____ the board.

3. Is the bulletin board in front of the globe?

   No. It's _____ the globe.

4. Where's the computer keyboard?

   It's _____ the mouse and the monitor.

5. Where are the students?

   They're all _____ their seats.

6. Where's the map?

   It's to the _____ the chalkboard.

7. Is there a projector in the classroom?

   Yes. It's _____ the screen.

8. Where's the bookcase?

   It's _____ the bulletin board.

C WHAT'S WRONG WITH THIS CLASSROOM?

There are 8 things that are strange about this classroom.

____The wastebasket is on the desk.____

_____

_____

_____

_____

_____

_____

A WHICH WORD?

1. It's time to get (dressed (undressed)) and go to bed.
2. I like to put on (makeup   my hair) before going out.
3. Where's the toothpaste? I need to brush my (hair   teeth).
4. Don't forget to (take   make) your bed before you go to school!
5. Jonathan is still in the bathroom. He's (taking a shower   eating lunch).
6. Before she goes to bed every night, Maria likes to (sleep   take a bath).
7. It's 7:00 P.M., and Michael is making (dinner   breakfast) for his children.
8. Timothy has a very short haircut because he doesn't like to (comb   shave) his hair very often.
9. Alice and Ron share the household chores. They each (make   have) dinner three nights a week.
10. Benjamin likes to get to work by 8 A.M. That's why he (goes to bed   gets up) at 6 A.M. every day.

B LISTENING

Listen and choose the best answer.

☐ brush her hair	☐ get up
☐ have lunch	1 go to bed
☐ shave	☐ get undressed
☐ wash his face	☐ put on her makeup

C IT'S TIME TO GET UP!

teeth	breakfast	shave	bed
hair	face	up	shower

It's time to get ____up____ ¹, wash my

_____ ², brush my _____ ³, take

a _____ ⁴, _____ ⁵, comb my

_____ ⁶, make the _____ ⁷, eat

_____ ⁸, and go to work!

A WHAT'S THE ACTIVITY?

cleaning	feed the baby	ironing	take the bus
do the laundry	feed the cat	leave work	walk
drives	go to the store	studying	washes the dishes

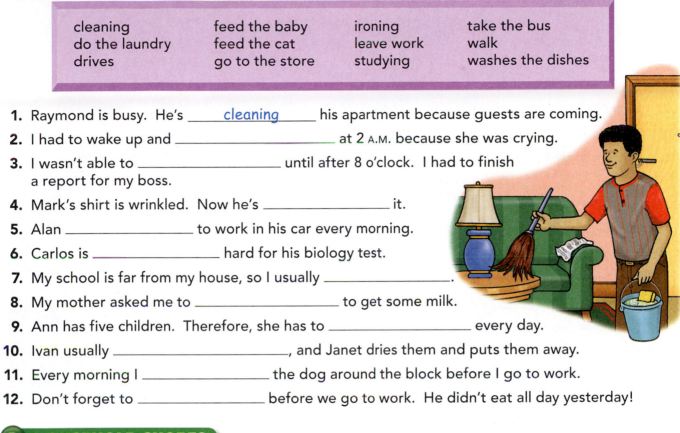

1. Raymond is busy. He's _____cleaning_____ his apartment because guests are coming.

2. I had to wake up and _____ at 2 A.M. because she was crying.

3. I wasn't able to _____ until after 8 o'clock. I had to finish a report for my boss.

4. Mark's shirt is wrinkled. Now he's _____ it.

5. Alan _____ to work in his car every morning.

6. Carlos is _____ hard for his biology test.

7. My school is far from my house, so I usually _____.

8. My mother asked me to _____ to get some milk.

9. Ann has five children. Therefore, she has to _____ every day.

10. Ivan usually _____, and Janet dries them and puts them away.

11. Every morning I _____ the dog around the block before I go to work.

12. Don't forget to _____ before we go to work. He didn't eat all day yesterday!

B HOUSEHOLD CHORES

What chores have you already done this week? What chores haven't you done yet?

I've already ....done the laundry.......... .

I haven't ....ironed.................... yet.

....

....

....

....

....

....

....

....

....

....

C JOURNAL

In your household, who cleans? Who washes the dishes? Who does the laundry? How often? Who does other chores?

....

....

....

....

A KEEPING BUSY

Complete the story with the correct form of each verb.

exercise	plant flowers	read	swim
listen	play cards	relax	write

Lisa tries to keep busy all the time. She likes to stay in shape, so every morning she _____exercises_____ **1** in her apartment for thirty minutes. Then, while she eats breakfast, she _____ **2** to the radio to find out what's going on in the world. At lunch, if she isn't busy, she _____ **3** to her family and friends to let them know how she's doing. After work, she goes to the pool to _____ **4** for a while. When she finally gets home, she _____ **5** on the sofa and _____ **6** a book or a magazine. On the weekend, she often _____ **7** in her garden, and in the evening she _____ **8** with a few friends who like to play games.

B WHAT'S THE ACTIVITY?

1. My father likes to _____relax_____ in his favorite chair after a hard day at work.
2. Danny always stays up late to _____ when his favorite shows are on.
3. Fernando wants to lose weight, so he _____ every morning.
4. Vivian has to _____ for four hours every day because she's a concert pianist.
5. Sheila's grandson is teaching her how to _____ so she can send him e-mails.
6. Jimmy _____ every afternoon. He can jump very high!
7. I'm glad it's springtime because now I can go outside and _____.
8. My uncle doesn't like TV so he _____ the newspaper to find out what's happening in the world.

C JOURNAL

What's your favorite leisure activity? How often do you do it? Why do you enjoy it?

....
....
....
....

A WHAT'S THE RESPONSE?

_e_ **1.** Thanks.

2. See you later.

3. What's new?

4. How are you?

5. This is my sister.

6. Nice to meet you.

7. May I please speak to Tom?

a. Fine, thanks.

b. Nice to meet you, too.

c. Yes. Hold on a moment.

d. See you soon.

e. You're welcome.

f. Not much.

g. Nice to meet you.

B CAN YOU REMEMBER?

Without looking at pages 12 and 13 of the Picture Dictionary, can you remember . . . ?

1. 2 ways to express gratitude

Thank you.

_____

2. 2 ways to say good-bye

_____

_____

3. 2 ways to ask someone to repeat something

_____

_____

4. 2 ways to say hello

_____

_____

5. 2 ways to say you don't understand

_____

_____

6. 2 ways to introduce yourself to someone

_____

_____

A WEATHER TALK

Celsius	drizzling	lightning	smoggy	sunny
cloudy	foggy	muggy	snowstorm	thunderstorm

1. It isn't raining very hard. It's just _____drizzling_____.

2. Water boils at 100 degrees _____.

3. It's a clear _____ day. Let's go to the beach!

4. It looks like it might rain. The sky is gray and _____.

5. It's so hot and uncomfortable on _____ days like this.

6. My children always hold their ears when there's a loud _____.

7. It's hard to breathe on _____ days like today.

8. Look up at the sky! Did you see that flash of _____?

9. It's dangerous to drive on a _____ day like this. I can't see anything!

10. I hear it's going to be freezing tomorrow and we're going to have a big _____.

B GOOD IDEA OR BAD IDEA?

1. It's freezing. I'll turn on the heat.
   a. Yes. Please do.
   b. I don't think that's a good idea.

2. It's a windy day. I think I'll fly my kite.
   a. Great idea!
   b. I don't think you should.

3. It's hailing! Let's go sailing!
   a. Sure. I'd love to.
   b. That's not a very good idea.

4. They're predicting a thunderstorm this afternoon. We should cancel our picnic.
   a. You're right. I guess we should.
   b. Why should we do that?

5. It's 25 degrees Fahrenheit. Do you want to go to the beach today?
   a. What a nice idea!
   b. I don't think that's a very good idea.

6. Do you want to go skiing after the snowstorm tomorrow?
   a. Sure. That sounds like fun!
   b. That doesn't sound like a good idea.

7. It's hailing. Do you want to have a picnic?
   a. That's a wonderful idea!
   b. I don't think that's a good idea.

8. Get the suntan lotion! It's drizzling!
   a. I'll get it right away.
   b. Suntan lotion?! We need an umbrella!

9. It's a clear night. Let's look at the stars.
   a. What a good idea!
   b. We won't be able to see them!

10. It's hazy today. You'll definitely need your raincoat and umbrella.
    a. I agree. I will.
    b. I don't think I'll need them.

11. If this heat wave continues, we can turn off our air conditioning.
    a. Please don't.
    b. I agree.

12. There's going to be a dust storm today. Let's go out and watch it!
    a. What a great idea!
    b. I think we should stay indoors.

A ORDINALS

Change the cardinal numbers in parentheses into ordinal numbers.

1. William, is that your (4) _____fourth_____ piece of cherry pie?
2. Evelyn Wong came in (2) _____ in this year's race for mayor.
3. Olga just finished her (6) _____ marathon.
4. My grandmother is celebrating her (85) _____ birthday today.
5. Mr. and Mrs. Lopez just celebrated their (40) _____ wedding anniversary.
6. My doctor's appointment is on November (1) _____.
7. On the (30) _____ of September, we're going to Canada for a vacation.
8. Timothy! This is the (3) _____ time I've told you to clean up your room!

B WHAT'S THE NUMBER?

1. I live on the tenth floor and Peter lives on the twentieth floor. His apartment is on a (higher   lower) floor.
2. I'm going to graduate from high school soon. I'm in the (twelfth   twentieth) grade.
3. Now that I'm (sixteenth   sixteen) I can learn how to drive.
4. The government spent 40 (billion   billionth) dollars on the new highway.
5. Fourteen is a (higher   lower) number than forty.
6. This is the (ten   tenth) time I've told you to take out the garbage, Howard!

C LISTENING: *Same or Different?*

As you listen, read the sentences below. Write S if the sentences are the same or D if the sentences are different.

__D__ 1. Amanda lives at 759 Central Avenue.
____ 2. Our town has a population of 5500.
____ 3. My zip code is 29209.
____ 4. Bernardo's new computer costs $1,599.
____ 5. Susan's phone number is 365–0751.
____ 6. My social security number is 050–23–1029.

D ROMAN NUMERALS

I = 1	IV = 4	VII = 7	X = 10	XXX = 30	C = 100
II = 2	V = 5	VIII = 8	XV = 15	XL = 40	D = 500
III = 3	VI = 6	IX = 9	XX = 20	L = 50	M = 1000

1. VIII _____8_____
2. XIV _____
3. XXV _____
4. XLIII _____
5. LIV _____
6. CLXXV _____
7. MX _____
8. LXVI _____
9. XIX _____
10. LXXVII _____
11. XLVIII _____
12. CI _____

A   WHAT TIME IS IT?

Write the time under each of the following clocks. If there is more than one way to tell the time, give both ways.

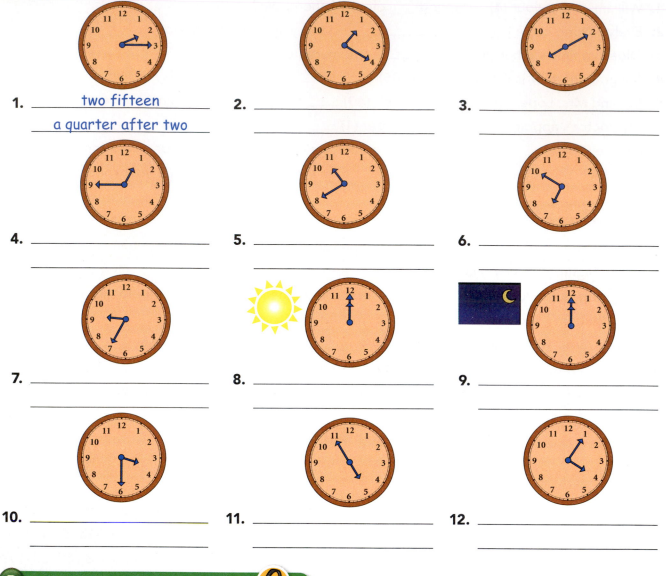

1. ___two fifteen___
   ___a quarter after two___

2. _____

3. _____

4. _____

5. _____

6. _____

7. _____

8. _____

9. _____

10. _____

11. _____

12. _____

B   LISTENING: *True or False?*

Listen and decide whether the following statements are True (T) or False (F).

__T__ **1.** Anthony's plane will arrive in London at 5:20 A.M.

_____ **2.** I usually have lunch at noon.

_____ **3.** My mother had to wait until 5:45 to see her doctor.

_____ **4.** My daughter finally went to bed at 10:50.

_____ **5.** William's bus will arrive from Seattle at 2:38 P.M.

_____ **6.** I have an appointment to see my professor at 3:10.

_____ **7.** Roger works at the convenience store from 10:00 A.M. until 11:30 P.M.

A LISTENING 🎧

Listen and write the amount of money you hear.

1. $29.50
2. _____
3. _____
4. _____
5. _____
6. _____
7. _____
8. _____
9. _____

B HOW MUCH DO THEY COST?

Match the following items with the appropriate prices.

_c_ 1. a slice of pizza   **a.** $15,000

____ 2. a computer   **b.** $1,500

____ 3. a new car   **c.** $1.50

____ 4. a can of soda   **d.** $100.00

____ 5. a cell phone   **e.** $30.00

____ 6. a pair of gloves   **f.** 75¢

C ANOTHER WAY OF SAYING IT

Replace the underlined amounts of money with other ways of saying them.

1. This only costs a dime.   _____ten cents_____

2. I lost a nickel.   _____

3. "Find a penny, pick it up. All day long you'll have good luck."   _____

What do you think these mean?

4. Can you lend me a buck?   _____

5. If I had a few grand, I'd buy a used car.   _____

D GETTING CHANGE

What change will you receive if you give a cashier . . .

1. a twenty-dollar bill for $16.75 in groceries?   _____$3.25_____

2. a dollar bill for a 75¢ piece of candy?   _____

3. a dollar and a quarter for a $1.20 magazine?   _____

4. fifty dollars for a $40 dinner?   _____

5. two dollars for a $1.35 bottle of water?   _____

6. a twenty-dollar bill and a ten-dollar bill for $22.50 of gas?   _____

A U.S. CALENDAR QUIZ

What do you know about the following U.S. dates?

1. Sweethearts celebrate Valentine's Day with cards, candy, and flowers in _____February_____.

2. Many people make resolutions and promises of what they will do differently on the first day of _____, or New Year's Day.

3. On the _____ of _____, Americans celebrate their independence with fireworks and parades.

4. For most people, _____ is the first day of the work week.

5. "_____ showers bring _____ flowers" is a famous saying.

6. In _____, Americans celebrate Thanksgiving with a festive holiday meal.

7. Americans honor workers on Labor Day and autumn officially begins in _____.

8. On the first day of _____, people often play tricks and jokes on each other.

9. Summer begins in _____, and many people celebrate Father's Day in this month.

10. People say that if _____ comes in like a lion, it goes out like a lamb. But if it comes in like a lamb, the opposite is true.

B IN MY COUNTRY . . .

1. .... is usually the hottest month of the year and .... is usually the coldest.

2. It typically rains the most in ....

3. We celebrate our independence on the .... of ....

4. The school year begins in .... and ends in ....

5. We honor and celebrate mothers on a day in ...., fathers on a day in ...., and children on a day in ....

6. The work week for most people ends on ....

7. We remember and honor the dead on the .... of ....

8. Most people take vacations in .... because ....

9. On the weekend, people usually ....

C IMPORTANT DATES IN MY LIFE

What are some important dates in your life—such as your birthday, your anniversary, the date you moved to a new city or country, or the date you started a new job?

Important Dates	The Occasion
....	....
....	....
....	....
....	....

A COMPLETE JULIE'S SCHEDULE

Read the story about Julie. Fill in her schedule with the correct activities.

dancing lesson	guitar lesson	singing lesson	concert	doctor	play
exercise class	piano lesson	Spanish class	dentist	party	

Sun 4	Mon 5	Tue 6	Wed 7	Thu 8	Fri 9	Sat 10
	piano lesson	singing lesson				

Sun 11	Mon 12	Tue 13	Wed 14	Thu 15	Fri 16	Sat 17
					dancing lesson	

Julie is on vacation for the next two weeks, and she's going to be very busy. Today is Sunday the 4th. She has a singing lesson this Tuesday afternoon and a dancing lesson next Friday morning. She has a piano lesson tomorrow evening and a guitar lesson next Wednesday afternoon. Her exercise class starts this Thursday evening, and her first Spanish class is next Monday afternoon. She has a doctor's appointment this Wednesday morning and a dentist appointment next Tuesday afternoon. She's really looking forward to the next two weekends. She's going to see a play this Saturday afternoon, and she's going to a concert next Friday evening. And next Saturday evening her parents are having a party to celebrate their thirtieth wedding anniversary.

B LISTENING: *True or False?*

Listen and decide whether the following statements are True (T) or False (F).

__T__ **1.** Bob called his brother before he called his sister.

_____ **2.** Marie hasn't seen the play yet.

_____ **3.** Thomas swims more often than he jogs.

_____ **4.** The Baxters haven't driven to the beach yet.

_____ **5.** Mabel has already seen her doctor.

_____ **6.** Michael hasn't taken French yet.

_____ **7.** The Garcias went to Canada before they went to Alaska.

_____ **8.** Kevin has already bathed his dog.

A WHAT'S THE WORD?

condominium	house	nursing home	the city
dormitory	houseboat	ranch	the country
farm	mobile home	shelter	town

1. Our _____ town _____ is small, but it has everything people need—a bank, a post office, a library, and some shops.

2. Most people who live in the suburbs live in a _____.

3. Max wanted to own his own apartment, so he decided to look for a _____.

4. Anna lives in a building for students of her university. She lives in a _____.

5. Our friends enjoy the water very much. That's why their new _____ is perfect for them.

6. When our house was damaged in the earthquake, our family had to go to a _____ for a while.

7. When Mr. and Mrs. Yamamoto retired, they sold their house, and now they travel around the country in their _____.

8. Abigail lives on a _____. She gets up every morning at 5:00 A.M. to milk the cows.

9. Mrs. Park is eighty years old and is too weak to take care of herself. Her doctor thinks she should live in a _____.

10. Our son wants to leave the farm and go to _____ to find a job. He also wants to have more excitement in his daily life.

11. We've been living on this _____ for many years. We raise horses and cattle.

12. Jason and his wife love living in _____. It's quiet, peaceful, and they never have to worry about traffic or parking.

B LISTENING: *What Are They Talking About?*

Listen and decide what kind of housing these people are talking about.

1. a. an apartment building
   b. a ranch

2. a. a duplex
   b. a dormitory

3. a. the city
   b. the country

4. a. the suburbs
   b. a ranch

5. a. a mobile home
   b. a nursing home

6. a. a dormitiory
   b. a mobile home

A CAN YOU FIND . . . ?

Look at the picture on page 21 of the Picture Dictionary and see if you can find . . .

7 Things to Put Other Things On or In

bookcase
_____
_____
_____
_____
_____
_____

5 Things that Are Decorative

_____
_____
_____
_____
_____

7 Things that Use Electricity

_____
_____
_____
_____
_____
_____
_____

3 Things We Sit On

_____
_____
_____

5 Things that Are Part of the Structure of the House

_____
_____
_____
_____
_____

2 Things that Lower Light

_____
_____

B WHICH WORD?

1. How do you like my new floor (chair   (lamp))?
2. We need something to hang over the (rug   mantel).
3. We recently bought a new wall (unit   table).
4. Do you think the (lamp   stereo) is on too loud?
5. We enjoy making fires in our (fireplace   fireplace screen).
6. That throw pillow looks very nice on your (drapes   loveseat).
7. The sun is in my eyes. Would you mind closing the (ceiling   drapes)?
8. That's a beautiful (photograph   painting) on the wall. Who's the artist?
9. Veronica just got a new CD to play on her (stereo system   television).
10. Let's get a new (wall unit   DVD player) so we can watch movies at home.
11. My mother took that (photograph   painting) of me when I was young.
12. That's a very unusual picture on the (ceiling   wall). Where did you get it?
13. Would you please turn on the (lamp   lampshade)? It's dark in this room.
14. I think we should buy (a coffee table   an end table) to put next to our couch.
15. Do you think this (fireplace   bookcase) is big enough to hold all these textbooks?

17

A CAN YOU FIND . . . ?

Look at the picture on page 22 of the Picture Dictionary and see if you can find . . .

5 Things that Hold Hot Beverages and Foods

china
_____
_____
_____
_____

6 Things that Hold Cold Beverages and Foods

_____
_____
_____
_____
_____

5 Things Used to Decorate a Table

_____
_____
_____
_____
_____

2 Things that Hold Food Seasonings

_____
_____

3 Pieces of Furniture

_____
_____
_____

2 Things that Give Light

_____
_____

B WHICH WORD?

1. Oops! I'm sorry. I just spilled some tomato sauce on your clean white (chandelier (tablecloth))!
2. We need to put the turkey on a (bowl   platter).
3. We keep our dishes in the china (cabinet   tray).
4. Let's put some fresh flowers in the (chandelier   vase).
5. Mom, could you please pass the butter (dish   bowl)?
6. This (tray   serving dish) is perfect for serving tea.
7. You can use this (spoon   knife) to cut your meat.
8. This is a very comfortable dining room (chair   table).
9. When you set a table, the fork goes on the (napkin   plate).
10. Please light the (candles   candlesticks). We're ready to eat.
11. We're serving tea now. Would you like a cup and (mug   saucer)?
12. When I have guests, I like to serve lemonade in my crystal (platter   pitcher).
13. This coffee smells wonderful! Where's the creamer and (sugar   coffee) bowl?
14. There are still some potatoes in the serving (dish   tray). Would you like some?
15. When Mr. and Mrs. Cardoza have people over for dinner, they put the food on the (buffet   china cabinet) so people can serve themselves.

A WHAT IS IT?

1. This tells you the time and wakes you up.   ___alarm clock___
2. You can keep your clock and lamp next to your bed on this.   _____
3. This is the first thing that goes on an unmade bed.   _____
4. This keeps you warm in the winter and has a cord.   _____
5. This holds earrings, bracelets, and rings.   _____
6. You rest your head on this.   _____
7. You use this to look at yourself.   _____
8. You turn this on when you want to read at night.   _____
9. You open these in the morning to let the sunshine in.   _____
10. The box spring and mattress are kept in place by this.   _____

B LISTENING: *Frannie's Furniture Store*

Listen to the following advertisement and write the prices you hear.

C WHAT'S THE WORD?

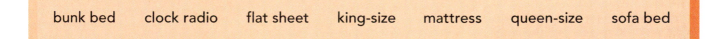

bunk bed   clock radio   flat sheet   king-size   mattress   queen-size   sofa bed

1. Uh-oh! I forgot to plug in the ___clock radio___.
2. Our bed has a very comfortable box spring and _____.
3. The _____ goes on top of the fitted sheet.
4. I'm looking for something larger than a _____ bed. Do you have a _____ bed?
5. Our kids enjoy having a _____. Bobby sleeps on the top, and Billy sleeps on the bottom.
6. This _____ is very convenient. We sit on it during the day and sleep on it at night.

19

A CAN YOU FIND . . . ?

Look at the picture on page 24 of the Picture Dictionary and see if you can find . . .

5 Things to Cook Food With

_____microwave (oven)_____

_____

_____

_____

_____

5 Things You Use When You Wash Dishes

_____dish rack/dish drainer_____

_____

_____

_____

_____

12 Appliances

_____(electric) can opener_____

_____

_____

_____

_____

_____

_____

_____

_____

_____

_____

_____

B ANALOGIES

1. coffee : coffeemaker *as* boiling water : _____tea kettle_____
2. garbage : garbage disposal *as* paper towel : _____
3. potholder : stove *as* dish towel : _____
4. cook : stove *as* cut : _____
5. slow baking : oven *as* rapid baking : _____
6. toaster : toaster oven *as* blender : _____
7. dishes : cabinet *as* spices : _____
8. dishwashing liquid : sink *as* dishwasher detergent : _____

C WHAT THE OBJECT?

_____e_____ **1.** toaster   **a.** detergent

_____ **2.** dishwashing   **b.** pail

_____ **3.** cutting   **c.** liquid

_____ **4.** garbage   **d.** holder

_____ **5.** can   **e.** oven

_____ **6.** paper towel   **f.** opener

_____ **7.** dishwasher   **g.** board

Listen and choose the best answer.

1. a. oven
   b. freezer

2. a. dish rack
   b. trash compactor

3. a. can opener
   b. potholder

4. a. cookbook
   b. refrigerator

5. a. an electric can opener
   b. a cutting board

6. a. faucet
   b. burner

7. a. cabinet
   b. kitchen table

8. a. toaster
   b. freezer

9. a. dish racks
   b. dishwashing liquid

E **WHICH WORD DOESN'T BELONG?**

1. toaster   freezer   burner   oven
2. faucet   dishwasher   oven   sink
3. coffeemaker   blender   electric can opener   tea kettle
4. spice rack   canister   garbage pail   kitchen table
5. dishwasher   placemat   dish rack   dishwasher detergent
6. electric mixer   toaster   food processor   blender

F **WHAT'S WRONG WITH THIS KITCHEN?**

Find 12 things wrong with this kitchen.

The microwave is sideways.

_____   _____
_____   _____
_____   _____
_____   _____
_____   _____
_____   _____

A   BABYTOWN

Carol and Dan are looking for the following items at Babytown, a store that sells everything families need for a new baby. In which department will they find the following items?

baby backpack	cradle	night light
baby carriage	crib	potty
booster seat	diaper pail	rattle
car seat	doll	stuffed animal
changing table	food warmer	teddy bear
chest of drawers	intercom	walker

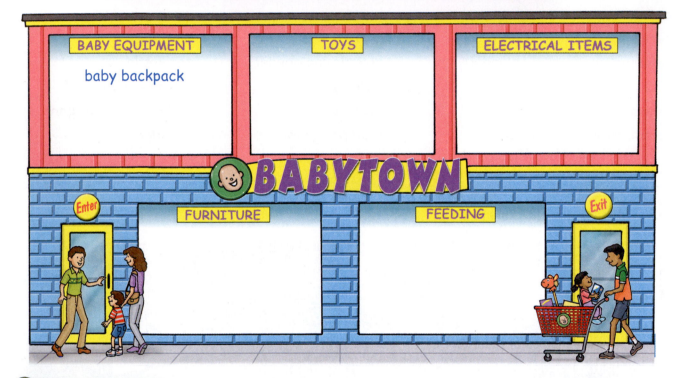

BABY EQUIPMENT

baby backpack

TOYS

ELECTRICAL ITEMS

BABYTOWN

Enter

FURNITURE

FEEDING

Exit

B   WHICH WORD?

1. We hung a (potty   **mobile**) over our baby's crib.
2. I keep all my baby's clothes in this (chest   playpen).
3. We keep our baby's toys in the (diaper pail   toy chest).
4. Hi, honey! Let's go for a walk in your (mobile   stroller)!
5. Our baby sits in a (baby frontpack   high chair) while she eats.
6. My baby just loves to play with this (stuffed animal   bumper pad).
7. When our baby goes to sleep, we always turn on the (night light   crib).
8. Today I think I'll dress the baby in this cute new (toy chest   stretch suit).
9. Whenever we take our baby for a ride, we put her in a (portable crib   safety seat).
10. You can hear everything in the baby's room with our new baby (monitor   carriage).

A LIKELY OR UNLIKELY?

Put a check in the best column.

	Likely	Unlikely
1. When Mark has guests, he always puts fresh towels in the hamper.	_____	✓
2. The plumber tried using a plunger to fix the toilet.	_____	_____
3. Ed slipped and fell because there wasn't a bath mat in the bathroom.	_____	_____
4. Vicky usually keeps a bar of soap in the soap dispenser.	_____	_____
5. The plumber told us we needed a new drain for our shower.	_____	_____
6. My washcloth is larger than my bath towel.	_____	_____
7. Joan turned on the air freshener because the bathroom was hot.	_____	_____
8. I weigh myself every day on my scale.	_____	_____
9. George cleans the toilet with toilet paper.	_____	_____
10. Gwen dries her hair with a fan.	_____	_____
11. My doctor says it's important to take this medicine cabinet every day.	_____	_____

B COMPLETE THE SENTENCES

1. I clean my teeth every day with an electric ___toothbrush___ .
2. There's liquid soap to wash your hands in the soap _____.
3. I protect my bathroom from getting wet with a shower _____.
4. After I wash my hands, I dry them with a hand _____.
5. I keep my toothpaste and medicines in the medicine _____.
6. You should hang your towel on the towel _____.
7. I keep my toothbrush in a toothbrush _____.

C WHAT'S THE ACTION?

Decide which actions are associated with the following objects. There may be more than one possible answer.

a. air freshener	e. mirror	i. toothpaste
b. cup	f. scale	j. towel
c. drain	g. sponge	k. tub
d. faucet	h. toilet	l. washcloth

__f__ 1. weigh	_____ 6. brush	_____ 11. spray
_____ 2. look at	_____ 7. clog	_____ 12. fold
_____ 3. leak	_____ 8. flush	_____ 13. turn off
_____ 4. drink	_____ 9. wash	_____ 14. squeeze
_____ 5. sit	_____ 10. turn on	_____ 15. bathe

23

A WHAT'S THE OBJECT?

1. A. What's a _____doorbell_____ used for?
   B. It lets you know that someone is at the door.

2. A. What does a _____ do?
   B. It lights up the front walk of your house.

3. A. What's a _____ used for?
   B. It's used to cook food outside the home.

4. A. What's a _____ used for?
   B. It keeps the grass from getting too high.

5. A. Why is a _____ useful to have?
   B. It's a good place to store garden equipment.

6. A. What's a _____ used for?
   B. It's a place to keep your car.

7. A. What's a _____ for?
   B. It carries rain water to the drainpipe.

8. A. What's the purpose of a _____?
   B. It carries smoke from the fireplace outside.

9. A. Why do many houses have _____s?
   B. They're used as a window decoration.

10. A. Why do people have a _____ on their roof?
    B. To watch TV channels from all over the world.

11. A. Why do houses in northern climates have a _____?
    B. It helps keep the cold air out.

12. A. Why do people like having _____s or _____s in their backyards?
    B. They're great places to relax outside and enjoy the fresh air.

B HOME REPAIRS

To get ready for summer, I have a lot of work to do on my house. First, I have to fix the _____screen_____ [1] door so flies don't come in the house. Then I have to repair the _____ [2] door because it hasn't been able to open properly for my car. I'd love to be able to put a fresh coat of paint on the front _____ [3] to match the front steps. I also have to repair the front _____ [4] so people can see better at night. The last thing I need to do is clean the _____ [5] so I can start cooking hamburgers and hot dogs outside. I'll certainly be busy over the next few weeks!

1. Last night's storm knocked the TV antenna off the ((roof)   doorknob).
2. It's such a warm evening. Let's have a barbecue on the (deck   driveway).
3. During the winter months we keep the (front walk   storm door) closed.
4. You'd better close the (garage   screen). Bugs are coming in the window!
5. Rain water goes into the gutter, down the (drainpipe   patio), and onto the ground.
6. My daughter lost her house key, so I left the (side door   window) unlocked for her today.

Listen and decide what's being talked about.

1. (a.) chimney
   b. patio

2. a. back door
   b. front walk

3. a. front door
   b. front light

4. a. front porch
   b. tool shed

5. a. lamppost
   b. roof

6. a. screens
   b. shutters

List 12 things that are very strange about this house.

_____The satellite dish is on the porch._____ _____
_____ _____
_____ _____
_____ _____
_____ _____
_____ _____

A OUR NEW PLACE

Complete the following conversation using words from pages 28 and 29 of the Picture Dictionary.

A. I'm exhausted! My wife and I just finished moving into our new apartment yesterday!

B. Really? What kind of place is it?

A. It's a two-bedroom apartment on the _____third_____ 1 floor of a big apartment building. It's really nice, but our _____ 2 above us on the fourth floor are noisy sometimes.

B. That's too bad. Was the move difficult?

A. It was terrible! First, we couldn't get a _____ 3 to carry our things until the last day. Then, the _____ 4 couldn't meet us to give us our _____ 5 so we couldn't open the door until the evening. And finally, the _____ 6 was broken, so we had to carry everything up the _____ 7!

B. That sounds awful. How did you find the apartment in the first place?

A. That wasn't easy either. We looked through the _____ 8 in the newspaper, and we even drove around the neighborhood looking for _____ 9 on buildings. When we finally found a place, the _____ 10 wouldn't sign the _____ 11 until we paid a three-month _____ 12. He said it was the policy for all new _____ 13.

B. That's unbelievable! Well, tell me about the apartment itself.

A. The place itself is great. First of all, there's an Olympic-size _____ 14 and heated _____ 15 to swim and relax in. Also, I don't need to worry about parking because there's a _____ 16 behind the building. Each tenant has his or her own _____ 17.

B. That's good to hear. Is there a _____ 18 to watch the entrance?

A. Yes, there is. The building is very secure. If people come to visit, they have to ring the _____ 19 and I talk to them through the _____ 20. There's also a _____ 21 alarm and an _____ 22 in case of fire. And the _____ 23 just installed new _____ 24 on the ceilings in all the rooms.

B. That's a relief. Is there a storage room in the building?

A. Yes. Each tenant has a _____ 25 for storing extra things, and there's also a _____ 26 room so we can wash our clothes whenever we need.

B. That's wonderful. You'll have to invite me over sometime!

A. Sure! We can have dinner out on the _____ 27 if the weather is nice!

A WHO SHOULD THEY CALL?

Judy and Don Jackson bought a very old house that needs a lot of work. Tell them who to call when . . .

1. their stove doesn't work.   appliance repairperson
2. black smoke comes out of the fireplace when it's being used. _____
3. their house is infested with mice.   _____
4. the steps to their porch need to be repaired.   _____
5. their house paint is chipped and peeling.   _____
6. their power is out.   _____
7. their front door key doesn't work.   _____
8. their house isn't warm enough during cold weather. _____
9. their kitchen sink gets clogged.   _____
10. their roof leaks during a rainstorm.   _____
11. their cable TV isn't working.   _____
12. the tiles in their bathroom are loose.   _____

B LISTENING: *Who to Call?*

Listen and write the number under the appropriate home repairperson to call.

A WHAT DOES HE NEED?

Miguel is cleaning his apartment. Decide what he needs in order to do his chores.
(There may be more than one possible answer.) What does he need . . . ?

a. ammonia	e. dust cloth	i. paper towels	m. vacuum cleaner
b. broom	f. dust mop	j. scrub brush	n. whisk broom
c. bucket	g. dustpan	k. sponge	o. window cleaner
d. cleanser	h. hand vacuum	l. sponge mop	

__e__ **1.** to dust his furniture

_____ **2.** to sweep his floors

_____ **3.** to clean his wall-to-wall carpet

_____ **4.** to mop his kitchen floor

_____ **5.** to clean his bathroom

_____ **6.** to clean his windows and mirrors

B WHICH WORD?

1. Ned, can you please sweep the kitchen floor? Here's a ((broom)   dust mop).

2. Don't forget to put the empty bottles into the (recycling   garbage) bin.

3. Your floor looks beautiful! Did you just (vacuum   wax) it?

4. Try not to smell the fumes from the (ammonia   hand vacuum).

5. I got a new bucket and (dust   sponge) mop. It's time to mop the floors.

6. Here. Use this (scrub brush   sponge mop) to clean the inside of the toilet.

7. After you finish cleaning the windows, could you (take out   clean) the trash?

8. Those windows will never get clean unless you use some window (cleaner   cleanser).

9. This vacuum isn't picking up any dust. We need to change the vacuum (cloth   bag).

C LISTENING

Listen and choose the appropriate cleaning item to complete the conversation.

1. a. dust mop
   (b.) broom

2. a. ammonia
   b. cleanser

3. a. recycling bin
   b. trash can

4. a. buckets
   b. cleanser

5. a. sponges
   b. dust cloths

6. a. floor wax
   b. ammonia

A ASSOCIATIONS

_i_	**1.** step ladder	**a.**	holding things together
____	**2.** spray gun	**b.**	making wood smooth
____	**3.** work gloves	**c.**	painting
____	**4.** duct tape	**d.**	insects
____	**5.** extension cord	**e.**	hands
____	**6.** yardstick	**f.**	the toilet
____	**7.** plunger	**g.**	measuring
____	**8.** mousetrap	**h.**	plug
____	**9.** sandpaper	**i.**	reaching high places
____	**10.** fly swatter	**j.**	seeing in the dark
____	**11.** flashlight	**k.**	mice

B WHICH WORD?

1. This lamp doesn't reach the plug. We need (a lightbulb   (an extension cord)).
2. Oh, no! The electricity went out! Do we have any extra (fuses   oil)?
3. Put (masking tape   paint thinner) on the windows before you paint them.
4. You need to use (paint   sandpaper) on this bookcase before you paint it.
5. Can you help me finish painting the walls? Here's a paint (roller   thinner).
6. This (paint pan   paintbrush) is too big to do the trim around the door frame.
7. That squeaky old door just needs some (fuses   oil) and it'll be like new again.
8. It's a good idea to wear (masking tape   work gloves) when you do home repairs.
9. We need (a tape measure   electrical tape) to see if the sofa will fit through the door.
10. When there are a lot of bugs around, it's necessary to have a good (step ladder   fly swatter).

C WHAT'S THE OBJECT?

1. You catch rodents with this. _____mousetrap_____
2. A portable radio won't work without these. _____
3. You might wrap this around a broken wire. _____
4. This is useful if the electricity goes out. _____
5. This helps unclog a toilet. _____
6. This helps you reach high places. _____
7. This holds pieces of wood together. _____
8. You kill flies with this. _____
9. You use this to find the length of something. _____ or _____

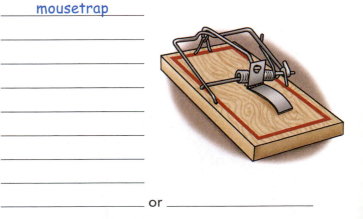

A   CAN YOU FIND . . . ?

Look at the picture on page 34 of the Picture Dictionary and see if you can find . . .

3 Tools for Making Holes

(drill) bit
_____
_____

3 Tools for Cutting

_____
_____
_____

12 Tools and Supplies for Fastening and Unfastening

_____   _____
_____   _____
_____   _____
_____   _____
_____   _____
_____   _____

B   WHICH WORD?

1. I use (a mallet   (an ax)) whenever I chop wood.
2. Be careful with that (saw   nut)! You might cut yourself.
3. Hand me the (level   hammer). I need to bang in this nail.
4. You can tighten that (plane   bolt) with this (chisel   wrench).
5. The best way to fasten that is to use a (pipe wrench   router).
6. Here. You can get the paint off with this (scraper   wire stripper).
7. Would you please cut this metal rod with your (hacksaw   handsaw)?
8. The best way to make this piece of wood smooth is to use a (router   plane).
9. This wood is too rough to smooth by hand. Do you have a power (saw   sander)?
10. The only way to clamp these two pieces of wood together is by using a (washer   vise).

C   LISTENING: _Which Tool Do You Hear?_

Listen to the sounds. Write the number next to the tool you hear.

☐ electric drill	☐ saw
☐ sandpaper	☐ hammer
☐ scraper	1 power saw

A WHICH WORD?

1. We should use a ((rake)   weeder) to gather up all these leaves.
2. This flower bed is so dry! I need the (watering can   vegetable seeds).
3. On a hot summer day, my children like to run through the (trowel   sprinkler).
4. It must have snowed a foot last night. We'd better get the (wheelbarrow   shovel).
5. The bushes are starting to block the window. I'll cut them with our new (hoe   hedge clippers).
6. We love our new (garden hose   leaf blower). It's long enough to reach every part of the lawn.

B WHAT'S THE OBJECT?

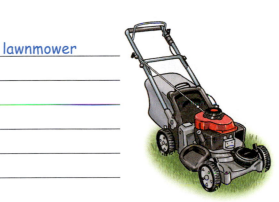

1. This keeps the grass low. _____lawnmower_____
2. The sprinkler is attached to this. _____
3. You can fill this up with leaves and take it away. _____
4. It's usually at one end of a hose. _____
5. You use this to dig a hole. _____
6. This makes things that grow become healthier. _____

C PROBABLE OR IMPROBABLE?

Put a check in the best column.

	Probable	Improbable
1. I mowed the lawn with a rake.	_____	✓
2. I used a trowel to plant some flowers.	_____	_____
3. I cleaned up the leaves with the leaf blower.	_____	_____
4. I cut my hedges with a line trimmer.	_____	_____
5. After I raked, I put the leaves in a gas can.	_____	_____
6. I watered the flowers with a hoe.	_____	_____
7. I used pruning shears to trim my front bushes.	_____	_____
8. I filled the wheelbarrow with dirt.	_____	_____
9. I put a nozzle on the end of the weeder.	_____	_____
10. I mowed the flowers and pruned the lawn.	_____	_____

D LISTENING: *What Are They Talking About?*

Listen and write the number next to the correct gardening word.

____ leaf blower		____ garden hose	
____ yard waste bag		____ lawnmower	
1 hedge trimmer		____ fertilizer	

A WHERE CAN I GET . . . ?

Answer the questions using the places on pages 36 and 37 of the Picture Dictionary.

Where can I get . . .

1. a new dress?   clothing store/department store/discount store

2. a quart of orange juice?   _____

3. some cough medicine?   _____

4. a shave and haircut?   _____

5. the oil in my car changed? _____

6. a pound of roast beef?   _____

7. a birthday cake?   _____

8. a dozen roses?   _____

9. a new car?   _____

10. the latest bestselling novel? _____

11. a blood test or physical exam? _____

12. prescription sunglasses?   _____

13. a suit cleaned and pressed? _____

14. a laptop?   _____

15. a cup of coffee?   _____

16. traveler's checks?   _____

B WHICH WORD DOESN'T BELONG?

1. candy shop   coffee shop   (barber shop)   convenience store
2. card store   donut shop   book store   copy center
3. car dealership   service station   florist   gas station
4. drug store   pharmacy   clinic   delicatessen
5. computer   drug   department   service
6. barber   donut   electronics   coffee
7. convenience store coffee shop   child-care center   fast-food restaurant

C ANALOGIES

1. books : book store *as* fresh rolls : _____ bakery _____

2. florist : flower shop *as* optician : _____

3. cole slaw : deli *as* donuts : _____

4. computers : computer store *as* TVs : _____

5. pharmacist : drug store *as* doctor : _____

6. clothing : dry cleaners *as* children : _____

A WHERE CAN I GET . . . ?

Answer the questions using the places on pages 38 and 39 of the Picture Dictionary.

Where can I get . . .

1. my hair cut and styled? _____hair salon_____
2. airplane tickets? _____
3. a manicure and pedicure? _____
4. a pair of sneakers? _____
5. a box of cereal? _____
6. a hammer and nails? _____
7. a kitten? _____
8. a workout? _____
9. a stuffed animal? _____
10. a hot fudge sundae? _____
11. a book for research? _____
12. emergency health care? _____
13. a fancy dinner? _____
14. a movie to take home and watch? _____
15. a book of stamps? _____
16. a silver bracelet? _____

B WHERE CAN I . . . ?

1. wash and dry my clothes? _____laundromat_____
2. see a new action film? _____
3. sit and feed the birds? _____
4. get something quick to eat? _____
5. sleep when I'm away from home? _____
6. get some film developed quickly? _____
7. buy a dress for my pregnant sister? _____
8. buy a new CD? _____

C ANALOGIES

1. earrings : jewelry shop *as* poodle : _____pet shop/pet store_____
2. shoes : shoe store *as* videos : _____
3. shop : shopping mall *as* study : _____
4. teacher : school *as* waiter : _____
5. grocery store : supermarket *as* motel : _____
6. film : photo shop *as* packages : _____

A WHAT'S THE WORD?

Complete the following using words from pages 40–41 of the Picture Dictionary.

1. My daughter works on the top floor of a modern _____office building_____. Lawyers, dentists, doctors, and accountants all work there.

2. It's raining very hard. We're lucky the bank has a _____ so we don't have to get out of the car.

3. When drivers see _____s at _____s, they should stop and let them walk across the street.

4. Did we leave our car on the second or third floor of the _____?

5. Sam is over an hour late! I don't have my cell phone with me. Let's call him on that _____.

6. One of my uncles robbed a bank and had to go to _____ for five years.

7. I hope the _____ didn't give us a ticket. I forgot to put money in the _____.

8. These streets are dark and dangerous at night. I think the city needs to install more _____s.

9. The _____ is where judges and lawyers work on legal cases.

10. You should always park your car close to the _____.

11. We stopped at the _____ to buy a magazine.

12. I smell smoke! Where's the nearest _____?

13. Does that _____ say Central Avenue?

B GOOD IDEA OR BAD IDEA?

Put a check in the best column.

	Good Idea	Bad Idea
1. Let's park in front of that fire hydrant!	_____	✓
2. You should always wear a helmet when you ride a motorcycle.	_____	_____
3. I don't usually walk on the sidewalk. I prefer to walk on the street.	_____	_____
4. We should ask that police officer where the bus stop is.	_____	_____
5. Always cross the street at a crosswalk.	_____	_____
6. I want to open that manhole cover to see what's underneath.	_____	_____
7. Jody takes the subway to work instead of driving her car into the city.	_____	_____
8. I always throw old newspapers into the sewer.	_____	_____
9. I want to get experience working in government, so I got a job at city hall.	_____	_____

A WHICH WORD DOESN'T BELONG?

1. Her hair is . . .	wavy.	long.	(elderly.)
2. My nephew is . . .	pregnant.	slim.	young.
3. That girl is . . .	young.	tall.	middle-aged.
4. His mustache is . . .	curly.	shoulder length.	black.
5. Those women are . . .	long.	elderly.	tall.
6. That senior citizen is . . .	thin.	wavy.	hearing-impaired.
7. That toddler is . . .	a boy.	a girl.	a teenager.
8. His beard is . . .	slim.	brown.	short.

B LISTENING: *Who Are They Talking About?*

Listen and decide who is being talked about.

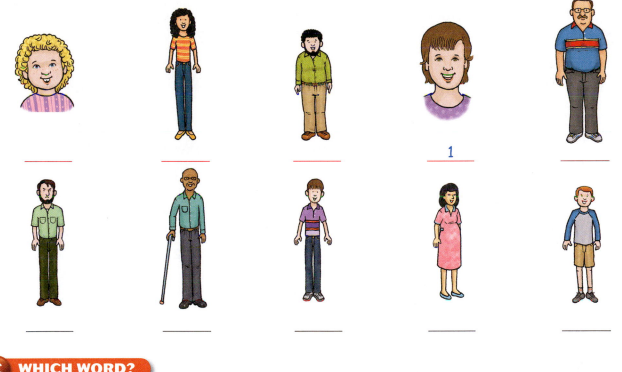

C WHICH WORD?

1. Is your sister the one with the (tall (long)) black hair?

2. He's only a teenager and he already has (hair   a mustache).

3. I love your new haircut! (Long   Short) hair looks good on you.

4. My brother is (hearing   vision) impaired. He needs special glasses.

5. If you want to look younger, you should color your hair (gray   black).

6. How did your baby get so much hair? My baby girl is still (bald   young).

7. I'd love to be as (slim   tall) as you. I've been trying to lose weight for years.

8. My grandmother is (hearing   physically) challenged. She needs help when she gets on a bus.

DESCRIBING PEOPLE AND THINGS

A WHAT'S THE CATEGORY?

___d___ 1. height
_____ 2. price
_____ 3. speed
_____ 4. sound
_____ 5. weight
_____ 6. age
_____ 7. temperature
_____ 8. texture
_____ 9. thickness
_____ 10. attractiveness

a. noisy–quiet
b. young–old
c. beautiful–ugly
d. tall–short
e. thick–thin
f. rough–smooth
g. expensive–cheap
h. heavy–thin
i. fast–slow
j. hot–cold

B THE RIGHT WORD

Choose the adjective that best describes each of the groups below.

bad	dry	heavy	hot	sharp
comfortable	fast	high	loud	soft
difficult	full	honest	messy	thick

1. _____soft_____
- skin
- mattress
- toothbrush

2. _____
- train
- runner
- sports car

3. _____
- weather
- coffee
- iron

4. _____
- music
- noise
- party

5. _____
- weather
- grades
- luck

6. _____
- sofa
- temperature
- clothing

7. _____
- fog
- accent
- line

8. _____
- heels
- voice
- bridge

9. _____
- room
- hair
- desk

10. _____
- test
- problem
- situation

11. _____
- person
- shopkeeper
- salesperson

12. _____
- knife
- pencil
- ax

13. _____
- glass
- gas tank
- room

14. _____
- box
- suitcase
- weights

15. _____
- skin
- climate
- dishes

C SYNONYMS

Match the following synonyms. Each word in the box may have more than one synonym in the list below.

a. beautiful	d. dirty	g. neat	j. thin
b. clean	e. heavy	h. small	k. ugly
c. closed	f. hot	i. tall	l. wide

<u>d</u> **1.** filthy

____ **2.** scalding

____ **3.** slender

____ **4.** immaculate

____ **5.** petite

____ **6.** chubby

____ **7.** shut

____ **8.** hideous

____ **9.** broad

____ **10.** lanky

____ **11.** diminutive

____ **12.** tidy

____ **13.** gorgeous

____ **14.** meticulous

____ **15.** repulsive

____ **16.** stout

____ **17.** expansive

____ **18.** fastidious

D "ICE COLD!"

See if you can figure out the correct combination of the following words. The meaning is always "very." For example, "ice cold" means "very cold."

boiling	chock	filthy	razor	soaking
bone	dirt	ice	skin	squeaky
brand	feather	pitch	sky	stick

1. "____ice____ cold"

2. "_____ cheap"

3. "_____ high"

4. "_____ dry"

5. "_____ clean"

6. "_____ tight"

7. "_____ hot"

8. "_____ light"

9. "_____ wet"

10. "_____ new"

11. "_____ rich"

12. "_____ sharp"

13. "_____ full"

14. "_____ straight"

15. "_____ dark"

E LISTENING

Listen and choose the best answer.

1. a. shiny
   b. dull

2. a. hard
   b. easy

3. a. wet
   b. dry

4. a. sharp
   b. dull

5. a. light
   b. heavy

6. a. open
   b. closed

7. a. loose
   b. tight

8. a. empty
   b. full

9. a. wide
   b. narrow

10. a. straight
    b. crooked

11. a. comfortable
    b. uncomfortable

12. a. honest
    b. dishonest

A   WHICH WORD DOESN'T BELONG?

1. lonely	miserable	(excited)	homesick
2. mad	bored	angry	furious
3. exhausted	sleepy	confused	tired
4. surprised	annoyed	frustrated	upset
5. hungry	thirsty	homesick	full

B   ANALOGIES

1. scared : afraid *as* sick : _____ill_____
2. food : drink *as* hungry : _____
3. mad : furious *as* tired : _____
4. unhappy : miserable *as* happy : _____
5. exciting : excited *as* frightening : _____

C   THE NEXT WORD

See if you can figure out which prepositions these adjectives are followed by.

1. angry   ____b, c, e____
2. confused   _____
3. worried   _____
4. jealous   _____
5. shocked   _____
6. excited   _____
7. furious   _____

```
a. of
b. about
c. at
d. by
e. with
```

D   SYNONYMS

Match the following synonyms.

_h_	1. exhausted	a.	bloated
____	2. afraid	b.	famished
____	3. confused	c.	perplexed
____	4. disgusted	d.	petrified
____	5. cold	e.	seething
____	6. hungry	f.	shivering
____	7. furious	g.	repulsed
____	8. full	h.	wiped out

1. We felt very ((proud)   disappointed) when our daughter graduated from medical school.
2. Don't be (exhausted   embarrassed) if you don't know the answer. We all make mistakes.
3. Many college students feel (homesick   jealous) living in the dormitory for the first time.
4. I'm so (annoyed   happy)! I can't enjoy this picnic with all of these mosquitoes.
5. Greg feels (lonely   confused) when his English teacher speaks too quickly.
6. Jenny is stuck in heavy traffic. She's feeling very (surprised   frustrated).
7. Ivan felt (exhausted   confused) after swimming in the ocean all day.
8. After eating several helpings of spaghetti, Carlos was (full   hungry).
9. I can't believe you did that! I'm really (exhausted   shocked)!
10. I felt (sick   hot) after eating the spoiled fruit.

F   **LISTENING:** *How Are They Feeling?* 🎧

Listen and choose the best description of the person's feelings.

1. a. He's extremely happy.
   (b.) He's absolutely furious.
2. a. She's sick.
   b. She's confused.
3. a. He's nervous.
   b. He's disappointed.
4. a. She must be sleepy.
   b. She must be thirsty.

5. a. He's lonely and miserable.
   b. He's nervous and homesick.
6. a. She's probably bored.
   b. She's probably worried.
7. a. She's jealous.
   b. She must be excited.
8. a. He's completely confused.
   b. He's totally disgusted.

G   **"RAGING MAD!"**

See if you can figure out the following expressions. The meaning is always "very." For example, "deathly ill" means "very ill."

a. dead
b. freezing
c. raging
d. deathly
e. thoroughly

1. "__c__ mad"
2. "_____ disgusted"
3. "_____ cold"
4. "_____ tired"
5. "_____ ill"

6. "sick __i__"
7. "shocked _____"
8. "proud _____"
9. "hungry _____"
10. "scared _____"

f. as a peacock
g. out of my mind
h. as a bear
i. as a dog
j. to death

A WHAT'S THE FRUIT?

1. These are small and dry and have a hard shell that has to be cracked open. _____nuts_____
2. This citrus fruit is high in Vitamin C and makes a popular breakfast juice. _____
3. This very sour, yellow citrus fruit can be used to flavor iced tea. _____
4. This soft, yellow fruit is eaten by both people and monkeys. _____
5. This oval-shaped fruit is red inside with black seeds and popular in summer. _____
6. This red-orange and yellow fruit has fuzzy skin and a large seed inside. _____
7. This fruit comes in bunches and may be green, purple, or red. _____
8. These are small, dark brown fruits made by drying plums. _____
9. This rough-skinned fruit is sweet and yellow inside and is grown in Hawaii. _____
10. Many people like to drink the *milk* inside this tropical fruit. _____

B WHICH FRUIT?

1. When you're at the grocery store, please pick up a few bunches of ((grapes)   raspberries).
2. I like eating (pineapples   pears) because they're soft and only have small seeds inside.
3. I almost can't tell the difference between a peach and (an apricot   a plum).
4. The best way to eat (plantains   cherries) is to slice them and fry them in oil.
5. If you like dried fruit, you'll like these (raspberries   prunes).
6. If you like citrus fruit, you'll love this (orange   papaya).
7. I need to peel this (apricot   tangerine) before eating it.
8. I was so hungry I ate half of the (raisin   watermelon).
9. Can I have a piece of that (avocado   blueberry) pie?
10. Try squeezing some (lime   nuts) into your drink.

C "SOUR GRAPES!"

1. That's just sour grapes!
   a. That tastes terrible.
   b. You're doing that because you're jealous.

2. She's the top banana.
   a. She's very tall.
   b. She's the boss.

3. He's a real peach.
   a. He's a wonderful person.
   b. His skin is soft.

4. You're the apple of my eye.
   a. You bother me.
   b. You're my favorite.

5. Irene got the plum job at her office.
   a. She got the best job.
   b. She got the worst job.

6. My new car is a real lemon!
   a. It's a terrible car.
   b. It's brand new and shiny.

A TOSSED SALAD

The letters in the following salad ingredients are all mixed up. Put the letters in their correct order to find out what's in the salad.

1. matoot   _tomato_
2. elutcte   _____
3. nereg preepp   _____
4. cryele   _____
5. rucemubc   _____

6. rtorac   _____
7. shrummoos   _____
8. driahs   _____
9. oekatrihc   _____
10. clsaniols   _____

B WHICH VEGETABLE DOESN'T BELONG?

1. mushroom	potato	(tomato)	turnip
2. spinach	acorn squash	butternut squash	yam
3. zucchini	carrot	brussels sprout	cucumber
4. sweet	red	chili	kidney
5. kidney	beet	black	lima
6. cauliflower	lettuce	bok choy	cabbage

C TRUE OR FALSE?

Write T if the sentence is true and F if the sentence is false.

_F_ 1. Zucchini, acorn, and sweet are all types of squash.

____ 2. Pickles are made from cucumbers.

____ 3. Celery should be cooked before eating.

____ 4. Another name for lima beans is kidney beans.

____ 5. Some mushrooms can be poisonous.

____ 6. Scallions are baby onions.

____ 7. Garlic tastes best when eaten raw.

____ 8. Peeling carrots can make you cry.

D CAN YOU REMEMBER?

Without looking at the Picture Dictionary, see if you can remember . . .

3 Kinds of Squash	4 Kinds of Beans	3 Kinds of Peppers
acorn	_____	_____
_____	_____	_____
_____	_____	_____
	_____	

41

A CATEGORIES

Circle the word that doesn't belong. Then write the category of each group.

Category

1. (chops)	wings	thighs	drumsticks	chicken
2. oysters	crabs	tripe	scallops	_____
3. lamb	pork	ribs	shrimp	_____
4. flounder	duck	trout	catfish	_____
5. roast	duck	turkey	chicken	_____
6. bacon	ham	salmon	sausages	_____
7. shrimp	filet of sole	clams	lobster	_____

B WHICH WORD?

1. Our poultry special today is ((turkey)   liver).
2. Let's grill chicken (chops   breasts) for dinner tonight.
3. This (roast   ground) beef is great for making hamburgers.
4. Stewing (beef   ham) should always be cooked thoroughly.
5. I'm allergic to shellfish, so I can't have the (mussels   haddock).
6. Which type of fish would you prefer—halibut or (catfish   tripe)?
7. You have to use the freshest (poultry   seafood) when you make sushi.
8. Let's go to that new restaurant. I hear their pork (chops   steaks) are delicious.
9. Grandma made a wonderful dinner with rice, vegetables, and leg of (chicken   lamb).
10. My doctor says I should avoid red meat. Is there any (sausage   poultry) on the menu?

C LISTENING

Listen and choose the best response.

1. a. Okay. Do we have any stewing beef?
   b. Sure. Do we have any roast beef?

2. a. My favorite is tripe.
   b. I like trout.

3. a. Okay. I hear they have excellent lobster.
   b. Good idea. Their liver is great!

4. a. I recommend one of our poultry dishes.
   b. I recommend our excellent steaks and ribs.

5. a. I like the wings.
   b. Chops. They're definitely my favorite.

6. a. Not really. Can you get some lamb chops?
   b. Not really. Can you buy some pork chops?

7. a. Drumsticks.
   b. Eggs and sausages.

8. a. Yes. You should try our scallops.
   b. Yes. I recommend our ham.

9. a. Yes. We have legs and wings.
   b. Yes. We have bacon and sausages.

10. a. Then you should definitely order the clams.
    b. Then you shouldn't order the scallops.

A LIKELY OR UNLIKELY?

Put a check in the best column.

	Likely	Unlikely
1. Melanie served cheese for her guests to drink last night.	____	✓
2. You'll need some water for that powdered drink mix.	____	____
3. I'm a vegetarian so I eat a lot of tofu.	____	____
4. I usually add sour cream and sugar to my coffee.	____	____
5. Cocoa tastes great on a cold winter day.	____	____
6. I'm on a diet so I'm only drinking whole milk.	____	____
7. When you're sick, drinking herbal tea might make you feel better.	____	____
8. It's healthy to eat eggs without cooking them.	____	____
9. You can find soda in the dairy section.	____	____

B WHICH WORD?

1. Many people switch to skim (eggs   (milk)) when they go on a diet.
2. Would you like some (chocolate   orange) juice with your breakfast?
3. Let's get some powdered (drink   coffee) mix to make for the picnic.
4. Have you ever tried fresh fruit with (sour   cottage) cheese?
5. Do want regular or (diet   skim) soda?
6. Can I have a toasted bagel with cream (cheese   paks)?
7. Be careful! That (grapefruit juice   tea) is very hot!
8. I like to put (margarine   sour cream) on my toast in the morning.
9. I'm trying to avoid caffeine, so I'm only drinking (decaf   low-fat) coffee.
10. The water from the faucet isn't very clean, so I only drink (herbal   bottled) water.

C CATEGORIES

Circle the word that doesn't belong. Then write the category of each group.

				Category
1. low-fat	skim	(apple)	chocolate	milk
2. coffee	diet soda	bottled water	grape juice	____
3. cheese	tea	butter	milk	____
4. herbal tea	fruit punch	hot chocolate	coffee	____
5. eggs	yogurt	cottage cheese	orange juice	____
6. apple	diet	pineapple	grapefruit	____
7. low-fat milk	skim milk	grape juice	diet soda	____

A WHICH WORD?

1. I don't have time to cook tonight. Let's just heat up some frozen ((dinners)   lemonade).
2. What kind of cheese do you prefer—(pastrami   provolone) or mozzarella?
3. I'm allergic to shellfish, so I can't have any (seafood   macaroni) salad.
4. Does (Swiss   cheddar) cheese really come from Switzerland?
5. Would you like to try some of this potato (salad   slaw)?
6. Let's have corned (cheese   beef) sandwiches for lunch.
7. Is there any (cole slaw   ice cream) for dessert?

B WHICH FOOD DOESN'T BELONG?

1. ice cream | (nuts) | frozen dinners | frozen vegetables
2. Swiss | ham | American | mozzarella
3. potato chips | potato salad | cole slaw | pasta salad
4. nuts | popcorn | seafood salad | pretzels
5. bologna | corned beef | salami | turkey

C A PICNIC

A. Some friends are having a picnic in the park next weekend. Would you like to come?

B. Sure. I'd love to. What can I bring?

A. Well, let's see. Bob says he'll bring the snacks. So I guess he'll bring some _____potato_____ 1 chips and _____ 2 chips. I'm going to bring the drinks since I already have some frozen _____ 3 and frozen _____ 4 juice in my freezer.

B. Is someone bringing sandwiches?

A. Yes. Samantha is bringing _____ 5 beef and _____ 6 beef. Armando likes poultry, so he's bringing _____ 7. Amy is bringing different kinds of cheese for sandwiches. I think she's bringing some _____ 8 cheese, some _____ 9 cheese, and some _____ 10 cheese.

B. Should I bring some _____ 11? My mother gave me a great recipe that uses potatoes, mayonnaise, and some herbs and spices.

A. That sounds great. And it will go together well with the _____ 12 salad Alex is bringing. I hope you like fish.

B. Yes, I do. The salad sounds delicious. See you next weekend!

44

A WHICH WORD DOESN'T BELONG?

1. jam	peanut butter	(mayonnaise)	jelly
2. rolls	muffins	cake	flour
3. macaroni	rice	spaghetti	noodles
4. mustard	relish	soup	ketchup
5. sugar	pepper	salt	pickles
6. olive oil	soup	soy sauce	relish

B WHAT'S THE WORD?

bread	flour	oil	soy sauce
cookies	ketchup	salad dressing	tuna fish
crackers	mustard	salsa	vegetables

1. This hot dog would taste perfect if I only had some _____mustard_____.
2. I can't eat french fries without _____.
3. Let's have some chocolate chip _____ for dessert!
4. Put some _____ in the pan and fry some onions.
5. I've stopped eating fish. Do you want these cans of _____?
6. The perfect appetizer for this meal would be cheese and _____.
7. For breakfast I usually just have tea and jam on toasted _____.
8. If you don't have sugar, _____, and eggs, you can't make cookies.
9. This salad is too dry—do you have any _____?
10. Do you think it's okay if I use canned _____ for this stew?
11. Let's eat some tortilla chips and _____ while we watch the game.
12. Can you order some Chinese food? Don't forget to ask for extra _____ for dipping.

C LISTENING

Listen and choose the best answer.

1. a. vegetables 　(b.) fruit	**4.** a. cereal 　b. salt	**7.** a. cake mix 　b. flour	**10.** a. cereal 　b. pita bread
2. a. soy sauce 　b. soup	**5.** a. cake 　b. vinegar	**8.** a. oil 　b. pepper	**11.** a. relish 　b. olive oil
3. a. jelly 　b. sugar	**6.** a. tortilla chips 　b. mustard	**9.** a. rolls 　b. muffins	**12.** a. cake 　b. cake mix

A WHAT'S THE WORD?

aluminum foil	dog food	paper plates	soap	tissues
diaper	paper cups	paper towels	straw	trash bags

1. Do we have any more ____trash bags____? We have a lot of things to throw away.
2. Uh-oh. It looks like we have to change the baby's _____.
3. Wash your hands with _____ and water.
4. We have to get some more _____ for the puppies.
5. Here. Blow your nose with these _____.
6. I don't want to do any dishes tonight. Let's just use _____.
7. When we go on a picnic, we drink lemonade out of _____.
8. I prefer to drink soda through a _____.
9. You can use _____ to wrap cooked meats, but don't put it in the microwave!
10. Oh, no! I spilled juice on the kitchen floor. Can you hand me some _____?

B WHICH WORD DOESN'T BELONG?

1. cat food	sandwich bags	dog food	baby food
2. toilet paper	tissues	plastic wrap	napkins
3. aluminum foil	waxed paper	wipes	plastic wrap
4. diapers	soap	liquid soap	wipes
5. paper plates	paper cups	aluminum foil	straws
6. baby cereal	formula	cat food	diapers

C ANALOGIES

baby food	cat food	paper cups	trash bags	wipes	wrap

1. dogs : dog food *as* cats : _____cat food_____
2. eating : paper plates *as* drinking : _____
3. adults : toilet paper *as* babies : _____
4. waxed : paper *as* plastic : _____
5. sandwiches : sandwich bags *as* trash : _____
6. newborn babies : formula *as* older babies : _____

A LIKELY OR UNLIKELY?

Put a check in the best column.

	Likely	Unlikely
1. Since I only had five things, I got into the express checkout.	✓	___
2. There were seven shoppers working at the checkout line.	___	___
3. Cooking oil? It's in the beverage section over there.	___	___
4. You'll find disposable diapers in the produce section.	___	___
5. The bottle-return machine helps us to recycle.	___	___
6. The customer is stocking the shelves.	___	___
7. You can find the manager in Aisle 7.	___	___
8. I used a shopping cart to carry my groceries home.	___	___
9. I read magazines while I was waiting at the checkout counter.	___	___

B WHICH WORD DOESN'T BELONG?

1. coupons	(candy)	cashier	cash register
2. shopper	scanner	cashier	packer
3. customer	manager	clerk	bagger
4. basket	cart	bag	aisle
5. magazine	tabloid	scale	candy

C WHAT'S THE WORD?

1. This person helps you when you pay for your groceries. _____cashier_____

2. Use this when you buy produce to see how much you want to buy. _____

3. This person asks you if you'd like paper or plastic. _____

4. You can buy this sweet snack in the checkout line. _____

5. Use these to get discounts on groceries that you buy. _____

6. You can find fruits and vegetables in this section. _____

7. This person can help you find items in the store. _____

8. If you only need to get a few things, use this. _____

D ASSOCIATIONS

_d_	**1.** "This is getting heavy to push!"	**a.**	tabloid
___	**2.** "I like *Time* and *Newsweek*."	**b.**	shopper
___	**3.** "Look at the headline: PEOPLE ON MARS!"	**c.**	express checkout
___	**4.** "It's not good for your teeth."	**d.**	shopping cart
___	**5.** "I just have a few things."	**e.**	gum
___	**6.** "Excuse me. Where can I find dog food?"	**f.**	magazines

A WHAT'S THE CONTAINER?

Write the correct container or quantity.

1. butter	cheese	hamburger	_____pound_____
2. sugar	flour	chips	_____
3. toilet tissue	plastic wrap	paper towels	_____
4. cereal	cookies	raisins	_____
5. tomatoes	tuna fish	soup	_____
6. grapes	carrots	bananas	_____
7. eggs	milk	orange juice	_____
8. yogurt	cottage cheese	sour cream	_____

B WHICH WORD IS CORRECT?

1. We need a few (boxes   (cans)) of soup.
2. Would you like a (stick   six-pack) of gum?
3. We need a (roll   pack) of toilet paper for our bathroom.
4. Abigail bought a (head   bunch) of grapes for dessert.
5. Should I bring a (six-pack   bag) of soda to the party?
6. Jonah went to the bakery to buy two (liters   loaves) of bread.
7. Do you think one (half-gallon   jar) of ice cream will be enough?
8. Could you please buy a (dozen   pound) eggs on your way home?
9. I'll pick up a (tube   bag) of toothpaste when I go to the supermarket.
10. Can you please pick up a (pack   container) of yogurt at the supermarket?
11. We bought a (jar   bag) of mustard and a (can   bottle) of ketchup at the store.
12. Kelly bought three (rolls   packages) of rolls and two (rolls   cartons) of paper towels when she went shopping this morning.

C LISTENING: *What Are They Talking About?*

Listen and decide what's being talked about.

1. a. beans
   b. blueberries

2. a. jam
   b. milk

3. a. beef
   b. toilet tissue

4. a. tuna fish
   b. salsa

5. a. eggs
   b. butter

6. a. cabbage
   b. bread

7. a. butter
   b. soda

8. a. salad dressing
   b. cereal

9. a. toothpaste
   b. soap

A   TRUE OR FALSE?

*Write **T** if a statement is true and **F** if it is false.*

__T__   **1.** There are four cups in a quart.

_____   **2.** Sixteen ozs. is the same as one lb.

_____   **3.** There are three tablespoons in a teaspoon.

_____   **4.** A quart is bigger than a gallon.

_____   **5.** There are eight ounces in a cup.

_____   **6.** A quarter pound contains twelve ounces.

_____   **7.** Two tsps. equals one fl. oz.

_____   **8.** A half pint holds twelve fluid ounces.

_____   **9.** Two tablespoons is the same as six teaspoons.

_____   **10.** A gallon contains more ounces than a quart.

_____   **11.** There are two pints in a cup.

_____   **12.** A ten-gallon hat holds 640 fluid ounces.

B   WHICH WORD?

1. Can I have two ((pounds)   fluid ounces) of stewing beef, please?

2. Would you like one or two (teaspoons   gallons) of sugar in your tea?

3. I'd like a (quart   half pound) of cheddar cheese, please.

4. Could you pick up some bread and (an ounce   a quart) of milk?

5. Let's just get a (gallon   pint) of ice cream. There's only the two of us.

C   RECIPES

1. Alan's recipe calls for a pint of heavy cream, so he should put in (a cup   (2 cups)).

2. Sam doesn't like food that's too spicy, so he should add only (1 tablespoon   2 teaspoons) of pepper to the chili.

3. Don't forget to add a (tsp.   fl. oz.) of salt to your stew.

4. This cake recipe calls for 8 (Tbsps.   cups) of sugar.

5. If you're making soup for six people, you'll need at least 8 (cups   gallons) of water.

6. If you don't want the sauce to be too thin, you should add only (1/2 cup   8 ounces) of water.

7. The recipe says I need four ounces of cheese and eight ounces of meat, so I guess I should buy (1/3   1/4) lb. of provolone and (3/4   1/2) lb. of ham.

FOOD PREPARATION AND RECIPES

A WHAT SHOULD I DO?

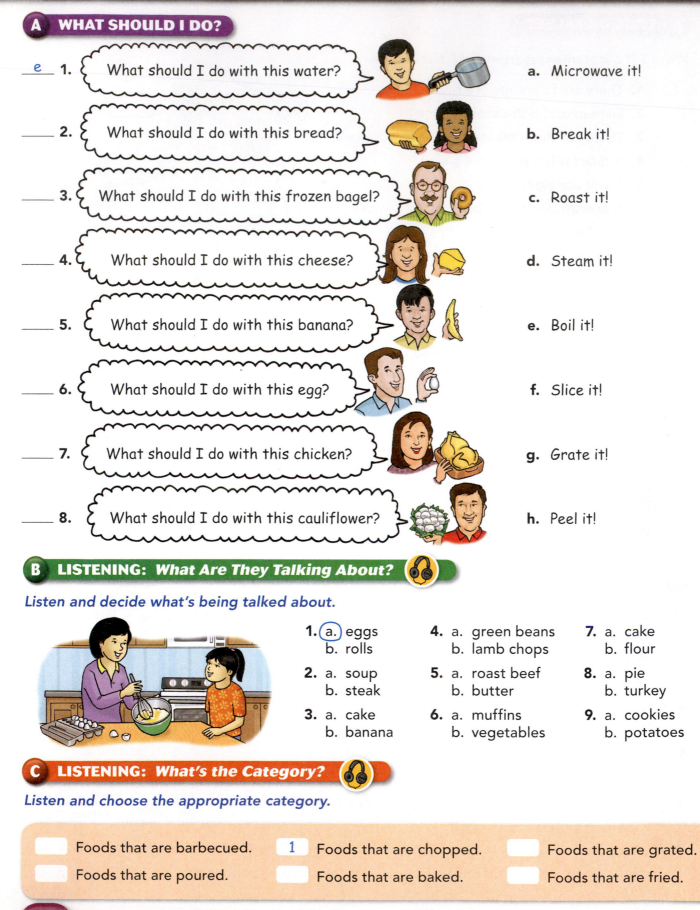

_e_ 1. { What should I do with this water? }

_____ 2. { What should I do with this bread? }

_____ 3. { What should I do with this frozen bagel? }

_____ 4. { What should I do with this cheese? }

_____ 5. { What should I do with this banana? }

_____ 6. { What should I do with this egg? }

_____ 7. { What should I do with this chicken? }

_____ 8. { What should I do with this cauliflower? }

a. Microwave it!

b. Break it!

c. Roast it!

d. Steam it!

e. Boil it!

f. Slice it!

g. Grate it!

h. Peel it!

B LISTENING: *What Are They Talking About?*

Listen and decide what's being talked about.

1. a. eggs
   b. rolls

2. a. soup
   b. steak

3. a. cake
   b. banana

4. a. green beans
   b. lamb chops

5. a. roast beef
   b. butter

6. a. muffins
   b. vegetables

7. a. cake
   b. flour

8. a. pie
   b. turkey

9. a. cookies
   b. potatoes

C LISTENING: *What's the Category?*

Listen and choose the appropriate category.

[ ] Foods that are barbecued.   [1] Foods that are chopped.   [ ] Foods that are grated.

[ ] Foods that are poured.   [ ] Foods that are baked.   [ ] Foods that are fried.

A WHICH KITCHENWARE WORD IS CORRECT?

1. I always use a ((colander)   peeler) when I make spaghetti.
2. Here's the soup! Where's the (grater   ladle)?
3. I use a (double boiler   skillet) whenever I fry chicken.
4. I'll bake these cookies on this cookie (cutter   sheet).
5. I'm making pancakes, and I can't find the (steamer   spatula).
6. If you're going to make a pie, you'll need a (rolling pin   strainer).
7. I'll cut the turkey with this (carving knife   can opener).
8. Use this (timer   steamer) so we know how long to bake the cake.
9. When you make sauces, you should use a (beater   wooden spoon) to stir.

B WHAT'S THE OBJECT?

__d__ 1. measuring	a. cutter		___ 7. egg	g. pan
___ 2. roasting	b. press		___ 8. vegetable	h. scoop
___ 3. garlic	c. knife		___ 9. cake	i. beater
___ 4. kitchen	d. cup		___ 10. paring	j. pin
___ 5. carving	e. timer		___ 11. rolling	k. peeler
___ 6. cookie	f. rack		___ 12. ice cream	l. knife

C WHICH WORD DOESN'T BELONG?

1. beater   whisk   (double boiler)   wooden spoon
2. saucepan   cake pan   pie plate   cookie sheet
3. wok   saucepan   skillet   grater
4. ice cream scoop   can opener   ladle   measuring spoon
5. cookie sheet   casserole dish   garlic press   roasting pan

D LISTENING

Listen and choose the best answer.

1. a. frying pan
   (b.) wok

2. a. egg beater
   b. colander

3. a. ladle
   b. spatula

4. a. paring knife
   b. grater

5. a. roasting rack
   b. carving knife

6. a. lid
   b. saucepan

A WHAT'S THE FOOD?

a. burrito	d. frozen yogurt	g. mayonnaise
b. chili	e. hamburger	h. paper cup
c. fried chicken	f. ketchup	i. pizza

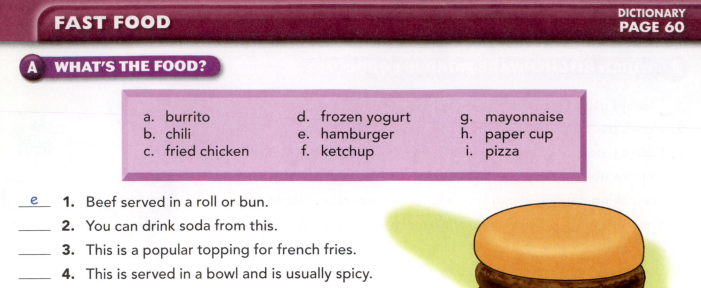

__e__ **1.** Beef served in a roll or bun.

_____ **2.** You can drink soda from this.

_____ **3.** This is a popular topping for french fries.

_____ **4.** This is served in a bowl and is usually spicy.

_____ **5.** This is a popular topping for fish sandwiches.

_____ **6.** This is sweet and is sometimes eaten by people on a diet.

_____ **7.** It's made with tomato sauce, and we often order this by the slice.

_____ **8.** This is made with beans, rice, some vegetables, and some kind of meat.

_____ **9.** An order usually contains two or three pieces, and it often tastes greasy.

B WHICH WORD DOESN'T BELONG?

1. ketchup | (taco) | mustard | relish
2. frozen yogurt | ice cream | milkshake | soda
3. pizza | nachos | taco | burrito
4. plastic utensils | napkins | straws | lids
5. hot dog | hamburger | chicken sandwich | fish sandwich

C WHICH WORD?

1. I'd like a slice of (chili (pizza)), please.

2. Let's have (frozen yogurt   tacos) for dessert!

3. I usually put (lids   ketchup) on my hamburger.

4. I'll have (soda   nachos) to drink with my fish sandwich.

5. You'll need (paper cups   plastic utensils) to use with your salad.

D LISTENING: *What Food Are They Talking About?*

Listen and decide what food is being talked about.

1. (a.) salad
b. nachos

2. a. chili
b. ice cream

3. a. fried chicken
b. burrito

4. a. mustard
b. salad dressing

5. a. cheeseburger
b. pizza

6. a. chicken sandwich
b. fish sandwich

A WHAT'S THE FOOD?

a. bagel	d. kinds of bread	g. pita
b. danish	e. lemonade	h. submarine
c. hot chocolate	f. muffin	i. waffle

_f_ **1.** A typical one is blueberry or bran.

_____ **2.** Pumpernickel, whole wheat, and rye.

_____ **3.** This is a refreshing natural summer drink.

_____ **4.** This is usually eaten with butter and syrup.

_____ **5.** This roll is the name of an underwater vehicle.

_____ **6.** This has a hole in the middle and is often toasted.

_____ **7.** This sweet breakfast treat has jam or cheese on it.

_____ **8.** This is often called pocket bread because of its shape.

_____ **9.** This sweet drink is usually enjoyed during cold weather.

B WHICH WORD?

1. I'd like a chicken salad sandwich on (a donut   (white bread)), please.

2. I'd like lettuce and tomato on my (tuna fish sandwich   croissant).

3. I'll have pancakes with two or three (sausages   home fries).

4. Would you like a corned beef (bread   sandwich)?

5. My favorite kind of sandwich is (roast beef   rye).

6. I'd like a cup of (decaf coffee   eggs).

7. I'll have a medium-size (roll   tea) to drink.

8. I like (danish   toast) because it's sweet.

9. I'd like an order of (pancakes   iced tea).

10. I'll have (a BLT   bacon) with my eggs.

C LISTENING: *What Food Are They Talking About?*

Listen and decide what food is being talked about.

1. a. pancakes
   b. egg salad sandwich

2. a. chicken salad sandwich
   b. roast beef sandwich

3. a. coffee
   b. lemonade

4. a. hot chocolate
   b. iced tea

5. a. milk
   b. coffee

6. a. tuna fish sandwich
   b. corned beef sandwich

A WHAT'S THE VERB?

1. At a restaurant, the customer (leaves   (pays)) the check at the end of the meal.

2. When you (serve   set) the meal, make sure everyone has enough to drink.

3. Before you (leave   take) the order, make sure you greet the customers.

4. Wait until customers leave before you (clear   set) the table.

5. Anthony, could you please (seat   take) the new customers?

6. Oh, no! I think I forgot to (pay   leave) a tip!

B WHICH WORD?

1. Uh-oh! Here comes the ((dessert cart)   check). And I'm on a diet!

2. Could we please have a (dining   booster) seat for our young child?

3. The (waiter   hostess) took our order but forgot to fill our bread basket.

4. The (dishwasher   busperson) needs to pour water in the customers' glasses.

5. Can we have another (server   table), please? It's too noisy next to the kitchen.

6. This restaurant's (salad bar   dishroom) is great! There are so many fresh vegetables.

7. There is a new (waiter   chef) at the French restaurant in town. I hear the food is wonderful.

8. My husband and I prefer to sit in a (booth   high chair). It's more comfortable than a table.

C LISTENING

Listen and circle the best answer.

1. meal   (order)   **3.** salad bar   menu   **5.** knife   spoon

2. server   customer   **4.** customer   table   **6.** tip   check

D WHAT'S WRONG WITH THIS PLACE SETTING?

Without looking at the place setting on Picture Dictionary page 63, see if you can find 6 things that are wrong with the place setting below.

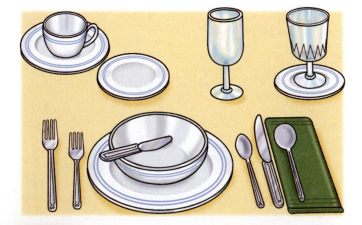

The cup is on the salad plate.

_____

_____

_____

_____

_____

A ORDERING DINNER

Put the following conversation in the correct order.

_____ Would you like a salad?

_____ Yes. I'd like an ice cream sundae.

_____ Yes. I'll have the garden salad.

_____ French fries, please.

__1__ What kind of appetizer would you like?

_____ Would you care for some dessert?

_____ Yes. I'd like the broiled fish.

_____ Are you ready to order your main course?

_____ I'll have the chicken wings.

_____ What side dish would you like with that?

B YOUR SERVER HAS A FEW QUESTIONS

What foods are these waiters and waitresses referring to?

What kind of dressing would you like with that?

a

How would you like that done—rare, medium, or well-done?

b

Would you like that mashed or baked?

c

Do you prefer white, brown, or wild?

d

You can choose to have either breast or thigh.

e

Do you prefer blueberry, apple, or cherry?

f

__c__ 1. potato   _____ 3. baked chicken   _____ 5. pie

_____ 2. rice   _____ 4. prime rib   _____ 6. salad

C LISTENING 🎧

Listen and decide what food is being talked about.

1. a. mixed vegetables
   b. tossed salad

2. a. cake
   b. fruit cocktail

3. a. antipasto
   b. french fries

4. a. jello
   b. noodles

5. a. nachos
   b. rice

6. a. pudding
   b. veal cutlet

A COLOR ASSOCIATIONS

What colors describe the following objects?

1. a carrot   _____orange_____
2. grass   _____
3. clouds   _____
4. a tomato   _____
5. daisies   _____

6. pine trees   _____
7. the sky   _____
8. a cucumber   _____
9. eggplant   _____
10. tires   _____

B MIXING COLORS

1. Red and blue make _____purple_____.
2. Black and white make _____.
3. Blue and yellow make _____.
4. Red and white make _____.
5. Green and red make _____.
6. Green and white make _____.
7. Red and yellow make _____.

C COLORFUL EXPRESSIONS

| black | gold | green | silver | yellow |
| blue | gray | red | white | |

1. Nicholas feels _____green_____ with envy because his best friend just got a new bicycle.
2. Jimmy's eye is completely _____ and blue after somebody punched him.
3. My girlfriend broke up with me so I'm feeling kind of _____.
4. Whenever I blush, my face turns bright _____.
5. In many countries people wear _____ clothes to a funeral.
6. Do you know George Gershwin's "Rhapsody in _____?"
7. On a cloudy day, everything looks so _____ and drab.
8. If the other side shows a _____ flag, that means they surrendered.
9. When someone is afraid to do something, we say that person is _____.
10. "All that glitters is not _____" means that not all things are as good as they seem.
11. When Billy thought there was a burglar in the house, he turned _____ as a ghost.
12. "Every cloud has a _____ lining" means that there is always something positive to see in every situation."

A WHO WEARS WHAT?

Decide whether the following clothing is typically worn by women (W), by men (M), or by both (B).

1. blazer _B_
2. blouse ____
3. bow tie ____
4. dress ____
5. gown ____
6. jeans ____

7. jersey ____
8. jumper ____
9. leggings ____
10. maternity dress ____
11. pants ____
12. shirt ____

13. skirt ____
14. suit ____
15. sweater ____
16. turtleneck ____
17. tuxedo ____
18. vest ____

B WHICH WORD?

1. Which tie should I wear with this ((shirt)   jersey)?
2. The groom looks very handsome in his (tuxedo   gown).
3. When most people play tennis, they wear (shirts   shorts).
4. I think I'll wear my new (suit   T-shirt) to my job interview.
5. Your little girl looks so cute in her (jumpsuit   jumper).
6. It's chilly out. You should wear (leggings   shorts) with that skirt.
7. I'm going to wear my new (shirt   skirt) and blouse today.
8. When I work in my yard, I usually wear (overalls   a vest).
9. I think I'll wear my new (pants   blazer) and sport jacket to the party.
10. Carl is a nurse. When he's at work, he always wears a (maternity dress   uniform).

C LISTENING

Listen and choose the best answer.

1. a. uniform
   b. sport jacket
2. a. overalls
   b. a blazer
3. a. sport shirt
   b. necktie
4. a. dress
   b. blouse
5. a. jeans
   b. a tuxedo

6. a. leggings
   b. shorts
7. a. jumper
   b. evening gown
8. a. sweater
   b. uniform
9. a. maternity dresses
   b. overalls
10. a. turtleneck
    b. T-shirt

A WHICH WORD DOESN'T BELONG?

1. hat   (gloves)   cap   baseball cap
2. poncho   trench coat   sweater jacket   umbrella
3. windbreaker ear muffs   down jacket   ski mask
4. gloves   mittens   ear muffs   coat
5. ski mask   rain boots   sunglasses   ear muffs

B SHOPPING FOR WINTER CLOTHES

| down jacket | gloves | parka | raincoat | ski hat |
| ear muffs | jacket | rain boots | scarf | |

A. Can I help you?

B. Yes. I'm from Kenya, and I just moved to Chicago. I need some clothes for the winter.

A. Okay. Well, what do you have already? Do you have a coat?

B. No. I only have a leather _____jacket_____ [1].

A. You'll probably need something much warmer, like a _____ [2] or a _____ [3].

B. Does it snow all winter?

A. No. Sometimes it rains, so you'll also need a _____ [4] and probably some _____ [5] to keep your feet dry.

B. And what about the snow?

A. For that you'll need a _____ [6] for your head, a _____ [7] for your neck, and _____ [8] for your hands. You might want _____ [9] for your ears, too.

B. Will I really need all of that?

A. You probably will. It's usually cold here during the winter.

C WHICH WORD?

1. When it's bright outside, I always wear ((sunglasses)   ear muffs).
2. It's not very cold today. I think I'll wear just a (down   sweater) jacket.
3. Oh, no! I found my right (mask   glove), but I can't find my left one!
4. This (muffler   cap) will keep your neck warm on cold winter days.
5. It's raining. Don't forget to take your (windbreaker   umbrella).
6. Remember to wear (mittens   tights) if you're going to play in the snow.

A WHICH WORD DOESN'T BELONG?

1. camisole   stockings   (boxers)   tights
2. pajamas   knee-highs   nightshirt   sleeper
3. bra   underpants   boxers   jockstrap
4. stockings   pantyhose   knee socks   panties
5. slip   nightgown   jockey shorts   half slip

B WHICH WORD?

1. I need to buy my son a new pair of ((socks)   stockings).
2. Where is the baby's (slip   blanket sleeper)?
3. Do you sell bikini (hose   panties) in this department?
4. Ricky, put on your (socks   pajamas). It's bedtime!
5. I wear briefs and a (nightshirt   T-shirt) under my clothes.
6. I can't find my jockey (shorts   briefs)!
7. I always wear a (half slip   nightgown) when I wear a skirt.
8. Where is my (camisole   jockstrap)? It's time for football practice.
9. You should wear your (long johns   robe). It's cold outside today.
10. In the evening when I get undressed, I put on pajamas, a bathrobe, and (tights   slippers).

C FINISH THE SENTENCE

___d___ 1. I like this dress. To wear under it, I think I'll buy a new _____.   a. jockstrap
_____   2. Your feet must be cold. Put on a pair of _____.   b. boxers
_____   3. When my son plays sports, he always wears a _____.   c. long johns
_____   4. For my wife's birthday, I think I'll get her a new _____.   d. half slip
_____   5. It's very cold out. I think I should wear my _____.   e. nightgown
_____   6. Some men like to wear jockey shorts, and others prefer _____.   f. slippers

D LISTENING: *What's Being Described?*

Listen and decide what's being described.

	athletic supporter		blanket sleeper
	knee socks	1	bathrobe
	T-shirt		boxer shorts

A WHAT KIND OF SHOES DO THEY NEED?

Decide which shoes would be most appropriate for the following people and situations. There may be more than one possible answer.

a. boots	d. high-tops	g. pumps	j. sneakers
b. flip-flops	e. hiking boots	h. running shoes	k. tennis shoes
c. high heels	f. moccasins	i. sandals	l. work boots

1. Diane is going to play basketball this morning.   _____d, j_____
2. It's snowing, and George has to go to the post office.   _____
3. My husband and I are going to the beach today.   _____
4. Jerry is going to jog this afternoon.   _____
5. I'm going to play tennis tomorrow morning.   _____
6. Jenny and Sarah are going to go mountain climbing.   _____
7. My sister has an important job interview tomorrow.   _____

B WHICH WORD DOESN'T BELONG?

1. swimming trunks   swimsuit   bathing suit   (cover-up)
2. running   bike   tank   lycra
3. work   moccasins   hiking   cowboy
4. swimsuit   bathing suit   pumps   thongs
5. high heels   sneakers   tennis shoes   running shoes

C A DAY AT THE LAKE

| bathing | hiking | sandals | sweatpants | work |
| flip-flops | running | shirt | trunks | |

A. Do you want to go to the lake today?

B. Good idea! We can hike around the lake in the morning and then swim in the afternoon.

A. Okay, but I don't have _____hiking_____ [1] boots.

B. No problem. Just wear your _____ [2] boots. Do you have a pair of _____ [3] for walking on the beach?

A. No, but I have some _____ [4]. Do you have a pair of _____ [5] for swimming?

B. I do. But what should I wear for the hike?

A. You can wear a T-_____ [6] and _____ [7]. I'll probably just wear a _____ [8] suit with my _____ [9] suit underneath.

B. That sounds good. Let's go!

A LIKELY OR UNLIKELY?

		Likely	Unlikely
1.	Lisa carries all her important papers in her briefcase.	✓	____
2.	Howard wore bright red suspenders around his waist.	____	____
3.	Elaine has a picture of her daughter in her locket.	____	____
4.	Ivan keeps his credit cards in a tote bag in his left pants pocket.	____	____
5.	I wanted something to hold my hair in place, so I got a barrette.	____	____
6.	Carol wears a beautiful gold key ring on her left hand.	____	____
7.	Maria always keeps an extra handkerchief in her pocketbook.	____	____
8.	James fastened his tie with his belt.	____	____
9.	When Sam and Rita got married, they exchanged wedding bands.	____	____
10.	Joanne looked lovely. She wore a beautiful gold pin on her wrist.	____	____
11.	Ben always carries extra money in his wallet.	____	____
12.	Francine wore a beautiful backpack around her neck.	____	____

B WHAT IS IT?

1. You use this to keep a small picture in.   _____locket_____
2. You use this to keep your hair in place.   _____
3. You keep credit cards and money in this.   _____
4. You carry books in this.   _____
5. You use this to keep makeup in.   _____
6. You use these to keep your pants up.   _____
7. You use these to connect the cuffs of shirts.   _____
8. You use this to keep keys together.   _____
9. You keep coins in this.   _____

C LISTENING: What Is It?

Listen and decide what's being described.

☐ bracelet	☐ beads	☐ wedding ring	☐ backpack
☐ pearls	1 change purse	☐ wrist watch	☐ belt
☐ earrings	☐ briefcase	☐ engagement ring	☐ book bag

A   NEW CLOTHES

1. What do you think of my new (V-neck   (denim)) jacket?
2. I wish I could afford some new (linen   leather) boots.
3. I need to buy some (cotton   wool) T-shirts.
4. How do you like my new (corduroy   knee-high) pants?
5. Can you help me pick out some new (crew   sleeveless) socks?
6. Charles bought me a beautiful (silk   straw) shirt for my birthday.
7. Stephanie bought her husband some new (clip-on   short-sleeved) shirts.
8. I think I should get some new turtleneck (sweaters   scarves) for winter.

B   LISTENING: *Shopping for Clothes*

Listen and choose the best answer.

1. a. the solid shirt
   b. the floral shirt

2. a. a medium size
   b. an extra-small size

3. a. the polka-dotted blouse
   b. the checked blouse

4. a. the polyester sweater
   b. the wool sweater

5. a. the ankle socks
   b. the knee socks

6. a. pierced earrings
   b. clip-on earrings

C   SUMMER OR WINTER?

Decide whether the following clothing is typically worn in the summer (S), the winter (W), or both (B).

1. short-sleeved shirt   ___S___
2. turtleneck   _____
3. cotton shirt   _____
4. corduroy pants   _____
5. linen dress   _____
6. straw hat   _____
7. cardigan sweater   _____
8. sleeveless shirt   _____
9. nylon stockings   _____

D   LISTENING: *The Fashion Show*

Match the description you hear with the appropriate design.

A CLOTHING REPAIRS

1. A. I need to shorten the sleeves on this jacket.
   B. I agree. They're much too ((long)   short)!

2. A. Is there a problem with your new pants?
   B. Yes. The zipper is (ripped   broken).

3. A. I like the suit, but the pants are a little long.
   B. You need to (shorten   lengthen) them.

4. A. The jacket feels a little baggy.
   B. You should definitely (take   let) it in.

5. A. It looks like you'll need to take your shirt to the cleaners.
   B. I know. The collar is (missing   stained). I spilled coffee on it.

B SHOPPING

1. A. How do you like this fancy tie?
   B. Actually, I prefer that _____plain_____ one.

2. A. The heels on these shoes are too high to be comfortable at work.
   B. I agree. Try to find some shoes with _____ heels.

3. A. Do you think I should buy this long skirt?
   B. It's okay. But I think you should try on that _____ one.

4. A. This coat is too light. It won't keep you warm during the wintertime.
   B. You're right. I really need to find a nice _____ coat.

5. A. Can I wear this light shirt with this suit?
   B. No. A _____ shirt would look better.

6. A. I don't like this lapel. It's too wide.
   B. I don't like it either. Let's find a jacket with a _____ one.

C LISTENING: *Gossip at a Family Picnic*

Listen and complete each nasty sentence of this couple gossiping at a family picnic.

		a.	b.
1.	Kelly	a. take it in	(b.) lengthen it
2.	Tim	a. ripped	b. narrow
3.	Aunt Maxine	a. loose	b. tight
4.	Uncle Frank	a. baggy	b. missing
5.	Thelma	a. heavy	b. light
6.	Cousin Janice	a. wide	b. narrow
7.	Cousin Bob	a. dark	b. light

A DOING THE LAUNDRY

Eduardo is in college. He needs to do his laundry and is calling his mother for some advice.

bleach	fabric softener	light	load	sort	unload
dark	laundry detergent	lint trap	put	static cling remover	

A. Hello, Mom? I've got a few questions about doing my laundry. Can you help me?

B. Of course I can help you. The first thing you have to do is _____sort_____ [1] your laundry into _____ [2] and _____ [3] clothing.

A. Okay. I can do that.

B. Then, you have to _____ [4] the washer. Do you have _____ [5]?

A. Yes. I just got some. I also got some _____ [6] to keep my clothes soft and some _____ [7] for stains.

B. Good. Okay. When the washing machine is done, _____ [8] it, and then put the wet clothes in the dryer. Before you start the dryer you should clean the _____ [9].

A. Should I put a few sheets of _____ [10] in the dryer, too?

B. Yes. And when you're finished, _____ [11] everything away as soon as possible.

A. Okay. Thanks, Mom!

B ANALOGIES

closet	drawer	ironed clothing	ironing board	shelves

1. laundry bag : laundry basket *as* drawer : _____shelves_____
2. clothespin : clothesline *as* hanger : _____
3. wet clothes : dryer *as* wrinkled clothes : _____
4. hang up clothes : closet *as* put away clothes : _____
5. dirty laundry : clean clothing *as* wrinkled clothing : _____

C LISTENING

Listen and choose the best answer.

1. a. clothespins
   b. clothesline
2. a. sort the laundry
   b. fold the laundry
3. a. dryer
   b. ironing board
4. a. clothespins
   b. hangers
5. a. laundry basket
   b. lint trap
6. a. spray starch
   b. static cling remover

A GOING SHOPPING

In which department would you find the following?

1. a CD player   <u>Electronics</u>
2. a silk blouse   _____
3. a microwave oven   _____
4. a three-piece suit   _____
5. a frying pan   _____
6. a gold chain   _____
7. a bottle of cologne   _____
8. a loveseat   _____
9. a blanket sleeper   _____

DIRECTORY	
Children's Clothing	2
Electronics	3
Furniture	4
Household Appliances	3
Housewares	3
Jewelry Counter	1
Men's Clothing	1
Perfume Counter	1
Women's Clothing	2

B LISTENING: *Attention, Shoppers!*

Match the following announcements to the appropriate department.

☐ Perfume Counter	☐ Men's Clothing	☐ Furniture Department
1 Jewelry Counter	☐ Women's Clothing	☐ Household Appliances
☐ Housewares	☐ Children's Clothing	☐ Electronics Department

C DEPARTMENT STORE MATCH

<u>d</u> 1. "Where can I get something to eat?"
_____ 2. "Where's the Men's Department?"
_____ 3. "I need to return something I bought here."
_____ 4. "I'm very thirsty!"
_____ 5. "I need to have my purchases wrapped."
_____ 6. "Can I get upstairs with this wheelchair?"

a. There's an elevator over there.
b. Go to the Gift Wrap Counter.
c. There's a water fountain over there.
d. Go to the snack bar!
e. Go to the Customer Service Counter.
f. Look at the store directory.

D LISTENING: *Where Are They?*

Listen and decide in which departments or areas of a department store you would most likely hear the following conversations.

☐ elevator	☐ escalator	☐ Gift Wrap Counter
☐ Housewares	☐ Customer Service	☐ customer pickup area
☐ Furniture Department	1 Men's Clothing	☐ snack bar

A LIKELY OR UNLIKELY?

Put a check in the best column.

	Likely	Unlikely
1. The shoes were on sale, so Angela decided to buy them.	✓	___
2. George's new pants didn't fit, so he decided to exchange them.	___	___
3. Marie tried on the dress right after she paid for it.	___	___
4. Harry didn't need a receipt to return his purchases.	___	___
5. Mona got a lot of information about the computer before she bought it.	___	___
6. There was a big discount on CDs, so Mohammed bought three.	___	___
7. I didn't read the care instructions on my shirt, and it was ruined in the laundry.	___	___
8. The sale price on the suit was a little higher than the regular price, so I bought it.	___	___

B SHOPPING FOR CLOTHES

> buy   price tag   sale   sales tax   tried on
> pay for   regular   sale sign   size

Monica went to the department store because she needed to ___buy___ [1] some new clothes for an upcoming job interview. First, she _____ [2] a dress she really liked that fit perfectly, but it was too expensive. Then she saw a blouse that looked nice, but she couldn't find one in her _____ [3]. All of them were either too big or too small. Then, she noticed a _____ [4] that said, "All suits 25% off." Then she saw that the _____ [5] on the suit said "Additional 10% off!" The _____ [6] price was $250, and the _____ [7] price was $168.75, not including _____ [8]. She found one that fit and decided to buy it and _____ [9] it in cash. Now she's ready for her interview!

C WHAT SHOULD THEY DO?

1. A. I bought this blouse yesterday, and then I noticed it has a missing button!
   B. You should (pay for   (exchange)) it.

2. A. Look at those TVs! I wonder how expensive they are.
   B. Look at the (price tag   receipt).

3. A. This coat is beautiful. Do you think it'll fit me?
   B. You should (pay for it   try it on).

4. A. Feel this material! I wonder what it's made from.
   B. Look at the (label   size).

5. A. I don't really like this necklace I bought yesterday.
   B. You should (exchange   return) it and get your money back.

A WHAT IS IT?

battery charger	DVD player	remote control	turntable
camcorder	hand-held video game	shortwave radio	TV
clock radio	headphones	speaker	VCR

1. With this, you can control your TV from the sofa. _____remote control_____

2. This lets you watch programs such as the news and game shows. _____

3. This helps you wake up on time. _____

4. This enables you to record TV programs. _____

5. With this, you can record live events such as birthday parties. _____

6. This allows you to rent movies and watch them at home. _____

7. This recharges batteries for portable equipment. _____

8. You connect this to your stereo to hear sounds. _____

9. This allows you to play video games anywhere you go. _____

10. This plays records. _____

11. You put these over your ears to listen to music. _____

12. With this, you can listen to stations in other countries. _____

B LISTENING: *A Sale at Ace Electronics*

Listen to the commercial and fill in the correct information.

1. Suny 48" plasma TV: ___25___% off

2. Sandstone DVD player: _____% off

3. personal digital audio player: as low as $_____

4. portable CD players: _____ to _____% off

5. video games: _____% off

6. stereo systems: starting at $_____

C WHICH WORD DOESN'T BELONG?

1. DVD	LCD	(shortwave)	camcorder
2. microphone	speaker	headphone	portable TV
3. DVD	plasma	projection	LCD
4. tape deck	tuner	VCR	CD player
5. digital audio player	CD player	cassette player	stereo system

A CROSSWORD

Across

2. If there isn't enough light to take a picture, you can use a _____.

5. This lets you adapt electronic equipment to a different style of electrical outlet.

7. You need this for your 35 millimeter camera to take photographs.

8. This focuses objects in the camera.

Down

1. This tells you when someone is trying to call you.

3. This gives power to portable devices.

4. This sends copies by phone.

6. This is a stand with three legs for a camera.

9. You show slides and movies on this.

B WHICH WORD?

1. I'm old-fashioned. I prefer a ((35 millimeter) digital) camera.

2. I need to make a call. Do you have a (pager cell phone)?

3. The (battery voltage) isn't ready yet. It's still charging.

4. I'm doing my taxes this weekend. Can I borrow your (PDA calculator)?

5. I use a (camera case flash) to protect my expensive photography equipment.

6. My electronic (cordless phone personal organizer) helps me be on time for meetings.

7. My camera is full. I need a new (memory disk zoom lens) if I want to take more pictures.

8. My daughter wants to be an accountant, so I'm going to buy her an (adding answering) machine.

C LISTENING

Listen and choose the best answer.

1. a. pager
   b. zoom lens

2. a. flash attachment
   b. memory disk

3. a. camera
   b. machine

4. a. slide projector
   b. calculator

5. a. digital camera
   b. 35 millimeter camera

6. a. answering machines
   b. adapters

7. a. screen
   b. tripod

8. a. portable phone
   b. camera case

9. a. a pager
   b. an adapter

10. a. slide projector
    b. voltage regulator

A WHICH WORD DOESN'T BELONG?

1. CPU	desktop computer	(computer game)	printer
2. floppy disk	printer	disk	CD-ROM
3. cable	track ball	mouse	joystick
4. printer	monitor	keyboard	disk drive
5. word-processing	flat panel	spreadsheet	educational software

B AT THE COMPUTER STORE

CD-ROM drives	desktop	joystick	software
CD-ROMs	flat panel screens	modem	spreadsheet
computer game	floppy disk	monitor	

A. Hello. Welcome to our store.

B. Hi. I'm interested in upgrading my home _____desktop_____ ¹ computer.

A. Certainly. How can I help?

B. Well, my _____ ² takes up a lot of desk space.

A. Hmm. You should take a look at these new _____ ³. They're on sale, and they save a lot of space because they aren't very deep. What else are you trying to upgrade?

B. Well, my Internet connection is pretty slow.

A. Sounds like you might need a faster _____ ⁴. Is there anything else you're interested in?

B. Yes. Right now my computer only has a _____ ⁵ drive, so I can't run _____ ⁶.

A. You're in luck! We're having a big sale on _____ ⁷ this week. Are you also interested in any computer _____ ⁸?

B. Yes. Do you have anything that can help me with numbers—to do my taxes, for example?

A. Here's our latest _____ ⁹ program. And if you like entertainment, this _____ ¹⁰ is great, and it comes with a free _____ ¹¹ to play it with.

B. That sounds great. I'll take it!

C LISTENING

Listen and choose the best answer.

1. a. desktop computer
   b. notebook computer

2. a. monitor
   b. CPU

3. a. surge protector
   b. floppy disk

4. a. LCDs
   b. CD-ROMs

5. a. printer
   b. scanner

6. a. cable
   b. CPU

A WHICH TOY DOESN'T BELONG?

1. wagon   (kiddie pool)   tricycle   skateboard
2. crayons   markers   paint set   coloring book
3. hula hoop   puzzle   beach ball   rubber ball
4. inflatable pool   doll house   bicycle   swing set
5. stuffed animal   doll   toy truck   action figure

B BIRTHDAY PRESENTS

1. Alice likes building things, so she got a (train   (construction)) set.
2. Tommy likes small airplanes and cars, so he got a new (model   science) kit.
3. Juan is artistic and likes to make things with his hands, so he got some (clay   soap).
4. The Kim twins wanted to have a place to play outside, so they got a (doll   play) house.
5. My daughter likes to play inside, so we bought her some (jigsaw puzzles   jump ropes) and a (wagon   board game).

C A LETTER TO SANTA

Dear Santa,

    I have a big list this year because I'm writing for my brother and sister as well as myself. First of all, my dolls need a place to live. Could you give me a _____doll house_____ [1]? I would also like _____ [2] to go in it. Do you know that _____ [3]s are very popular? In case you don't know, they're plastic rings that you swing around your hips or waist. I think this would be a good present for my little sister, who always wants to play with mine. She also hates taking baths. I thought some _____ [4] instead of regular soap would make the tub more fun for her. My little brother would like a _____ [5] so that he and his friends can pretend they're police officers and talk to each other from a distance. He also likes science, so a _____ [6] might be a good idea for him. Also, we'll be spending a lot of time at the beach next summer. Could you send a _____ [7] and a _____ [8] to play with in the sand? A _____ [9] would also be a good thing to throw around the beach. I love to paint and draw, so color _____ [10], _____ [11], and a _____ [12] set would also be very nice presents. I think that's everything.

Thanks, Santa.

Love,
Carla

THE BANK

A BANKING ACTIONS

__c__ **1.** To put money into your account,

_____ **2.** When you need money from your account,

_____ **3.** When you need to borrow money,

_____ **4.** Before you can do business at a bank, you need to

_____ **5.** If you're planning to travel overseas, you should

a. you make a withdrawal.

b. open an account.

c. you make a deposit.

d. get traveler's checks.

e. you can apply for a loan.

B BANK SERVICES

| check | credit card | deposit slip | passbook | vault | withdrawal slip |

1. Use a ____withdrawal slip____ to take money from your account.

2. Use a _____ when you put money into your account.

3. You can keep valuable items locked at the bank in a _____.

4. Use a _____ to keep records of all your account transactions.

5. A _____ is made from plastic and lets you buy things that you pay for later.

6. If you want to pay someone without using cash, you can write them a _____.

C LIKELY OR UNLIKELY?

Put a check in the best column.

	Likely	Unlikely
1. I decided to apply for a loan to help pay for a new car.	✓	____
2. Jane had to show her ID to cash a check.	____	____
3. Most people keep their ATM card in a safe deposit box at the bank.	____	____
4. When I need to take money out of the bank, I fill out a withdrawal slip.	____	____
5. Manuel charged a new computer on his credit card.	____	____
6. ATMs are bank employees who help customers exchange currency.	____	____
7. Linda filled out a deposit slip and gave her deposit to the security guard.	____	____

D LISTENING: *A Bank Robbery*

Listen and decide whether the following statements are True (T) or False (F).

__F__ **1.** The robbers told the bank officer to put one thousand dollars into a bag.

_____ **2.** The teller didn't have the combination to the vault.

_____ **3.** The robbers took only the contents of the safe deposit boxes.

_____ **4.** A security guard was in the lobby and set off one of the ATM machines.

_____ **5.** The police weren't able to stop the robbery.

71

A WHICH WORD?

1. Alexandra was shocked when she looked at her ((monthly)   check) statement.
2. I love my new house, but the (car   mortgage) payments are very high.
3. After you enter your PIN, you need to (transfer   select) a transaction.
4. I didn't have any cash with me, so I wrote a (money order   check).
5. I once forgot to take my (ATM   receipt) card from the machine.
6. We always get (traveler's   credit) checks when we go abroad.
7. Susan wrote a check to pay her credit card (number   bill).
8. It's a good idea to (balance   write) your checkbook.

B SAVING MONEY

cable TV	oil
car	rent
credit card	telephone
electric	water

Peter had to pay a lot of money for his household bills last month so he's making some changes to save money. First, because his _____electric_____ [1] bill was so high, he's decided to turn off all lights and appliances he isn't using. Then, to save money on the _____ [2] bill, he's going to keep the heat a little lower than usual and wear a sweater to stay warm. Next, he's going to spend less time running the water in the shower to cut down on the _____ [3] bill. Then, he's going to minimize all his long-distance calls so he can reduce his _____ [4] bill. He's also going to cancel some television channels, which will lower his _____ [5] bill. Finally, he's going to stop buying new things he doesn't need so won't have to pay so much for his _____ [6] bill. Unfortunately, there isn't anything he can do about his _____ [7] or _____ [8] payment because those bills are the same every month. It's not easy living on a budget!

C LISTENING: *Household Bills*

Listen and decide which household bill these people are talking about.

1. a. electric bill
   b. telephone bill
2. a. water bill
   b. credit card bill
3. a. electric bill
   b. cable TV bill
4. a. car payment
   b. rent
5. a. credit card bill
   b. mortgage payment
6. a. gas bill
   b. oil bill

A WHICH WORD IS CORRECT?

1. I'd like to buy a ((sheet)   box) of stamps.
2. Please drop this (letter   worker) in the mail slot.
3. We bought some stamps at the (mail slot   stamp machine).
4. This (envelope   roll of stamps) will need some more postage.
5. You forgot to put the (book of stamps   zip code) on the envelope.
6. My Uncle Ben is a (postmark   postal clerk) at the local post office.
7. Do you want to send this (aerogramme   certified) or first class?
8. Please drop these in the mail (slot   carrier) for out-of-town mail.
9. Can you stop at the post office and pick up a (mailbox   roll of stamps)?
10. Put your package on the (scale   mail slot) to see how much it weighs.
11. The (change-of-address   passport application) form requires two small photos.
12. Oh, no! I forgot to put my (return address   postmark) on the package I just sent!
13. Excuse me, sir. Where is this package going? The (address   postage) isn't very clear.
14. I just received a certified (parcel   letter) from my brother. I hope everything is okay.
15. Howard's letter got returned to him because he forgot to put a (mail truck   stamp) on it.
16. If your package needs to get there overnight, you should send it (priority   express) mail.
17. Mindy just received a beautiful (air letter   postcard) from her niece in Colorado. It has a picture of the Rocky Mountains on it, and on the back it says, "Wish you were here!"
18. All eighteen-year-old males in the United States are required to register with the military by filling out a (selective service   passport) form.
19. I'm moving in a few weeks, so I'll need to fill out a (mailing address   change-of-address) form.

B LISTENING

Listen and choose the best answer.

1. a. mailbox
   b. mail carrier
2. a. zip code
   b. postmark
3. a. parcel
   b. parcel post
4. a. stamp machine
   b. roll of stamps

5. a. mail slot
   b. certified mail
6. a. letter
   b. money order
7. a. air letter
   b. overnight mail
8. a. mail
   b. class

A OUR TOWN LIBRARY

atlas	clerk	magazines	photocopier
author	dictionary	media	reference
card	DVDs	microfilm	shelves
CDs	encyclopedias	newspapers	tape
checkout	foreign language	online	title
children's	librarian	periodical	videotapes

We have a wonderful library in our town. Many people go there to take out books. If you want to find a book, you can look in the _____card_____ [1] catalog or the computerized _____ [2] catalog under the name of the _____ [3] or the _____ [4] of the book. You'll find information telling you where on the _____ [5] you can find the book. If you want to take the book out, you can bring it to the _____ [6] desk and a library _____ [7] will stamp the due date in your book so that you'll know when to return it.

The library isn't just a place for borrowing books. There is a very large _____ [8] section. This is the area where you can look up any information you need. If you want to find out the meaning of a word, you can look it up in a _____ [9]. If you're looking for information on any topic from A to Z, there are several _____ [10]. And if you need to locate a country, mountain range, river, or ocean, you can look in an _____ [11].

To keep up with current events both here and abroad, you can spend time in the _____ [12] section, where you can browse through daily _____ [13] and weekly and monthly _____ [14]. If you want to find an article from an old newspaper or periodical, you can look it up on the _____ [15] reader. If you want to take an article home, you can make a copy on the _____ [16].

You can also find entertainment in the library. In the _____ [17] section you'll find _____ [18] and books on _____ [19] to listen to and _____ [20] and _____ [21] to watch.

Just recently the library has added two new sections. First, the library now has a

_____ [22] section with books and materials for young readers. Second, there is a

brand new _____ [23] section with books and listening materials in several world

languages.

So the next time you're in the neighborhood, you should stop by and look around. Margaret

Chen is the reference _____ [24]. She would be happy to show you around the

library.

B LIKELY OR UNLIKELY?

Put a check in the best column.

		Likely	Unlikely
1.	People who want to take books out of the library need a library card.	✓	___
2.	If you're looking for a magazine, look in the media section.	___	___
3.	You can find encyclopedias in the reference section over there.	___	___
4.	If you want to find the meaning of a word, look it up in the atlas.	___	___
5.	All the computer software in this library is in the children's section.	___	___
6.	You'll find journals in the periodical section.	___	___
7.	If you want to know where something is, ask the person at the reference desk.	___	___
8.	You'll find all the books that the library has at the checkout desk.	___	___
9.	You can look at microfilm on the microfilm reader.	___	___
10.	Alice works as a photocopier at the local library.	___	___
11.	You'll find the title of the book and the author's name on your library card.	___	___
12.	It's a good idea to ask the online librarian if you have any questions.	___	___

C LISTENING: *What Are They Talking About?*

Listen and decide what's being talked about.

☐	atlas	☐	dictionary	☐	online catalog
☐	books on tape	☐	foreign language section	☐	periodical section
☐	checkout desk	1	library card	☐	reference librarian
☐	children's section	☐	media section	☐	reference section

A WHICH WORD DOESN'T BELONG?

1. police station   fire station   (church)   city hall
2. ambulance   emergency room   police car   fire engine
3. city manager   EMT   sanitation worker   recycling center
4. synagogue   mosque   child-care center   temple
5. police car   recreation center   hospital   game room

B LISTENING 🎧

Listen and choose the best answer.

1. a. game room
   b. gym

2. a. swimming pool
   b. dump

3. a. child-care center
   b. senior center

4. a. meeting room
   b. reycling center

5. a. EMT
   b. activities director

6. a. emergency operator
   b. emergency room

C WHICH WORD?

1. A. Help! My grandmother fell and has been hurt badly!
   B. I'll call to get (an ambulance   a senior care worker)!

2. A. Do you work at the recreation center?
   B. Yes. I'm the (activities director   sanitation worker).

3. A. Where should I take these old newspapers and paint cans?
   B. Take them to the (fire station   dump).

4. A. Would you like to go to the (nursery   swimming pool) after work today?
   B. I can't. I don't have my bathing suit with me.

5. A. Did you hear about the big fire at the church last night?
   B. Yes. At least three (fire engines   paramedics) rushed there to help put out the fire.

6. A. Are the election results in?
   B. Yes. Gary Matsumoto has been chosen to be our new (city hall   mayor).

7. A. I looked in the nursery, but I didn't see the child-care worker.
   B. She's here at the child-care center, but I think she's in the (playroom   emergency room).

8. A. What do you want to be when you grow up, Johnny?
   B. I want to be an (emergency operator   eldercare worker). I want to tell police cars where to go.

A THE EVENING NEWS

assault	burglary	chemical spill	gang violence	vandalism
blackout	car accidents	downed power lines	train derailment	water main break

Good evening. The top story of the evening is the citywide ___blackout___ [1] that left thousands without power for over twelve hours last night and today. Police report that there were also a number of crimes that occurred that may have been related.

A large number of teens were seen fighting in what police are calling the worst _____ [2] in over ten years. Many teens were also involved in numerous acts of _____ [3], damaging dozens of cars and buildings. Many citizens called the police to report _____ [4]s, and several people were hospitalized as a result.

Incidents of _____ [5] were also very high, with citizens all over the city reporting stolen items. Also related to the power outage, there were a large number of _____ [6] because drivers were unable to see the traffic signals. In one case, a truck carrying deadly liquid overturned and created a _____ [7] that forced residents to evacuate.

Finally, the electrical problems led to a _____ [8] when the A-line subway ran off the track. The situation was further complicated because the accident caused a _____ [9] and the entire downtown area was flooded for hours.

Police are urging everyone to stay at home because there are still a number of electrical problems around town such as _____ [10].

B LISTENING: *Help!*

Listen and choose the best answer.

1. a. fire
   b. explosion

2. a. kidnapping
   b. lost child

3. a. fire
   b. downed power lines

4. a. assault
   b. murder

5. a. burglary
   b. car jacking

6. a. vandalism
   b. mugging

C ANALOGIES

1. money : robbery *as* people : _____kidnapping_____
2. drugs : drug dealing *as* alcohol : _____
3. gas : gas leak *as* electricity : _____
4. at the bank : bank robbery *as* on the street : _____
5. things : vandalism *as* people : _____

assault
blackout
drunk driving
kidnapping
mugging

A WHICH WORD DOESN'T BELONG?

1. cornea   iris   (nerve)   pupil
2. gallbladder   nose   large intestine liver
3. chin   shin   thigh   leg
4. heel   toe   knuckle   ankle
5. palm   heel   finger   thumb
6. veins   lungs   pancreas   kidneys
7. lip   hip   gums   tooth

B WHICH WORD?

1. A. Does your whole arm hurt?
   B. No, just my ((elbow)   calf).

2. A. What happened to you?
   B. I sprained my (iris   neck).

3. A. Which part of your leg did you injure?
   B. My (shin   chin).

4. A. How does your hand feel?
   B. I'm having trouble moving my (toes   fingers).

5. A. My (leg   nose) is running!
   B. Here's a handkerchief.

6. A. Did you hurt your whole foot?
   B. No. Just my (ankle   palm).

7. A. Did the doctor check your eye?
   B. Yes. She thinks my (cornea   knuckle) is damaged.

8. A. Has your diet been successful?
   B. Yes. I've already taken two inches off my (wrist   waist).

9. A. My son broke his (thigh   jaw).
   B. That's a shame! He won't be able to eat for several weeks.

10. A. What does the chest X-ray show?
    B. It shows that you fractured your (ribcage   knee).

11. A. Please turn and face me so I can examine your (back   abdomen).
    B. Okay.

12. A. How did your husband break his (gums   shoulder)?
    B. He was playing volleyball.

13. A. Mrs. Miller, I'm going to have to remove your (gallbladder   bones).
    B. I just hope I feel better after the operation, Doctor.

14. A. Mr. Bell, I think you're going to need open (heart   head) surgery.
    B. Oh, no!

C WHAT'S THE ACTION?

Match the action with the correct part of the body.

a. arm	e. eyelid	i. knees	m. nose
b. brain	f. finger	j. legs	n. stomach
c. ears	g. fingernail	k. lips	o. throat
d. eyes	h. hair	l. lungs	p. teeth

__m__ **1.** smell

_____ **2.** see

_____ **3.** breathe

_____ **4.** bend

_____ **5.** think

_____ **6.** digest

_____ **7.** comb

_____ **8.** run

_____ **9.** hear

_____ **10.** swallow

_____ **11.** scratch

_____ **12.** point

_____ **13.** chew

_____ **14.** kiss

_____ **15.** throw

_____ **16.** blink

D GUESS THE WORD!

See if you can guess which parts of the body are used in the following expressions. Some words may be used more than once.

back	cheek	chin	face	heart	neck	shoulder	stomach	tongue
bone	chest	elbow	foot	leg	nose	skin	thumb	

1. The race was close. They ran "_____neck_____ and _____neck_____."

2. Be brave and "keep your _____ up"!

3. Don't say anything. Just "hold your _____"!

4. Stop bothering me! Just "get off my _____"!

5. Try hard and "put your best _____ forward"!

6. He "_____ed his way" into the crowd.

7. Aunt Martha is generous. She "has a big _____."

8. They danced together "_____ to _____."

9. Let's discuss this in person, "_____ to _____."

10. Another way of saying "hitchhike" is to "_____ a ride."

11. The president has to "_____ a lot of responsibilities."

12. I think I'll "_____ around" to find out what's happening.

13. My son has gotten so thin he's just "_____ and _____s"!

14. You'll feel better if you "get that off your _____" and talk about it.

15. I'm so upset with Beth's behavior. I don't think I can "_____ it" much longer.

16. In the theater, it is considered good luck before a performance to tell an actor or actress to "break a _____."

A WHAT'S THE DIAGNOSIS?

1. I'm concerned. It's over 102 degrees!

   a. She's bloated.
   b. She has a fever.

2. Ouch!! That bee just stung me!

   a. He has a wart.
   b. He has an insect bite.

3. I'm having trouble swallowing!

   a. You must have a bad sore throat.
   b. That's because you're itchy.

4. Ooh! I have a terrible toothache!

   a. You probably have a cavity.
   b. You probably have cramps.

5. My doctor says I shouldn't lift anything.

   a. She has a cough.
   b. She has a backache.

6. I hear a ringing sound!

   a. He has an earache.
   b. He has a sore throat.

7. Achoo! Quick! Hand me a tissue!

   a. She has a runny nose.
   b. She has a stiff neck.

8. It's all over my body!

   a. He has a cold.
   b. He has a rash.

9. I can't breathe at all!

   a. No wonder! You're exhausted.
   b. No wonder! You're congested.

10. Oh! My back! I was at the beach all day!

   a. He has a sunburn.
   b. He has a backache.

11. My head is spinning!

   a. She's swollen.
   b. She feels faint.

12. Quick! I need a Band-Aid™!

   a. He cut himself, and he's bleeding.
   b. He's itchy, and he's sneezing.

13. I'm having trouble talking.

   a. He has diarrhea.
   b. He has laryngitis.

14. My dentist is very concerned.

   a. She has the hiccups.
   b. She has a toothache.

B ABSOLUTELY MISERABLE!

I feel terrible! I was congested (hurt) [1] in a car accident the other day. Here's what happened.

I twisted my knuckle ankle [2], sprained my throat wrist [3], and dislocated my eyelid knee [4]. Also, I scraped my cornea nerves [5] and bruised my right hip waist [6]. On top of that, this morning I woke up with a bad case of the warts chills [7]. My feet have sunburn blisters [8] from walking home, my head is exhausted congested [9], my stomach is bloated dizzy [10], and I have a stiff lip neck [11]. I feel absolutely miserable! I hope I get better soon.

C LISTENING: What's the Problem?

Listen and choose the best answer.

1. a. He has a stomachache.
   b. He has a blister.

2. a. She's bloated.
   b. She's itchy.

3. a. He had shortness of breath.
   b. He got a temperature.

4. a. She developed a wart.
   b. She sprained her ankle.

5. a. He has a rash.
   b. He has a cavity.

6. a. She has a stiff neck.
   b. She feels nauseous.

7. a. He has a sunburn.
   b. He has laryngitis.

8. a. She just sneezed.
   b. She just burped.

D OH, MY ACHING BACK!

See if you can figure out how we describe the following ailments.

aching	hacking	high	itchy	pounding	scratchy	upset

1. I don't know what to do for my _____upset_____ stomach!

2. I'm miserable with this _____ cough!

3. I can't stand this _____ rash!

4. I have a _____ headache!

5. I've got a _____ fever!

6. I have a _____ throat!

7. Oh, my _____ back!

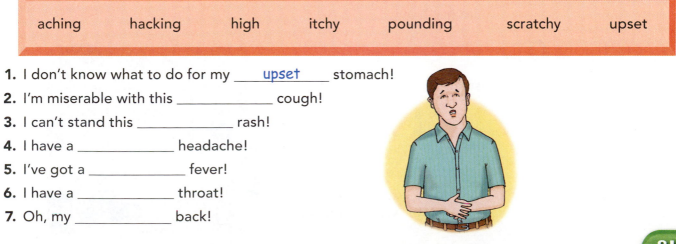

A GOOD IDEA OR BAD IDEA?

Decide whether the following first-aid treatments would be appropriate.

		Good Idea	Bad Idea
1.	When you have a sore throat, you should use antiseptic cleansing wipes.	____	✓
2.	If you have a headache, you should take some aspirin.	____	____
3.	I keep a first-aid kit in my bathroom.	____	____
4.	My friend was bloated, so I did the Heimlich maneuver.	____	____
5.	When my friend's heart stopped beating, I immediately did CPR.	____	____
6.	My throat was sore, so I used some antibiotic ointment.	____	____
7.	When someone has shortness of breath, you should do rescue breathing.	____	____
8.	When you scrape your arm, you should use a sterile dressing pad.	____	____
9.	When someone's arm is bleeding, you should put on a splint.	____	____
10.	If someone has no pulse, you should put an Ace™ bandage on the person's wrist.	____	____

B A DAY AT THE BEACH

I'm one of the lifeguards at the local beach. Today was a very busy day! In the morning, we had to pull a man out of the water. He wasn't breathing and I couldn't feel a pulse, so I had to do CPR   the Heimlich [1]. Then, a young boy cut his knee on a piece of glass. There was a lot of blood, so we had to make a   splint   tourniquet [2] right away. After that, a woman got stung by a bee. Luckily our first-aid   kit   manual [3] had some   antibiotic   antihistamine [4] cream in it. And just when we thought the day was over, a young girl got a tiny splinter of wood stuck in her finger. We had to use some   gauze   tweezers [5] to get it out.

C LISTENING

Listen and choose the best answer.

1. a. CPR
   b. the Heimlich maneuver

2. a. hydrogen peroxide
   b. Band-Aid™

3. a. aspirin
   b. tweezers

4. a. a tourniquet
   b. a splint

5. a. CPR
   b. rescue breathing

6. a. an Ace™ bandage
   b. some ointment

A ASK A DOCTOR!

1. A. Our son has shortness of breath frequently. What could it be?
   B. He may have _____ asthma _____.

2. A. Doctor, I've had a runny nose and fever for several days.
   B. It sounds like a case of _____.

3. A. Can you do something to help my earache?
   B. Hmm. You may have an _____.

4. A. My daughter has itchy red spots all over her body.
   B. She probably has _____.

5. A. I'm having trouble talking. I have laryngitis.
   B. Let's see. It looks like you have _____.

6. A. Nothing is wrong with me physically, Doctor, but I feel sad all the time.
   B. It sounds like you're _____.

7. A. Our son ate something and now he's having trouble breathing!
   B. He's having an _____. He needs immediate attention!

8. A. Doctor, I'm feeling strong chest pains!
   B. Get to the emergency room! You might be having a _____.

B HOW DID IT HAPPEN?

electric shock	frostbite	injured	shock
fell	heatstroke	overdosed on drugs	unconscious

1. I ____injured____ my back while I was moving some heavy furniture.
2. Louis got lost hiking in the mountains and he got _____ on his fingers and toes.
3. My grandfather was trying to climb a ladder to the roof but he _____ and broke his leg.
4. My sister was hurt in a car accident and was in _____.
5. When I fell, I hit my head on the table and became _____.
6. Uncle Stan fell asleep in the sun at the beach and had to go to the hospital for _____.
7. The lamp must be broken because I got an _____ when I turned it on.
8. Henry had been depressed for months before he _____ and was rushed to the emergency room.

C WHICH WORD DOESN'T BELONG?

1. measles   (poison)   mumps   chicken pox
2. electric shock   hurt   injured   unconscious
3. AIDS   TB   diabetes   heatstroke
4. heart disease   heart attack   hypertension   depression

A MY MEDICAL EXAM

| blood pressure | health | stethoscope |
| eye chart | height | weight |

I went to my doctor today for my yearly medical exam. First he asked me to step on the scale so he could measure my _____height_____ 1 and _____ 2. Then he checked my _____ 3 and told me it was a little higher than it should be. Then he asked me to read the _____ 4. I couldn't read it as well as before, so it looks like I'll need glasses. The last thing he checked was my heart with his _____ 5. When that was done, he asked me some questions about my _____ 6 and told me I needed to get some exercise. I'm certainly not getting any younger!

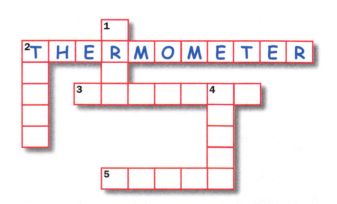

B LIKELY OR UNLIKELY?

	Likely	Unlikely
1. The doctor checked my pulse with a thermometer.	_____	✓
2. The doctor drew blood with a blood pressure gauge.	_____	_____
3. The doctor listened to my heart with a stethoscope.	_____	_____
4. The doctor took a chest X-ray of my eyes, ears, nose, and throat.	_____	_____
5. I waited in the examination room for almost 20 minutes.	_____	_____
6. The blood pressure gauge was broken, so the doctor just used a syringe.	_____	_____
7. I couldn't read the eye chart, so the doctor took my temperature.	_____	_____

C CROSSWORD

Across

2. Doctors take your temperature with this.
3. Doctors give medicine or take blood with this.
5. You step on this to measure your weight.

Down

1. A doctor uses this to look inside you.
2. You sit or lie on this when the doctor examines you.
4. Doctors check your blood pressure with this.

A WHICH WORD?

1. Andrew had to get a ((shot)   stitch) of antibiotics.
2. Let me use some (cotton balls   tape) to clean that cut.
3. You need to (dress   clean) the wound before you close it.
4. The doctor gave me (stitches   alcohol) to close my wound.
5. The doctor set my broken arm and put it in a (glove   cast).
6. I had to wear a leg (crutch   brace) when I broke my ankle.
7. This (ice pack   prescription) should help reduce the swelling in your ankle.
8. Janice filled out her (examination   medical history) form in the waiting room.
9. The dentist gave me a shot of (anesthetic   filling) before drilling my cavity.

B WHAT DID THE DOCTOR DO?

alcohol	crutches	examined	ice pack
cast	drilled	filled	medical history
cleaned	examination	gauze	tape

1. A. What did the doctor do for the bump on your head?
   B. He gave me an ___ice pack___.

2. A. What did the doctor do for your broken leg?
   B. She put it in a _____ and gave me some _____.

3. A. What did the dental hygienist do during your appointment?
   B. He _____ my teeth and then he _____ them.

4. A. What did the dentist do for your cavity?
   B. She _____ the cavity and then _____ the tooth.

5. A. What did the doctor do for the cut on your arm?
   B. He cleaned it with _____ and dressed it with _____ and _____.

6. A. What did the doctor do before your appointment?
   B. She looked at my _____ form and asked me to wait in the
   _____ room.

C LISTENING

Listen and choose the best answer.

1. (a.) Novocaine™
   b. injection

2. a. cotton balls
   b. gauze

3. a. waiting room
   b. receptionist

4. a. a prescription
   b. alcohol

5. a. a patient
   b. a hygienist

6. a. masks and gloves
   b. gauze and tape

A GOOD ADVICE OR BAD ADVICE?

Decide whether or not the following treatments would be appropriate.

	Good Advice	Bad Advice
1. Rest in bed for a few days, drink fluids, and your cold will be better soon.	✓	___
2. After Sandra stepped on a rusty nail, her doctor told her to take vitamins.	___	___
3. The doctor told Jim to exercise and go on a diet because he was overweight.	___	___
4. I was feeling tired and depressed, so my doctor recommended counseling.	___	___
5. I recommend surgery to take care of your virus.	___	___
6. If other treatments aren't working, you should try acupuncture.	___	___
7. I'll do some blood tests with this thermometer.	___	___
8. Are you still having problems with your arm? You should see a specialist.	___	___
9. Gargling is good if you're in a cast.	___	___
10. This is a bad cut. I think you need a walker.	___	___
11. When Gregory broke his leg, the doctor told him he needed braces.	___	___
12. I recommend physical therapy. That should help the psychological problems you're having.	___	___

B ASSOCIATIONS

_c_ 1. gargle		**a.** teeth
___ 2. humidifier		**b.** back
___ 3. heating pad		**c.** throat
___ 4. drinking fluids		**d.** weight
___ 5. diet		**e.** water
___ 6. braces		**f.** tests
___ 7. cane		**g.** moisture
___ 8. blood work		**h.** legs

C GIVING ADVICE

1. A. I've been having trouble breathing at night.
   B. I recommend (a cane   (an air purifier)).

2. A. I don't feel as energetic as I used to.
   B. You should probably start to (gargle   take vitamins).

3. A. My grandmother fell and broke her hip.
   B. That's too bad. Did she need to (have surgery   drink fluids)?

4. A. I've been lifting and carrying a lot of heavy boxes. My back is killing me!
   B. Get some rest and use (vitamins   a heating pad).

5. A. I've been gaining weight recently.
   B. Have you thought about (getting acupuncture   going on a diet)?

A AILMENTS AND REMEDIES

You're a doctor working in a busy health clinic. Today you're seeing a lot of patients. What will you suggest for the following ailments? More than one kind of medicine may be appropriate.

The Problem

Your Advice

1. a hacking cough   cough syrup, cough drops
2. dry skin
3. itchy eyes
4. a pounding headache
5. a scratchy throat
6. a stuffy nose
7. a burn
8. blood that's low in iron
9. an upset stomach
10. an aching back
11. a miserable cold
12. laryngitis

B INTERNAL OR EXTERNAL?

Decide how the following are taken—internally (I) or externally (E)?

____I____ 1. vitamins   _____ 4. cough syrup   _____ 7. throat lozenges

_____ 2. lotion   _____ 5. ointment   _____ 8. aspirin

_____ 3. cold tablets   _____ 6. nasal spray   _____ 9. antacid tablets

C TAKE OR USE?

1. Go home, get some rest, and (take   use) two non-aspirin pain relievers.
2. Harry ate too much for dessert and had to (take   use) antacid tablets.
3. For dry, itchy skin, I always (take   use) a moisturizing lotion.
4. Ahmed's doctor told him to (take   use) eye drops twice a day.
5. You need to (take   use) a decongestant spray.
6. To stay healthy, I (take   use) vitamins every day.

A WHICH SPECIALIST?

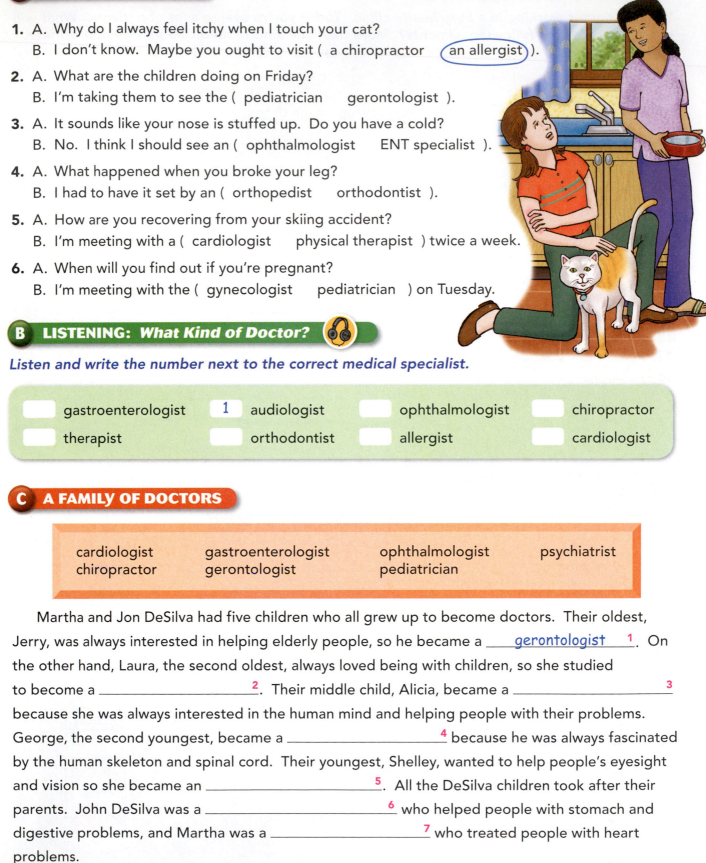

1. A. Why do I always feel itchy when I touch your cat?
   B. I don't know. Maybe you ought to visit (a chiropractor (an allergist)).

2. A. What are the children doing on Friday?
   B. I'm taking them to see the (pediatrician   gerontologist).

3. A. It sounds like your nose is stuffed up. Do you have a cold?
   B. No. I think I should see an (ophthalmologist   ENT specialist).

4. A. What happened when you broke your leg?
   B. I had to have it set by an (orthopedist   orthodontist).

5. A. How are you recovering from your skiing accident?
   B. I'm meeting with a (cardiologist   physical therapist) twice a week.

6. A. When will you find out if you're pregnant?
   B. I'm meeting with the (gynecologist   pediatrician) on Tuesday.

B LISTENING: *What Kind of Doctor?*

Listen and write the number next to the correct medical specialist.

	gastroenterologist	**1**	audiologist		ophthalmologist		chiropractor
	therapist		orthodontist		allergist		cardiologist

C A FAMILY OF DOCTORS

cardiologist	gastroenterologist	ophthalmologist	psychiatrist
chiropractor	gerontologist	pediatrician	

    Martha and Jon DeSilva had five children who all grew up to become doctors. Their oldest, Jerry, was always interested in helping elderly people, so he became a _____gerontologist_____ [1]. On the other hand, Laura, the second oldest, always loved being with children, so she studied to become a _____ [2]. Their middle child, Alicia, became a _____ [3] because she was always interested in the human mind and helping people with their problems. George, the second youngest, became a _____ [4] because he was always fascinated by the human skeleton and spinal cord. Their youngest, Shelley, wanted to help people's eyesight and vision so she became an _____ [5]. All the DeSilva children took after their parents. John DeSilva was a _____ [6] who helped people with stomach and digestive problems, and Martha was a _____ [7] who treated people with heart problems.

A WHICH WORD?

1. Mrs. Garcia, I need to put this (medical chart   (I.V.)) in your arm.
2. Use the bed (pan   control) to adjust the height of the bed.
3. Here, Mr. Chen. Please put on this (hospital gown   gurney).
4. If you press the (bed   call) button, a nurse or orderly will come.
5. The (dietitian   volunteer) has recommended that you eat more solid foods.
6. You can sit in the (waiting   operating) room while your wife is having surgery.
7. Your (vital signs   emergency) monitor indicates that your heart rate is normal.
8. The (X-ray   lab) technician will have the results of the blood test later this afternoon.

B LISTENING: *Where in the Hospital Are They?*

Listen and decide where these people are in the hospital.

	the operating room		the waiting room		a patient's room		the delivery room
	the nurse's station		the ER		the lab	1	the radiology department

C WHO ARE THEY?

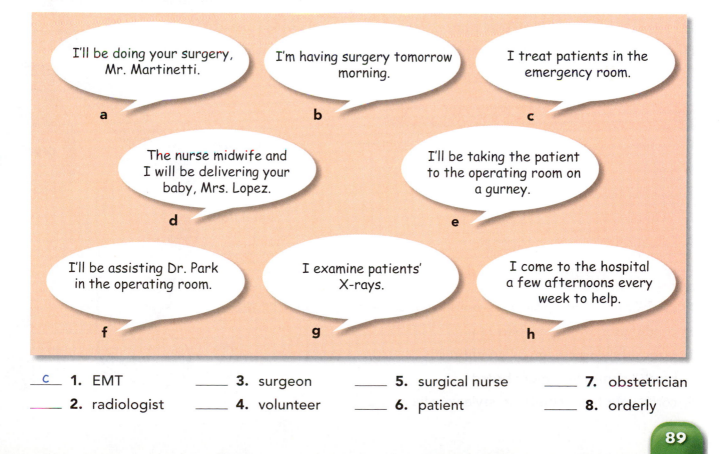

a. I'll be doing your surgery, Mr. Martinetti.

b. I'm having surgery tomorrow morning.

c. I treat patients in the emergency room.

d. The nurse midwife and I will be delivering your baby, Mrs. Lopez.

e. I'll be taking the patient to the operating room on a gurney.

f. I'll be assisting Dr. Park in the operating room.

g. I examine patients' X-rays.

h. I come to the hospital a few afternoons every week to help.

_c_ 1. EMT
____ 2. radiologist
____ 3. surgeon
____ 4. volunteer
____ 5. surgical nurse
____ 6. patient
____ 7. obstetrician
____ 8. orderly

89

A WHAT'S USED WHERE?

Match the following items with a part of the body. There may be more than one possible answer.

a. aftershave	e. bobby pins	i. emery board	m. moisturizer
b. barrettes	f. conditioner	j. eye shadow	n. nail polish
c. blow dryer	g. dental floss	k. lipstick	o. shampoo
d. blush	h. deodorant	l. mascara	p. sunscreen

___g___ 1. teeth   _____ 3. lips   _____ 5. fingernails   _____ 7. eyelashes

_____ 2. eyelids   _____ 4. hair   _____ 6. underarms   _____ 8. skin

B WHICH WORD?

1. What kind of mouthwash do you ((gargle)   brush) with?
2. Do you have any hair (gel   polish)? I'm trying to style my hair.
3. Ever since Brian grew a beard, he hasn't bought any (razors   cologne).
4. After her shower, Diane likes to put on some (body   aftershave) lotion.
5. Johnny, where's the toothpaste? It's time to (floss   brush) your teeth.
6. This razor isn't working very well. I think the (shaver   blade) is dull.
7. You should take the shoelaces out before you (polish   put on) your shoes.
8. Do you have a nail (brush   clipper) that I can use to cut the baby's fingernails?
9. This color is too bright. I need to take it off with nail (polish   polish remover).
10. Nancy wants her blond eyelashes to look darker, so she uses (mascara   makeup).
11. Your teeth look very bright! What have you been using to (wash   whiten) them?

C WHICH WORD DOESN'T BELONG?

1. lipstick	mascara	eyeliner	(bubble bath)
2. nail file	nail clipper	soap	scissors
3. electric shaver	aftershave	razor	blades
4. toothbrush	deodorant	mouthwash	dental floss
5. conditioner	foundation	brush	comb

D ANALOGIES

1. do your nails : nail polish as polish your shoes : _____shoe polish_____
2. conditioner : rinse as perfume : _____
3. razor : shaving cream as toothbrush : _____
4. brush : comb as emery board : _____
5. comb your hair : comb as style your hair : _____

A WHICH WORD?

1. A ((bib)   cubby) is important at mealtime.

2. Attach these cloth diapers with diaper (wipes   pins).

3. When a baby wants to suck, a (bib   pacifier) can help.

4. If your baby has a rash, use a little baby (powder   wipe).

5. Since I'm not nursing, my baby drinks (baby lotion   formula).

6. I feel that (cloth diapers   training pants) are better for the environment.

7. Remember to clean your infant's ears carefully with (cotton swabs   baby shampoo).

8. Some doctors recommend supplementing a baby's diet with (ointment   vitamins).

B OUR NEW BABY

baby shampoo	child-care center	feed	pacifier	rocking
bathe	cotton swabs	hold	play with	
change	disposable	nipple	rock	

My wife and I have a six-month-old baby girl. She's really cute, but it hasn't been easy taking care of her. For example, we have to _____change_____ 1 her diaper several times every day. And although we would like to be more environmentally conscious, we use _____ 2 diapers because we're so busy. And it's not easy to _____ 3 the baby either. She's very fussy about what she eats, and sometimes won't suck on the _____ 4 on the bottle. She seems the happiest when we _____ 5 her in the _____ 6 chair. It's a lot of work to _____ 7 the baby also. Of course we only use _____ 8 so that she won't cry if it gets in her eyes, but she doesn't like her ears to be cleaned with _____ 9.

It's difficult to leave our baby at the _____ 10 too because she doesn't like anyone else to _____ 11 her yet. She likes to _____ 12 her toys, but if she cries, then they give her a _____ 13 to suck on. It sure is a lot of work having a baby!

C LISTENING: *What Are They Talking About?*

Listen and decide which baby item these people are talking about.

1. a. disposable diapers
   b. cloth diapers

2. a. teething ring
   b. bib

3. a. baby shampoo
   b. toy

4. a. vitamins
   b. baby wipes

5. a. cotton swab
   b. diaper pins

6. a. baby food
   b. ointment

A CAREER GUIDANCE

1. Christine is in college now and hopes to eventually become a lawyer.

    She should go to _____law_____ school.

2. Jake is in high school. He'd like to become an electrician like his father.

    He should go to a _____ school.

3. Angela graduated from college with a degree in biology, and now she'd like to be a doctor.

    She should apply to _____ school.

4. Michael already has a full-time job, but he'd like to take Spanish classes.

    He should attend an _____ school.

5. Pamela needs a Master's degree so she can get a better position in her company.

    She should go to _____ school.

B ANALOGIES

1. lawyer : law school *as* doctor : _____medical school_____

2. three-year-old : preschool *as* twelve-year-old : _____

3. four years : college *as* two years : _____

4. adults : adult school *as* teenagers : _____

5. economics : university *as* automotive technology : _____

C AN "EDUCATED" FAMILY

community college	Elementary	graduate	high
Middle	nursery school	University	vocational

   Helen Jenkins has three children—May, Alex, and Marcus, and four grandchildren—Brandon, Alicia, Jenny, and Emily. Every one of them is studying in a different kind of school!

   Emily is four years old. She goes to __nursery school__ [1] every morning. Her older sister Jenny is eight. She's in second grade at Carter _____ [2] School. Alicia is the next oldest. She's in the eighth grade at Midtown _____ [3] School. And her older brother Brandon will be graduating from _____ [4] school next June and going to City _____ [5] to study psychology.

   Marcus Jenkins is the youngest of the Jenkins children. He's finishing _____ [6] school in order to work at his father's company, Jenkins Plumbing. Alex, on the other hand, is just starting at a new school. He's not sure what he wants to study, but he'll study for two years at the local _____ [7] and then transfer to a four-year college. And May Jenkins has been going to school the longest of everyone in the family. She's going to _____ [8] school to get her Ph.D. in physics. She's planning to become a professor.

THE SCHOOL

A WHICH WORD?

1. The best place at school to study and do homework is the (gymnasium (library)).
2. Most of our school's (offices lockers) are located in the hallway.
3. If you want to try out for the football team, you should speak with the (coach librarian).
4. The principal wants to see you in her (office hallway).
5. Maria doesn't feel well. She should go to the (guidance nurse's) office.
6. All the students gathered in the school (locker auditorium) for an assembly.
7. Careful! The floor is wet and slippery. We should call the (custodian clerk).
8. The members of the school's cross-country team run five miles around the (hallway track) every day.
9. The school (security lunchroom) officer makes sure everyone in the building is safe.
10. Our (P.E. science) teacher gives us a lot of homework every night.
11. Amanda is having trouble deciding what career she would like to go into. She should meet with the (cafeteria worker guidance counselor).
12. The principal is away at a conference. While she's away, the (clerk vice-principal) is in charge of the school.
13. The members of the football team get dressed in the (locker room lunchroom) and then go to the (cafeteria field) to warm up and practice.

B ASSOCIATIONS

_f_ 1. P.E. teacher
____ 2. lunchroom monitor
____ 3. teacher
____ 4. school nurse
____ 5. security officer
____ 6. librarian
____ 7. custodian
____ 8. science teacher

a. classroom
b. books
c. safety
d. cleaning
e. cafeteria
f. gym
g. science lab
h. sickness

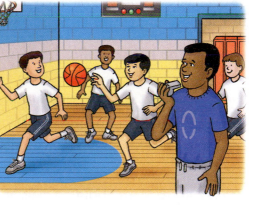

C LISTENING: Who's Talking?

Listen and decide who is talking.

1. a. custodian
   b. principal
2. a. librarian
   b. coach
3. a. principal
   b. vice-principal
4. a. school nurse
   b. cafeteria worker
5. a. teacher
   b. lunchroom monitor
6. a. guidance counselor
   b. coach

A WHICH COURSE?

Decide in which course you might hear the following.

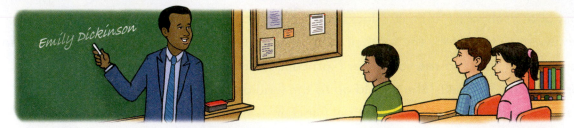

__d__	**1.** We're going to study Emily Dickinson's poetry next week.	**a.** history
_____	**2.** Where exactly is the Nile River located?	**b.** Spanish
_____	**3.** Subtract your costs from earnings to get your profit.	**c.** geography
_____	**4.** Today we're going to talk about the ancient Mayan Empire.	**d.** English
_____	**5.** We're going to study how plants and flowers reproduce.	**e.** health
_____	**6.** You're going to learn all the rules of the road.	**f.** French
_____	**7.** Let's talk about the importance of a balanced diet.	**g.** physics
_____	**8.** ¡Hola! ¿Cómo está usted?	**h.** government
_____	**9.** We're having a test tomorrow on atoms, neutrons, and protons.	**i.** driver's ed
_____	**10.** Let's write a program that will count all even digits under 99.	**j.** biology
_____	**11.** Bonjour. Comment allez-vous?	**k.** computer science
_____	**12.** In the US, there are three branches: executive, legislative, and judicial.	**l.** business education

B LIKELY OR UNLIKELY?

Put a check in the best column.

	Likely	Unlikely
1. We learn all about cooking and nutritious eating in our industrial arts class.	_____	✓
2. We draw and paint in our music class.	_____	_____
3. We learn the rules of the road in our driver's ed class.	_____	_____
4. We use graph paper and calculators in math class.	_____	_____
5. There is a lot to learn about animals and plants in chemistry class.	_____	_____
6. We learn about famous composers from around the world in music class.	_____	_____

C LISTENING: *Which Subject?*

Listen and choose the best answer.

1. a. math
   b. home economics

2. a. history
   b. geography

3. a. art
   b. music

4. a. home economics
   b. science

5. a. biology
   b. physics

6. a. P.E.
   b. health

A THEY CAN'T DECIDE

AV crew	cheerleading	chorus	drama	government	newspaper
band	chess	debate	football	literary magazine	orchestra

A. Have you decided what after-school activity you'd like to do?

B. Not yet. I can't decide what I'd like to do the most. Do you have any suggestions?

A. Well, if you like sports, then maybe you should try out for _____football_____ 1.

B. I don't think I'd like to do that. I'd prefer something that requires more thinking.

A. Then how about the _____ 2 club?

B. Well, I don't want to just play games. And I'd like to interact with more people.

A. Have you considered the _____ 3 club then?

B. I thought about that, but I get nervous giving speeches and talking in front of groups. Maybe I'd enjoy something with music.

A. Okay. How about the _____ 4?

B. Hmm. I don't really want to wear a uniform. Also, I would have to attend all the sports events.

A. Then how about the _____ 5?

B. No. I don't think so. You know how bad my voice is!

A. Then you should think about joining the _____ 6.

B. That might be the best suggestion. I've always wanted to learn to play the cello.

A. Great! Now you can help ME find something.

B. Okay. Do you have a lot of school spirit?

A. Of course!

B. Then why don't you do _____ 7?

A. I don't have energy to do that!

B. Okay. What about student _____ 8?

A. That's a good idea. But I don't think I would ever get elected.

B. Then how about the _____ 9 club?

A. I like that idea, but I get stage fright! I don't like performing in front of people.

B. You could do the _____ 10. They work on stage but only to set up for the plays and shows.

A. Hmm. That doesn't really appeal to me. I think what I really enjoy is writing.

B. Well, then. You should write for the school _____ 11.

A. I think I'd rather write fiction, like stories and poetry.

B. Then you should join the _____ 12.

A. That sounds great. Thanks for the suggestion.

A ARITHMETIC PROBLEMS

1. Six plus nine equals fifteen.
2. Forty-one minus eleven equals thirty.
3. Fourteen times five equals seventy.
4. Two hundred divided by four equals fifty.
5. Nine times seven equals sixty-three.
6. Ninety-nine minus nineteen equals eighty.
7. Eleven divided by eleven equals one.
8. Fifteen plus thirty-seven equals fifty-two.

6 + 9 = 15

B LISTENING: *Fractions*

Listen and decide whether the following statements are True (T) or False (F).

__T__ 1. The tank is less than 50% full.

_____ 2. The milk container is 2/3 full.

_____ 3. He only got 1/3 of the answers right on the test.

_____ 4. More students in their school are left-handed than right-handed.

_____ 5. She needs to read 25% of the book in order to complete it.

C PERCENTS

Barbara loves bargains! That's why she was so excited about the big sale at Big Buy Electronics Store last weekend. How much did she spend on the following items?

1. $90 clock radio—50% off   __$45__
2. $150 CD player—40% off   _____
3. $20 DVD—10% off   _____
4. $1600 plasma TV—25% off   _____
5. $20 CD—30% off   _____
6. $250 stereo system—40% off   _____
7. $290 set of speakers—half price   _____
8. $50 headphones—70% off   _____

D TYPES OF MATH

Can you figure out the correct type of math?

algebra	calculus	geometry	trigonometry	statistics

1. You have to master arithmetic before you can study _____algebra_____.
2. Rich is good at analyzing shapes and angles. He likes _____.
3. Janice likes to calculate percentages and probabilities. She likes _____.
4. _____ deals with sine, cosine, and tangent.
5. If you are integrating or differentiating, then you're using _____.

A SOLID SHAPES

| cone | cube | cylinder | pyramid | sphere |

1. The sides of a _____ pyramid _____ are triangles.
2. The two ends of a _____ are circles.
3. Each side of a _____ is a square.
4. The base of a _____ is a circle.
5. A _____ doesn't have a base or a side.

B WHAT'S THE WORD?

1. An inch equals 2.54 _____ centimeters _____.
2. Three feet is the same as a _____.
3. A line that isn't straight is _____.
4. A mile is equal to 1.6 _____.
5. There are twelve _____ in a foot.
6. The top part of a triangle is its _____.
7. The area of a _____ is its length times its width.
8. Two sides are of equal length in an _____ triangle.
9. The longest side of a right triangle is called its _____.
10. The orbit followed by the planets is shaped like an _____.
11. The distance around the outside of a circle is called the _____.
12. Two lines that intersect to form a right angle are called _____.
13. The _____ between the earth and the sun is 93 million _____.
14. Two lines that are always the same distance from each other are called _____.

C ANALOGIES

1. right angle : right triangle *as* obtuse angle : _____ isosceles triangle _____
2. square : straight line *as* circle : _____
3. square : rectangle *as* circle : _____
4. meter : kilometer *as* foot : _____
5. circle : sphere *as* square : _____
6. long : length *as* wide : _____
7. high : height *as* deep : _____

A A TEACHER'S COMMENTS

Marco's teacher, Mrs. Wong, sent him a note with comments on a history paper he turned in.

Marco,

Here is some (feedback) revision ¹ on the final first ² draft of your paper on the history of your family. The revised draft ³ paper isn't due until next week, but it looks like you have a number of marks corrections ⁴ to make.

First of all, I think you should spend some more time organizing writing ⁵ your ideas because they were a little confusing in some places. For example, in the second article paragraph ⁶, I'm not sure what the sequence of events is.

Second, it seems like you had some trouble with punctuation. For example, you forgot to put colons periods ⁷ at the ends of some of your sentences. And you also forgot to put quotation question ⁸ marks at the end of all of your interrogative imperative ⁹ sentences. It seems that you were also a little confused about whether or not to use semi-colons commas ¹⁰ between items in a list. I further recommend that you use fewer exclamation apostrophe ¹¹ points. You should just use declarative exclamatory ¹² sentences instead. As a final point, make sure you always put colon quotation ¹³ marks around things that people say.

Finally, I would like you to spend time brainstorming organizing ¹⁴ a better draft title ¹⁵ for the paper. It's the first thing people will see, and it should give a good idea of what the paper is about.

If you'd like some help, please talk with me after class.

B PARTS OF SPEECH

Read the sentence and identify the parts of speech.

Sally quickly hurried to the store last night so she could buy the new shoes she needed.
 1   2 3 4   5   6   7

1. _____adverb_____   3. _____   6. _____
2. _____   4. _____   7. _____
                      5. _____

A WHAT TYPE OF WRITING?

Which of the following kinds of writing would be appropriate for the situations described below? There may be more than one answer.

a. biography	h. note
b. editorial	i. novel
c. e-mail	j. poem
d. essay	k. postcard
e. invitation	l. report
f. letter	m. short story
g. memo	n. thank-you note

1. You received a graduation present from your grandmother. ___f, h, n___

2. Your supervisor wants to know the progress of your current project. _____

3. You're having a party and want to tell people about it. _____

4. Your son got a phone call while he was out and you want to make sure he knows about it. _____

5. Your English assignment is to write a few paragraphs giving your opinion about television in our lives. _____

6. Valentine's Day is coming up and you want to tell your girlfriend how you feel. _____

7. You want to tell the story of your father's life. _____

8. You want to send a message to your friend in another state. _____

9. You made up an interesting science fiction story and you want to write it down. _____

10. You work at a newspaper, and you and your co-workers want to tell readers your opinion about pollution. _____

11. You're visiting the pyramids of Egypt and want to say hello to your friends. _____

12. You have to write about your plant experiment and give it to your biology teacher. _____

B WHICH WORD?

1. According to this (novel   (newspaper article)), there was a power outage at the airport last night.

2. Look at this beautiful (postcard   instant message) we received from Jane! She says she's having a wonderful time in Brazil.

3. There's a (memo   report) in the International Medical Journal about new ways to treat heart disease.

4. Do you think this magazine (article   e-mail) will help? It gives ten ways to lose weight fast.

5. We received a very nice (short story   thank-you note) from our nephew. I guess he liked the sweater we sent him.

6. Mark and I will be sending out our wedding (essays   invitations) this week.

7. After I retire as president of this company, I plan to write my (biography   autobiography).

A GEOGRAPHY MATCH

_d_ 1. Niagara   **a.** Bay

____ 2. Walden   **b.** Canyon

____ 3. Appalachian   **c.** Desert

____ 4. Redwood   **d.** Falls

____ 5. Pacific   **e.** Forest

____ 6. Mississippi   **f.** Islands

____ 7. Mojave   **g.** Lakes

____ 8. Great   **h.** Mountains

____ 9. Hawaiian   **i.** Ocean

____ 10. San Francisco   **j.** Pond

____ 11. Death   **k.** River

____ 12. Grand   **l.** Valley

B WHICH WORD?

1. I love to hear the crashing sound of a ((waterfall) brook).

2. There's no sign of water in this (rainforest desert).

3. In the fairy tale *Hansel and Gretel*, the children get lost in the (forest ocean).

4. Even though I'm afraid of heights, I love hang-gliding off of (rivers cliffs).

5. When I was a child, I dreamed about tracking wild animals in the (jungle hill).

6. It's hard to believe that this little (meadow stream) was once a rushing river.

7. Some people like swimming in pools, but I prefer fresh-water (lakes canyons).

8. The hotel is located on (an island a peninsula), so you'll have to get there by boat.

9. We built our home in the (plains plateau) so our horses would be able to run freely.

10. My favorite place to go on vacation is the (dunes seashore) because I love the ocean and sand.

C LISTENING: *Sounds*

Listen to the sounds and identify the type of geography.

| | brook | 1 waterfall | | desert | | seashore | | jungle |

A WHICH WORD?

1. A. I'm growing bacteria in this (computer (Petri dish)).
   B. Can I look at it under the ((microscope) balance)?

2. A. Do you need to use the (dropper computer)?
   B. Yes. I have to look at the images of these (test tubes slides).

3. A. Did you use the (Bunsen burner prism) to heat that sample?
   B. Yes. It's very hot, so only hold it with the (magnet forceps).

4. A. Add just a small amount of that (test tube chemical).
   B. I know. That's why I'm using a (dropper beaker).

5. A. Have you finished (planning stating) your procedure?
   B. Yes. I've started making (problems observations).

6. A. How much water should I put in this (flask scale)?
   B. Only 500 ml. But be careful not to spill any. Use a (test tube funnel).

7. A. This (magnet prism) can attract a lot of metal!
   B. I know. Next we have to use a (scale balance) to measure the amount.

8. A. I'm going to pour the liquid from the (flask slide) now.
   B. Make sure you use the (graduated cylinder test tube) so you can record the correct amount.

B ASSOCIATIONS

_g_ **1.** prism	**a.** weigh
____ **2.** magnet	**b.** liquid
____ **3.** scale	**c.** magnify
____ **4.** forceps	**d.** heat
____ **5.** dropper	**e.** attract
____ **6.** Bunsen burner	**f.** hold
____ **7.** microscope	**g.** reflect

C LIKELY OR UNLIKELY?

Put a check in the best column.

	Likely	Unlikely
1. I drew my conclusions before I made my observations.	____	✓
2. I started with a question and then made a hypothesis.	____	____
3. I looked at the slides of bacteria using the prism.	____	____
4. I couldn't find a flask so I just used a funnel.	____	____
5. My observations weren't good because I planned a good procedure.	____	____

A CELESTIAL BODIES

comet	Mars	satellite	the moon
galaxy	Mercury	Saturn	the sun
Jupiter	meteor	telescope	Uranus
lunar eclipse	quarter moon	The Big Dipper	Venus

1. This is a celestial body made up of a solid head of ice and a long vapor tail. _____comet_____

2. This is made up of gas, stars, and dust. The one we live in is called the *Milky Way*. _____

3. This is the closest planet to the sun and the second smallest in our solar system. _____

4. This is the closest object to Earth in the solar system. Humans have traveled there. _____

5. This is a constellation of stars shaped like a saucepan. _____

6. Astronomers look through this to look at stars and planets. _____

7. Also known as a *shooting star*, this appears as a luminous trail in the sky. _____

8. This is the second largest planet. It is surrounded by a series of rings. _____

9. This is the seventh planet from the sun and almost the same size as its neighbor, Neptune. _____

10. This is anything that orbits a planet. It can be man-made or natural. _____

11. This planet is close to Earth and named after the Roman god of war. _____

12. This is what happens when the moon passes through the Earth's shadow. _____

13. This is the largest planet. _____

14. When the moon appears in the sky as a half circle, it is called this. _____

15. This is the largest object in the solar system. Without it, life on Earth would be impossible. _____

16. This planet is named after the Roman goddess of love. It is the hottest planet. _____

B WHICH WORD?

1. Have you ever seen a ((solar eclipse)   star)? They're quite rare.
2. There are many (asteroids   astronauts) traveling between Mars and Jupiter.
3. My uncle works at (a UFO   an observatory) in Puerto Rico.
4. Do you know the name of that (constellation   meteor)? It might be Orion.
5. When I was young, I wanted to be an (astronomer   astronaut) and go to the moon.
6. A new (space station   planet) was recently launched into space.
7. I can't see the moon at all tonight. It must be a (new   full) moon.
8. There must be millions and millions of (planets   stars) in the sky.
9. There are a lot of communication (satellites   moons) orbiting the Earth right now.

A   WHAT'S THE OCCUPATION?

1. I became a ____firefighter____ so I could rescue people and animals from burning buildings.

2. I have a job serving food as a _____ in the Veterans Hospital Cafeteria.

3. I pack boxes and maintain inventory as a _____ at the BigCo Plant.

4. I've worked at home as a _____ ever since our children were born.

5. We need to call a _____ to fix our broken wooden front door.

6. My compliments to the _____! This was an excellent meal!

7. I have an excellent _____ who helps with my tax returns.

8. The _____ who cut your husband's hair should be fired!

9. We need to find a new _____. All our rose bushes died!

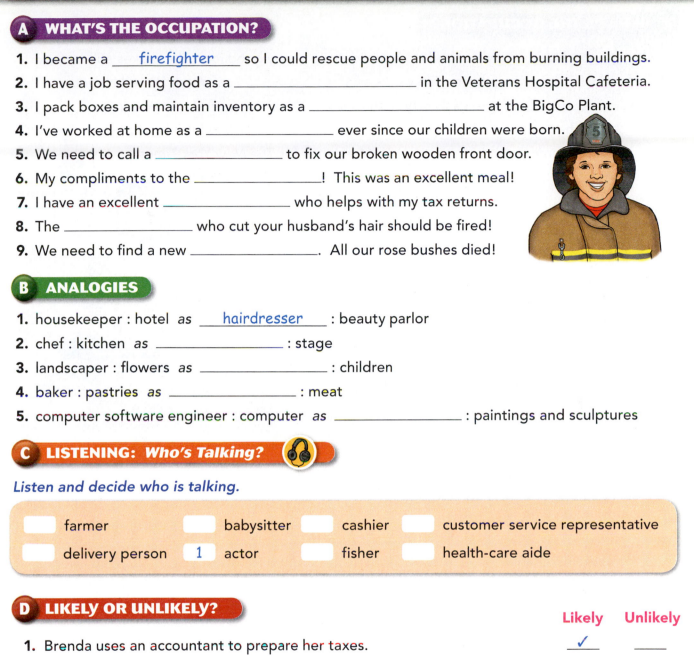

B   ANALOGIES

1. housekeeper : hotel *as* ____hairdresser____ : beauty parlor

2. chef : kitchen *as* _____ : stage

3. landscaper : flowers *as* _____ : children

4. baker : pastries *as* _____ : meat

5. computer software engineer : computer *as* _____ : paintings and sculptures

C   LISTENING: *Who's Talking?*

Listen and decide who is talking.

	farmer		babysitter		cashier		customer service representative
	delivery person	1	actor		fisher		health-care aide

D   LIKELY OR UNLIKELY?

		Likely	Unlikely
1.	Brenda uses an accountant to prepare her taxes.	✓	____
2.	Our wedding cake was baked by an excellent carpenter.	____	____
3.	I go to the butcher on Main Street when I want to buy good quality meat.	____	____
4.	Our gardener is very dependable. He takes very good care of our children.	____	____
5.	Arnold went to the dockworker up the street to get a haircut.	____	____
6.	The new factory was built by an excellent team of custodians.	____	____
7.	The painting over our mantel was done by a famous Japanese artist.	____	____
8.	Josephine is a housekeeper at the Parkview Hotel.	____	____
9.	Pay the foreman near the door when you leave the cafeteria.	____	____
10.	Martha is a garment worker at Blake's Department Store	____	____
11.	I call an assembler whenever we have problems with our front light.	____	____
12.	We need to call a mason to fix the front walk in front of our house.	____	____

A WHAT'S THE OCCUPATION?

1. The _____mechanic_____ who fixed this car didn't do a very good job. The brakes still squeak.
2. Carla speaks seven languages. She works as a _____ at the United Nations.
3. The _____ needs to retype this letter. There are several mistakes in it.
4. You have to have proper ID or the _____ won't let you pass.
5. My sister is a famous _____. She writes for *The New York Times*.
6. Ask the _____ how much of this medication you should take.
7. As your _____, I think it's important for you to have a will.
8. Susan is a _____. She flies airplanes for Trans-Global Air.
9. Let's call the _____ to fix our washing machine.

B ANALOGIES

1. supervisor : office *as* _____pharmacist_____ : drug store
2. letter carrier : mail *as* _____ : messages
3. musician : music *as* _____ : paintings
4. waiter : restaurant *as* _____ : courtroom
5. pilot : plane *as* _____ : telephone
6. mechanic : cars *as* _____ : fingernails

C LISTENING: *Who's Talking?*

Listen and decide who is talking.

	medical assistant		pilot		police officer		postal worker
	server		serviceman	1	teacher		travel agent
	receptionist		veterinarian		tailor		photographer

D LIKELY OR UNLIKELY?

	Likely	Unlikely
1. This suit was made by a very fine tailor.	✓	___
2. We called our travel agent when we decided to take a trip.	___	___
3. My cousin works as a musician at the bank.	___	___
4. When our cat is sick, we take him to a sanitation worker.	___	___
5. We always call a manicurist when we have heavy things to move.	___	___
6. The lawyer successfully defended her client.	___	___
7. The new welder arrested a burglar in our neighborhood last night.	___	___
8. The mechanic charged a lot of money to fix my car.	___	___
9. Alice works as a servicewoman at the new restaurant downtown.	___	___

A WHAT'S THE ACTION?

act	draw	mow	repair	speak
assemble	drive	operate	sell	take care of
clean	fly	paint	serve	translate
deliver	grow	play	sew	type
design	manage	prepare	sing	wash

1. I used to _____drive_____ a bus before I retired a few months ago.

2. I'm sorry. We don't _____ breakfast—only lunch and dinner.

3. I like to _____ dishes, but I don't like to dry them afterwards.

4. Do you want to _____ to Philadelphia or take the train?

5. Here. Let me show you how to _____ this machine.

6. My wife can _____ things around the house. She's very handy.

7. We _____ tomatoes and cucumbers in our garden.

8. Do you know how to _____ the saxophone?

9. I can't _____ at all! I have a terrible voice.

10. I'm a terrible artist. I can't even _____ a straight line!

11. I think I'll _____ the walls light green. What do you think?

12. Timothy, please _____ your room before our guests arrive!

13. I'm an architect. I _____ factories and office buildings.

14. I don't want to _____ dinner at home tonight. Let's go out to eat!

15. We need to _____ the lawn. The grass is getting very high.

16. My son has to _____ all his papers for school on the computer.

17. My daughter loves to _____. Maybe someday she'll be in the movies.

18. We can _____ this sofa next week. What day is convenient for you?

19. My daughter can _____ beautifully. She makes all her own clothes.

20. Dolan's Department Store is _____ing everything at half-price this week!

21. I need to find someone who can _____ this letter from English into Portuguese.

22. Two years ago I had no idea how to _____ a store. Now I supervise eight workers.

23. We have a lot of customers from Mexico, so if you can _____ Spanish, you're hired.

24. Manny can _____ components for circuit boards faster than anyone else in the factory.

25. If you like to _____ young children, you'd be perfect working at the child-care center.

(continued)

Decide what the actions below have in common.

> a. Things you do with a vehicle.
> b. Things you do with your voice.
> c. Things you do in an office.
> d. Things you do to buildings.
> e. Things you do with people.
> f. Things you do to food.
> g. Things you do to clothing.
> h. Things you do with your hands.

1. speak
   teach
   sing   b

3. bake
   prepare
   serve   ___

5. design
   construct
   guard   ___

7. type
   write
   file   ___

2. draw
   write
   paint   ___

4. assist
   take care of
   supervise   ___

6. deliver
   drive
   fly   ___

8. sell
   sew
   wash   ___

C   WHAT'S THE CATEGORY?

See if you can figure out which activities from Picture Dictionary pages 116–117 are associated with the following groups of words.

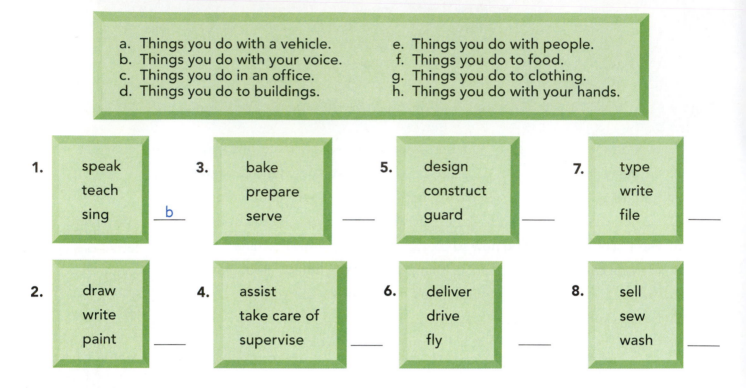

1. flowers   vegetables   crops   Things you ____grow____.
2. cars   trucks   buses   Things you _____.
3. poems   e-mails   your name   Things you _____.
4. airplanes   kites   spaceships   Things you _____.
5. houses   buildings   bridges   Things you _____.
6. breakfast   lunch   dinner   Things you _____.
7. the piano   football   games   Things you _____.
8. customers   people   patients   People you _____.
9. furniture   pizzas   mail   Things you _____.
10. food   drinks   tennis balls   Things you _____.
11. your face   your car   dishes   Things you _____.
12. biology   math   history   Things you _____.
13. cars   broken appliances   leaky roofs Things you _____.
14. machines   cash registers   equipment Things you _____.

A LOOKING FOR A JOB

A. Hi, Richard. How's the job search coming along? Have you gone to any ((interviews)   announcements)[1] yet?

B. No, not yet. I haven't even (requested   responded)[2] to any ads.

A. Why not?

B. Well, first, I don't know how to (prepare   fill out)[3] a good resume.

A. A good resume is important. I can help you.

B. Thanks. I appreciate that. But something else is bothering me.

A. What's that?

B. If I have an interview, I'm not sure how to (dress   talk)[4] appropriately.

A. I understand. I think you should wear your blue suit.

B. Okay. And I also feel nervous about what to say during the interview.

A. You should just relax and talk about your (skills and qualifications   salary and benefits)[5].

B. And should I write a (job notice   thank-you)[6] note?

A. It's always a good idea to do that if you really want to get (hired   requested)[7].

B. Thanks very much for your advice.

B LISTENING

Listen and choose the best answer.

1. a. FT, M–F
   b. PT, M–F

2. a. prev. exp. req.
   b. no exp. req.

3. a. PT, eves.
   b. PT, wknds.

4. a. excel. ben.
   b. excel. sal.

5. a. FT pos. avail. now
   b. FT pos. avail. 6/1

6. a. PT, W–F, eves.
   b. PT, M–W, eves.

C GOOD IDEA OR BAD IDEA?

Put a check in the best column.

	Good Idea	Bad Idea
1. Jerry was a few minutes late for his job interview.	_____	✓
2. Stanley is going to wear jeans and sneakers to his job interview.	_____	_____
3. Linda asked her friends to look over her resume before she sent it out.	_____	_____
4. Hugh doesn't have any experience, so he lied on the application.	_____	_____
5. Alice asked about the salary at the beginning of her interview.	_____	_____
6. Mohammed wrote a thank-you note after his interview.	_____	_____
7. Barbara is looking for a part-time job, so she looked in the classified ads.	_____	_____
8. Alan had a few grammar mistakes on his resume, but he sent it out anyway.	_____	_____
9. The restaurant needs more part-time staff, so the manager put up a help wanted sign in the window.	_____	_____
10. Susan is still in college, but she applied for a full-time position with an immediate opening.	_____	_____

A WHICH WORD?

1. The company's (boss   (receptionist)) usually greets people at the front desk.
2. We keep brooms, mops, and old equipment in the (file cabinet   storage room).
3. The office (manager   assistant) is the person who runs the office.
4. Please hang up your jacket on the (closet   coat rack) over there.
5. Put these confidential documents in the paper (shredder   cutter).
6. Oh, no! I lost my money in the (vending   adding) machine!
7. This is the (cubicle   lounge) where I work.
8. Help yourself to hot drinks from the (coffee machine   water cooler).
9. I can barely read this. The (presentation board   copier) must be out of toner.
10. Visitors to the company usually wait in the (employee lounge   reception area).
11. Can you (sort the mail   make some copies) and bring them to the conference room?
12. Are you almost finished? I'd like to use the (computer   photocopier) workstation soon.
13. There's an important meeting today in the (conference room   storage cabinet).
14. My back hurts. I need a new (typewriter   swivel chair) for my office.

B LISTENING: *Where Are They?*

Listen and decide where the conversation is taking place.

___ in the reception area	1 in the employee lounge	___ in the mailroom
___ in the supply room	___ in the work area	

C WHAT ARE THEY DOING?

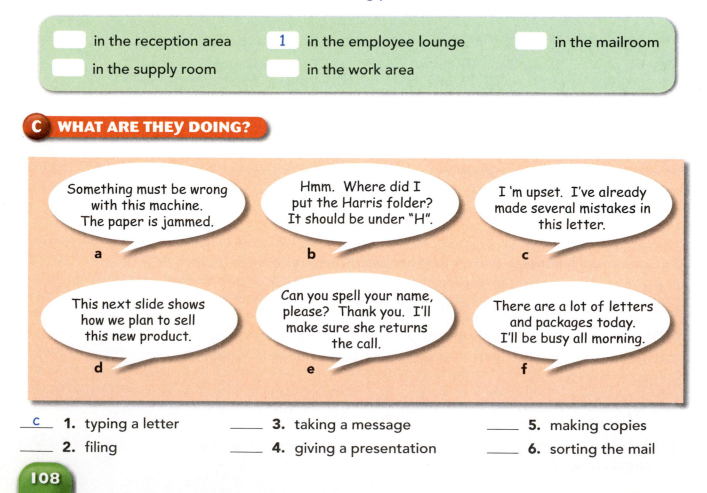

a. Something must be wrong with this machine. The paper is jammed.

b. Hmm. Where did I put the Harris folder? It should be under "H".

c. I'm upset. I've already made several mistakes in this letter.

d. This next slide shows how we plan to sell this new product.

e. Can you spell your name, please? Thank you. I'll make sure she returns the call.

f. There are a lot of letters and packages today. I'll be busy all morning.

__c__ 1. typing a letter   ___ 3. taking a message   ___ 5. making copies

___ 2. filing   ___ 4. giving a presentation   ___ 6. sorting the mail

A WHAT'S THE WORD?

glue stick	ink cartridge	mailer	packing tape
index card	letterhead	mailing label	pushpin

1. Use a _____pushpin_____ to fasten that notice to the bulletin board.
2. Use a _____ to attach the photographs to the paper.
3. Don't forget to put a _____ on this package.
4. These letters are difficult to read. You need a new _____.
5. Use _____ to make sure the package is sealed tightly.
6. You need to type this on official company _____.
7. I wrote her name on a 3 x 5 (three inch by five inch) _____.
8. A _____ is a padded envelope you can buy at the post office.

NOTICE

B MAXINE'S NEW JOB

*Maxine got a new job and needs some supplies from the supply closet. Help her make a list.
She needs . . .*

1. something to help her remember scheduled meetings. _____appointment book_____
2. a place to put incoming and outgoing mail. _____
3. something to help her plan her time. _____
4. something to write messages on and attach to surfaces. _____
5. something to attach papers and documents together. _____
6. something to sharpen pencils with. _____
7. something to remove typographical errors. _____
8. something to attach memos and papers to her bulletin board. _____
9. a place to put people's names, addresses, and phone numbers. _____

C GOOD IDEA OR BAD IDEA?

Decide whether or not the following bits of office advice are appropriate.

	Good Idea	Bad Idea
1. You should lean on a desk pad when you write.	✓	____
2. Keep your staples in a clearly marked file folder.	____	____
3. Use an ink cartridge with your rubber stamp.	____	____
4. Keep track of all your appointments in your personal planner.	____	____
5. Hold pens and pencils together with a rubber band.	____	____
6. Sharpen your pencils with rubber cement.	____	____

A WHAT'S THE WORD?

assembly line
forklift
line supervisor
loading dock
payroll office
personnel office
suggestion box
time clock
union notice
warehouse

1. You need to use a _____ forklift _____ to move those boxes.
2. Don't forget to punch in on the _____ at the start of your shift.
3. We keep all the finished products in the _____ before they're shipped.
4. Have you read the latest _____? It's posted in the employee lounge.
5. Meet me at the _____ to help empty the truck.
6. We'll be conducting interviews for new workers in the _____ today.
7. If you have an idea for improving the way we do things, put it in the _____.
8. You can pick up your checks in the _____ after four o'clock this afternoon.
9. The _____ watches over the production to make sure everything goes well on the _____.

B WHICH WORD DOESN'T BELONG?

1. line supervisor	shipping clerk	(dolly)	packer
2. worker	machine	conveyor belt	forklift
3. payroll office	time clock	time card	locker room
4. warehouse	dolly	forklift	freight elevator
5. locker room	suggestion box	work station	loading dock

C WHICH WORD?

1. Use this (freight elevator   (hand truck)) to take these boxes out to the dock.
2. There's a problem on the line. The (conveyor   machine) belt isn't moving.
3. The employees should go to the (suggestion box   payroll office) to pick up their checks.
4. We need to hire more (workers   packers) on the assembly line. We're falling behind schedule.
5. The fact that the products from our factory are so well-made is due in large part to our excellent (quality control supervisor   dollies).

110

A WHAT'S THE OBJECT?

| backhoe | cherry picker | dump truck | pneumatic drill | tape measure |
| bulldozer | crane | ladder | scaffolding | wheelbarrow |

1. This carries workers a few dozen feet off the ground to do work. ___cherry picker___
2. This is used to measure short distances. _____
3. This is used to carry small amounts of loose objects. _____
4. This is used to transport large amounts of dirt and stones. _____
5. Construction workers use this to break up hard cement. _____
6. This is used to push large piles of dirt or stones. _____
7. This is used to dig large holes. _____
8. This machine is used to work high above the ground. _____
9. Workers use this to climb to high places. _____
10. This is built around buildings under construction so workers can construct the outside. _____

B WHAT'S THE WORD?

| blueprints | concrete | girder | lumber | plywood | toolbelt |
| brick | drywall | insulation | pipe | shingle | wire |

1. The electrician couldn't complete the job because he didn't have enough ___wire___.
2. Our house has very good _____. That's why it always stays warm all winter.
3. Can your pickup truck hold enough _____ to build this wooden structure?
4. A sheet of _____ isn't very expensive because it's low quality lumber.
5. The workers made a new sidewalk in front of our house with _____.
6. One of our water _____s burst in the basement and we had a flood!
7. We use _____ to cover the interior walls of buildings and homes.
8. Our architect drew an excellent set of _____ for our new house.
9. Use a metal _____ as the main support in large structures.
10. Our carpenter always wears a _____ around his waist.
11. The _____s on our roof have to be replaced.
12. We have a lovely _____ home.

111

A   A SAFETY MEMO

back support	earplugs	glasses	masks
boots	emergency exits	goggles	respirators
defibrillators	fire extinguishers	hard hats	toe guards
earmuffs	flammable	latex gloves	vests

To: Employees at Brody Construction Company
From: Human Resources / Management
Date: January 19, 2012
Subject: Safety on the Job

There have recently been a number of accidents related to carelessness with equipment, machinery, and vehicles. Therefore, the management has prepared a list of safety precautions that must be followed at all times.

1. _____Hard hats_____ must be worn at all times on all construction sites to protect employees' heads from falling objects.

2. When operating noisy machinery, _____ or safety _____ must be used to protect against loss of hearing.

3. When lifting heavy objects such as boxes, a _____ must be worn for protection.

4. All employees working near moving machinery or vehicles must wear orange safety _____ to be easily seen.

5. Safety _____ and _____ must be worn to protect the feet and toes of workers on construction sites.

6. In dusty environments, _____ must be worn to protect from breathing small particles.

7. When working with toxic or poisonous gases, _____ must be used to prevent against breathing dangerous fumes.

8. When handling poisonous or dangerous liquids, rubber or _____ must be worn to protect employees' hands.

9. In environments with small flying particles, _____ or safety _____ must be worn to protect eyes from injury.

10. Extreme care must be taken when handling _____ materials to prevent fires from starting.

11. In case of fire, employees should know the location of _____ to leave buildings safely as well as the location of _____ to put out fires if possible.

12. All employees must be trained in the use of _____ for medical emergencies involving heart failure.

A DIRECTIONS TO GRANDMA'S HOUSE

Dear Cassandra,

I'm really looking forward to your visit with your grandfather and me next week. Since this is your first time taking the ((train) taxi)[1], I want to make sure you have the right instructions. First, the train (station ticket)[2] will probably cost about $45. You can get it at the ticket (window station)[3]. After that, check the arrival and departure (booth board)[4] to see which (route track)[5] your train will depart on. When you get on, put your suitcase in the baggage (compartment platform)[6]. If you don't know where that is, ask the (driver conductor)[7].

When you arrive, you'll have to take a local (bus ferry)[8] to the neighborhood near our house. Look for bus #87. Get off the bus at the Jefferson Street bus (stop transfer)[9]. From there you'll have to take a (meter taxi)[10] for a short trip. Give the (conductor driver)[11] our address.

If you have any trouble on the way, give us a call from your cell phone.

Love,
Grandma

B WHICH WORD DOESN'T BELONG?

1. subway   bus   (platform)   taxicab
2. taxi stand   bus stop   ferry   train station
3. driver   rider   meter   passenger
4. station   booth   counter   window
5. transfer   ticket   rider   token

C ANALOGIES

1. bus : bus stop as cab : _____taxi stand_____
2. ferry : water as train : _____
3. passenger : rider as schedule : _____
4. conductor : train as cab driver : _____
5. ticket widow : train station as fare card machine : _____

113

A WHICH VEHICLE?

1. A. What a beautiful sunny day! Let's put the top down.
    B. It's nice to have a ((convertible)   semi) on days like this.

2. A. Our car won't start. What can we do?
    B. Let's call (an R.V.   a tow truck).

3. A. Take a look at my new (jeep   sports car)!
    B. I can't wait to go camping in the mountains with it!

4. A. A (minivan   hatchback) has been very convenient for us.
    B. I'm not surprised. You have a large family.

5. A. How would you like to ride this (bicycle   motorcycle) around town?
    B. I can't. I don't have a license.

6. A. We have so much furniture! How are we ever going to get it to our new apartment?
    B. We'll have to rent a (moving   mini) van.

B LISTENING: *Which Type of Vehicle?*

Listen and decide which type of vehicle these people are talking about.

☐ moving van	☐ hybrid	☐ limousine
☐ motorcycle	1 hatchback	☐ camper

C VEHICLE MATCH

__b__ **1.** People usually rent this kind of car for weddings and big celebrations.

_____ **2.** This type of vehicle is good for the environment because it uses electricity.

_____ **3.** People use this vehicle for long road trips and camping. It usually has a bed inside.

_____ **4.** This is a small two-wheeled vehicle that's good for very short distances in the city.

_____ **5.** This large vehicle is used to transport goods and products across the country.

_____ **6.** Many carpenters and construction workers use this vehicle because it can hold a lot of wood, tools, and other materials.

a. hybrid

b. limousine

c. moped

d. pickup truck

e. recreational vehicle

f. tractor trailer

A WHICH WORD?

1. My battery is dead. Do you have any ((jumper cables)   fan belts) to help me get started?
2. Don't forget to take the key out of the (door lock   ignition) when you park your car.
3. We're lucky we have a (gearshift   navigation system). We could have gotten lost!
4. Our car isn't driving very well. There's a problem with the (transmission   seat belt).
5. The weather was wet and foggy, so I turned on my (windshield wipers   CD player) and (muffler   rear defroster).
6. Step on the (brake   gas pedal)! There's something in the middle of the road.
7. I'm not sure how fast we're going. I'll check the (odometer   speedometer)
8. To pump the gas, first take the (visor   nozzle) from the (gas   air) pump.
9. The car won't roll down the hill if you use the (accelerator   emergency brake).
10. I don't like a car with manual transmission because I'm not very good at using a (stick shift   gas pedal) and (dashboard   clutch).
11. I use a (dipstick   hubcap) to measure the amount of oil in the engine.
12. It was very sunny, so I lowered the (vent   visor) over the windshield.
13. Don't forget to use your (turn signal   horn) when you change lanes.
14. Make sure you tie down your luggage on the (roof rack   headrest).
15. I see that the car in front of us has a broken (headlight   taillight).
16. You'd better check the air in the rear left (backup light   tire).
17. The spare tire is in the (trunk   glove compartment).
18. I hit another car and dented my (hood   heater).

B LISTENING: *Calling About a Car*

Listen to the following telephone conversation and circle the answers as you listen.

1. a. The car costs $900.
   b. The car costs $1900.
2. a. The car is a sedan.
   b. The car is a hatchback.
3. a. A taillight is broken.
   b. A headlight is broken.

4. a. The car may need a new clutch.
   b. The clutch is new.
5. a. The fan belt is old.
   b. The battery stays cold.
6. a. The radiator hose should be replaced.
   b. The radiator hose can hurt you.
7. a. The alternator needs to be checked.
   b. The accelerator needs to be checked.
8. a. The brakes have been making noise.
   b. The brakes have been weak.
9. a. The heater works, but the horn doesn't.
   b. The heater and the horn don't work.
10. a. The radio and the muffler are okay.
    b. The radio is fine, but the muffler isn't.

A GOOD IDEA OR BAD IDEA?

Decide whether or not the following driving decisions are appropriate.

	Good Idea	Bad Idea
1. Take that entrance ramp to get onto the interstate.	✓	
2. We're approaching an intersection. You should speed up.		
3. Since I drive a little slowly, I usually drive in the left lane.		
4. I never pass a car in front of me when there's a solid line dividing the road.		
5. Drive through the divider to get from one side of the highway to the other.		
6. I prefer to drive on the shoulder of the highway.		
7. Look at the route sign to see what road we're on.		
8. Get into the right lane if you want to pass that car.		
9. Honk your horn while you're driving through the tunnel.		
10. Let's stop our car on the median and rest for a while!		
11. Since I had the correct amount of money, I got into the exact change lane at the tollbooth.		
12. If the speed limit is 40 miles per hour, then we should go 20 miles per hour to be safe.		

B LISTENING TO DIRECTIONS

Listen and put a check next to the correct directions

- ☐ Take the interstate south.
- ✓ Take the interstate north.
- ☐ Get off at Exit 16.
- ☐ Get off at Exit 6.
- ☐ Stay in the right lane.
- ☐ Turn onto First Avenue.
- ☐ Turn onto Third Avenue.
- ☐ Don't go through the intersection.
- ☐ Go past two traffic lights.
- ☐ Elm Street is at the fifth traffic light.
- ☐ Elm Street is at the third traffic signal.
- ☐ Go straight for two blocks.
- ☐ Blake Insurance is on the right.
- ☐ Blake Insurance is on a corner.

C WHICH WORD?

1. When you're walking, always cross the street in the ((crosswalk)   corner).
2. On the highway, a (yellow   broken) line means you can pass slower cars.
3. You have to accelerate quickly when you get on the (on   off) ramp.
4. I got a ticket for going the wrong way down a (speed limit   one-way) street.
5. When you see a (double yellow line   tollbooth), you have to pay some money.
6. That new very tall (bridge   tunnel) crosses over to the other side of the bay.

A WHICH PREPOSITION?

1. I'm too tired to ride my bicycle (**up** down) this hill!
2. Turn left after you drive (past   into) the museum.
3. Check for traffic before you get (down   out of) the car.
4. Take the subway and get (off   out of) at Park Street.
5. I can't figure out how to get (onto   into) Route 28.
6. Stop! You can't go (into   down) a one-way street!
7. You'll see the exit after you go (around   through) the tunnel.
8. When you get (out of   off) the bridge, you'll see a sign for Exit 12.
9. There's something in the road up ahead. Go (over   around) it slowly.
10. It's the first traffic light after you go (through   over) the intersection.
11. Always stay (in   on) the sidewalk unless you are crossing the street.
12. The bus station is easy to find. It's just (through   around) the block.
13. When you see the sign for Exit 57, get (out of   off) the interstate.
14. Do you recognize that famous person getting (out of   on) a taxi?
15. Go (over   through) the bridge when you get off the highway.
16. If you take a cab, make sure you get (in   on) the back seat.
17. You can take the ferry (into   across) the river.
18. Get (on   into) the bus at 18th and Washington Street.
19. Excuse me? Can you tell me how to get (into   onto) Interstate 87?
20. Take a left, and go (down   on) the hallway until you see the gymnasium.
21. Make sure you take a picture from the boat when you go (past   over) the Statue of Liberty.

B WHAT'S THE PREPOSITION?

Look at the words and decide which preposition goes with them. More than one answer may be possible.

1. Go _____over_____ bridges, mountains, and hills.
2. Go _____ streets, hills, and stairs.
3. Get _____ buses, subways, and airplanes.
4. Go _____ streets, rivers, and oceans.
5. Get _____ cars, taxis, and limousines.
6. Go _____ blocks, corners, and things in the road.
7. Go _____ tunnels, intersections, and traffic signals.

A WHICH WORD?

1. We can't turn right here. The sign says (only   (no)) right turn.
2. Make a (hand signal   detour) for a left turn.
3. The sign says there's no (outlet   U-turn). We should turn around.
4. Slow down! The sign says the road is (handicapped parking   slippery when wet).
5. The route sign says this is 99 North, but the (compass   hand signal) says we're going south.
6. They're doing construction on the highway. We have to follow the (detour   one-way) signs.
7. Watch out for the people walking! There's a (pedestrian   railroad) crossing at the next intersection.

B ROAD TEST

| detour | hand | one-way | railroad crossing | turn left |
| go straight | handicapped | parallel | 3-point turn | turn right |

A. Good morning. Are you ready for your test?

B. Yes. But I'm a little nervous.

A. Don't worry. I'll help you through it. First, I want you to head north on Main St. and _____go straight_____ 1 until the traffic signal at the intersection.

B. Okay.

A. Now, you can't turn right onto Kent Street because it's a _____ 2 street. So _____. 3

B. Should I use _____ 4 signals when I turn?

A. No. The car's turn signals are fine. Now, _____ 5 onto Perry Street and head north again.

B. Uh-oh! It looks like this part of Perry Street is under construction, and there's a _____ 6 sign. What should I do?

A. Stay on Perry Street for another block and then make a right turn. Now, stop at the _____ 7 sign and make sure there are no trains coming.

B. Okay. All clear.

A. I want you to turn around and head south now. Make a _____ 8 up ahead.

B. Okay.

A. Good. Now go straight for a few blocks and _____ 9 park the car on the street. Just don't park in the _____ 10 parking area.

B. Is that all? Am I finished?

A. Yes, you are. You passed!

A A FRUSTRATING DAY!

baggage	carry-on bag	metal detector	suitcases
baggage cart	customs	passport	ticket agent
boarding area	customs declaration	security checkpoint	ticket counter
boarding pass	immigration	security officer	X-ray

What a flight! From beginning to end it was a disaster!
I left my house with plenty of time to get to the airport, but
when I got there, I realized I had left my _____suitcases_____ [1]
with all my clothes in them at home! So I had to go back home
to get them. By the time I got to the airport, the line at the
_____ [2] was so long I didn't think I was going to
get to my flight on time. I had forgotten to get a _____ [3],
so I had to carry my heavy suitcases on my own. When I finally
got to the _____ [4], she told me that my _____ [5]
was too heavy and that I needed to pay extra.

I had trouble at the _____ [6] when my watch
and belt set off the _____ [7]. The _____ [8] also
said that the _____ [9] machine showed I had a sharp object in my
_____ [10], so he had to check everything in it.

By the time I got to the _____ [11], my flight had already finished boarding
and I almost missed the flight! I gave my _____ [12] to the flight attendant and
was the last person on the plane.

When we arrived, I had trouble at _____ [13] because I didn't have a proper visa
in my _____ [14]. And I also had a problem at _____ [15] because I had
some fruit in my bag that I didn't declare on my _____ [16] form.
What a frustrating day!

B WHICH WORD?

1. You need to show your ((baggage claim check)   boarding pass) when you pick up your
   luggage.

2. Look! The (arrival and departure monitor   check-in counter) isn't working! How will we
   know when Grandma's flight is arriving?

3. Always have your boarding pass ready when you reach the (counter   gate) to board the
   plane.

4. When I travel, my suits never get wrinkled because I hang them in a (suitcase   garment bag).

5. You need (a passport   immigration) in order to travel to a foreign country.

6. These suitcases are very heavy. I'm glad we have a (carousel   luggage cart).

A PROBABLE OR IMPROBABLE?

Decide whether the following are probable or improbable.

	Probable	Improbable
1. If you want a good view from the plane, you should ask for a window seat.	✓	
2. In case of emergency, turn on the air sickness bag.		
3. We sat in the aisle during the whole flight.		
4. The passenger pushed the call button to get the flight attendant.		
5. You can store this carry-on bag in the lavatory.		
6. The airplane landed on the runway inside the control tower.		
7. The passengers asked the pilot to turn on the No Smoking sign.		
8. Life vests are an important safety feature on airplanes.		
9. Tray tables are located in the overhead compartment.		
10. The passenger turned on the Fasten Seat Belt sign for the landing.		
11. The pilot sat in an aisle seat and the co-pilot sat in a middle seat.		
12. In case of emergency, there is a life jacket for every passenger.		
13. The pilot told the passengers to put on their emergency instruction cards.		

B WHICH WORD?

1. Please fasten your ((seat)   conveyor) belt before takeoff!
2. The jet was on the (cockpit   runway) for more than an hour.
3. Smoking is not allowed during this (flight   flight attendant).
4. If you can't check in at the ticket counter, then do it at the (gate   lavatory).
5. I carefully read through the emergency (exit   instruction card) before takeoff.
6. If there is turbulence during the flight, you can use the (carry-on   air sickness) bag.

C LISTENING

Listen and choose the best answer.

1. a.) walk through the metal detector
   b. check in

2. a. get your boarding pass
   b. fasten your seat belts

3. a. find the emergency exit
   b. find your seat

4. a. check in at the gate
   b. put your bag on the conveyor belt

5. a. stow your carry-on bags
   b. take off your shoes

6. a. fasten your seat belt
   b. put your computer in the tray

7. a. put on an oxygen mask
   b. board the plane

8. a. take off your shoes
   b. find your seat

A WHICH WORD?

1. A. Does the hotel have ((valet parking)   room service)?

   B. Yes. Just give your keys to the (concierge   parking attendant).

2. A. Is our (room   pool) on the nineteenth floor?

   B. Yes. We should definitely take the (elevator   hallway).

3. A. How long have you been the bell (attendant   captain) at this hotel?

   B. For a few years. Before that, I worked as a (bellhop   guest).

4. A. Do you know if the (gift shop   ice machine) sells cold drinks?

   B. I think so, but you should check with the (lobby   desk clerk).

5. A. I'm going to the (concierge   hall) desk to find out where to get something to eat.

   B. Why don't we just eat in the (meeting room   restaurant) at the hotel?

6. A. Oh, no! Our room is right next to the (ice machine   baggage cart).

   B. That will be noisy. Let's call the (front desk   bellhop) to see if we can change rooms.

B LIKELY OR UNLIKELY?

Put a check in the best column.

	Likely	Unlikely
1. I checked in at the front desk.	✓	
2. I opened the door for the doorman.		
3. The exercise room is a great place to have delicious food.		
4. Some of the guests are attending a conference in the meeting room.		
5. I gave my car keys to the parking attendant.		
6. The concierge took the bellhop's bags to the guest room.		
7. I felt very relaxed after swimming in the pool.		
8. Anna is a housekeeping cart at the Plaza Hotel.		
9. The guest rooms are clean because this hotel has excellent room service.		

C WHAT'S THE WORD?

1. __Room service__ is the service that allows guests to order food to be delivered to their rooms.

2. A _____ is a hotel worker who cleans guest rooms.

3. The _____ is the large room at the front of a hotel where people often meet.

4. _____ is the hotel service that takes care of guests' cars.

5. A _____ is what you need to enter a room. It can be either a plastic card or a piece of metal.

A WHAT'S THE WORD?

| bird-watching | cards | coins | photography | sewing |
| building | chess | knitting | pottery | stamps |

1. Let's go _____bird-watching_____ this weekend. I just bought a new pair of binoculars.

2. How long have you been _____? This wool sweater you made is beautiful.

3. I'm sure you can do some wonderful _____ with that expensive camera.

4. My wife and I enjoy playing _____. Our favorite game is bridge.

5. I'm frustrated. I have needles and thread, but my _____ machine is broken.

6. If you want to know more about collecting _____, talk with the manager of the post office.

7. Checkers and _____ are similar games. They're both played on a black and red square checkered board.

8. Many young people enjoy _____ models. With a kit, some glue, and some paint, they can create authentic miniature cars and planes.

9. My uncle's hobby is making _____. He has a gigantic wheel in the other room. He's made some beautiful painted clay dishes.

10. My nephew has been collecting _____ for many years. He has a complete collection of twentieth century silver dollars.

B WHICH WORD?

1. A. I wish I could afford a (deck of cards (telescope)).
   B. You can use mine. (Astronomy   Sewing) is my hobby, too.

2. A. It's your turn. Roll the (wheel   dice).
   B. Alright! (Scrabble   Monopoly) is a lot of fun!

3. A. I'd like to try (woodworking   painting), but the canvas, easel, and brushes are too expensive.
   B. You should try (drawing   embroidery) then. All you need is a pencil and sketch book.

4. A. Have you been playing (backgammon   woodworking) these days?
   B. No. I got a new computer, and now I'm going (online   bird-watching) all the time.

5. A. Do you know how to make (an origami   a woodworking) bird?
   B. No. But I have a wonderful bird (pattern   wheel) for needlepoint.

6. A. Can I borrow a (thimble   safety pin) to hold these pieces of cloth together?
   B. Sure. And I'd like to borrow your (oil paint   magnifying glass) so I can look at my new stamp.

A WHICH PLACE DOESN'T BELONG?

1. (museum)   park   beach   mountains
2. art gallery   amusement park   planetarium   museum
3. craft fair   swap meet   yard sale   play
4. amusement park   carnival   craft fair   fair
5. flea market   zoo   aquarium   botanical gardens
6. mountains   amusement park   national park   park

B WHERE SHOULD THEY GO?

aquarium	botanical gardens	historic site	planetarium	yard sale
beach	concert	movies	play	zoo

1. My daughter loves to look at fish and animals that live in the sea.
   You should take her to the _____aquarium_____.
2. Mohammed is interested in astronomy.
   He should go to the _____.
3. My friends and I want to go out and hear some music tonight.
   You should go to a _____.
4. Jason wants to go somewhere where he can swim and enjoy the sunshine.
   He should go to the _____.
5. Greta has always enjoyed nature and wildlife. She especially likes flowers.
   She should go to the _____.
6. Julie and Bob are going out on their first date tonight. They want to relax
   and see some famous people on the big screen.
   They should go to the _____.
7. Brian has some old furniture and appliances he'd like to get rid of.
   He should have a _____.
8. Lisa likes museums and history. She also likes being outside.
   She should go to a famous _____.
9. My son wants to go to a place where he can see a lot of animals.
   You should take him to the _____.
10. Miranda enjoys watching actors and actresses perform on a stage.
    She should go to a _____.

A WHAT'S THE WORD?

bench	climbing wall	picnic	tennis court
bicycle	duck pond	playground	trash can
carousel	jogging	sandbox	water fountain

1. Let's go to the _____ duck pond _____ and feed the ducks!

2. I'd rather sit on a _____ and feed the birds.

3. Throw that paper away in the _____.

4. Emily! Don't throw your toys out of the _____!

5. You can get a drink from that _____ over there.

6. Do you want to have lunch over there in the _____ area?

7. I think I'll run on the _____ path. I need some exercise!

8. Wait! I have to go back to the _____. I think I left my racket there.

9. The new _____ is wonderful. There's a seesaw, a slide, and swings.

10. Make sure you wear your helmet if you go riding on the _____ path.

11. I love to go around and around on the _____ and listen to the organ music.

12. Our son loves to play on the _____. He's only six, and he can already get to the top.

B LISTENING: *Where Are They?*

Listen and decide where these people are.

1. a. in the playground
   b. on the bike path

2. a. on a bench
   b. on the jogging path

3. a. at a picnic table
   b. at the duck pond

4. a. on the swings
   b. on the merry-go-round

5. a. at the ballfield
   b. on the tennis court

6. a. on the slide
   b. on the skateboard ramp

C WHICH WORD?

1. My grandfather likes to sit on a park ((bench) swing) and read the newspaper.

2. What a shame! It rained last night and now the (pond   sand) is all wet.

3. You should lock your bicycle when you leave it in the bike (rack   way).

4. Be sure to watch your child when he plays on the (sandbox   climber).

5. Let's go to the park and cook some hamburgers on the (grill   picnic table).

6. My friends and I enjoy playing on the (ballfield   fountain).

7. You went down very fast on that (path   slide)!

A WHICH WORD?

1. Look at that (rock   (kite)) up in the sky!
2. I love to use a (shovel   boogie board) in the water.
3. The lifeguard is sitting on the lifeguard (stand   seat).
4. Let's get something to eat at the (snack bar   sand castle).
5. If we put up the beach (chair   umbrella), we can have some shade.
6. Let's collect some (sunglasses   seashells) when we go to Hawaii.
7. We love to throw a beach (ball   umbrella) back and forth at the beach.
8. The water was freezing! Where's my (blanket   towel) so I can dry off?
9. Put on your (sunglasses   life preserver). The sun is very bright today.
10. Jimmy, if you're thirsty, look for the juice I put in the (cooler   vendor).
11. Michael is going very fast on that (kite   surfboard)! I hope he doesn't get hurt!
12. There are very strong (surfers   waves) in the ocean today. I think a storm is coming.
13. The (life preserver   lifeguard) is busy, so don't talk to her unless there's an emergency.

B LIKELY OR UNLIKELY?

Put a check in the best column.

	Likely	Unlikely
1. Alison worked as a sunbather at the beach last summer.	____	✓
2. My daughter and I spent time looking for seashells at the beach.	____	____
3. My husband was knocked over by an enormous wave.	____	____
4. To protect herself from the sun, Melissa always uses a cooler.	____	____
5. I stepped on a rock in the water and hurt my foot.	____	____
6. The sand dunes are very high in the water today.	____	____
7. I sat on a beach chair under a beach umbrella.	____	____
8. My wife and I live in a beautiful sand castle at the beach.	____	____

C WHAT'S THE ACTION?

_e_	1. collect	a.	vendor
____	2. fly	b.	surfboard
____	3. surf	c.	sunblock
____	4. put up	d.	shovel
____	5. throw	e.	shells
____	6. sell	f.	sand castle
____	7. build	g.	kite
____	8. dig	h.	beach umbrella
____	9. put on	i.	beach ball

A PLANNING A CAMPING TRIP

backpack	camping stove	GPS	matches	rope	tent
boots	compass	hiking	rock climbing	Swiss army knife	trail

A. Let's go camping this weekend!

B. Good idea! I love going camping. I also enjoy going _____hiking_____1!

A. We'll need special shoes for that.

B. I know. We need to take along some good hiking _____2.

A. I hate to admit it, but I sometimes get lost in the woods.

B. Don't worry. We'll take a _____3 and _____4 map with us.

A. What about a _____5 device?

B. That will work, too, but they're very expensive. Tell me, would you also be interested in going _____6?

A. That sounds like fun! I have some _____7 and harness equipment at home.

B. That's great. Now, how will we carry our supplies?

A. I can put everything in my _____8. But do we need to take a _____9?

B. Of course we do. How else can we cook our food?

A. One more question. Where will we sleep at night?

B. We'll bring along a _____10. We'll also bring _____11 to start a fire.

A. And don't forget to bring your _____12. It's a really handy tool, especially for cutting things.

B. Don't worry. I'll remember to take it. This trip is going to be great!

B WHICH WORD?

1. I think we're lost! We should have brought a ((GPS) canteen) instead of this old compass.

2. Here. Use this (canteen   hatchet) to chop this wood for the campfire.

3. I bought a great new mountain (bike   climb)! We should go riding soon.

4. Keep your (matches   hiking boots) tied tightly so you don't trip.

5. Do we have enough (stakes   hatchets) to pitch this tent?

6. Give me a match so we can light this (thermos   lantern).

C LISTENING

Listen and choose the best answer.

1. a. canteen
   b. repellent

2. a. helmet
   b. harness

3. a. backpack
   b. tent

4. a. insect repellent
   b. tent stakes

5. a. picnic basket
   b. thermos

6. a. picnic blanket
   b. sleeping bag

126

A WHICH SPORT DOESN'T BELONG?

1. bowling   (running)   ping pong   racquetball
2. boxing   martial arts   wrestling   bowling
3. Frisbee   badminton   table tennis   tennis
4. golf   Frisbee   wrestling   skateboarding
5. gymnastics   horseback riding   working out   weightlifting
6. horseback riding   cycling   skateboarding   archery

B ANALOGIES

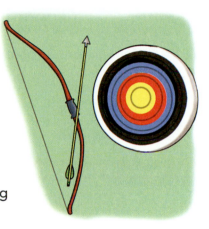

1. weights : weightlifting *as* ____bow and arrow____ : archery
2. club : golf *as* _____ : billiards
3. tennis shorts : tennis *as* _____ : boxing
4. racquet : badminton *as* _____ : ping pong
5. billiard balls : pool *as* _____ : badminton
6. safety goggles : racquetball *as* _____ : cycling
7. bowling shoes : bowling *as* _____ : inline skating

C NAME THE SPORT!

1. This sport is played with a big ball you put three fingers in.   ____bowling____
2. This sport is played on a green table with pockets.   _____
3. In this sport, you wear colored belts to show your level of skill.   _____
4. This sport requires excellent balance while you jump and do flips.   _____
5. This sport was first played on green grass in Scotland.   _____
6. This sport's most famous competition is called the "Tour de France."   _____
7. This sport requires you to shoot the center of a target.   _____
8. In this sport, two opponents punch each other.   _____
9. In this sport, two opponents try to pin each other down to a mat.   _____

D WHICH WORD?

1. I use the (exercise (rowing)) machine at the gym to exercise my back and legs.
2. I don't like running outside, so I use the (treadmill barbell).
3. I just recently got my black (belt gloves) in karate.
4. Tennis, ping pong, and badminton all use a (ball racket).
5. That gymnast is really skilled on the (horse saddle).
6. Hold the (bow reins) tightly or the horse might throw you!

127

TEAM SPORTS

A TRUE OR FALSE?

Write T if the statement is true or F if it is false.

F **1.** Football is played on a court.

____ **2.** Soccer players dribble the ball.

____ **3.** A hockey rink can melt.

____ **4.** A volleyball court has ice on it.

____ **5.** Lacrosse is played on a hardwood floor.

____ **6.** A football field sometimes has to be mowed.

B CORRECT OR INCORRECT?

Write C if the names of places are correct and I if they are incorrect.

I **1.** soccer rink   ____ **4.** basketball court   ____ **7.** volleyball rink

____ **2.** lacrosse field   ____ **5.** baseball field   ____ **8.** soccer field

____ **3.** hockey field   ____ **6.** hockey court

C WHAT'S THE SPORT?

| ballfield | basketball | football | rink | softball |
| baseball | court | hockey | soccer | volleyball |

1. ____Hockey____ is played on skates. It's played on a _____.

2. _____ is the most popular sport in the United States.

3. Baseball and _____ are played on a _____.

4. In the United States, this field sport is called _____.
In other countries, it's called _____.

5. _____ attracts very tall athletes. It's played on a _____.

6. _____ is also played on a court.

D LISTENING: *Team Sports Sounds*

Listen and identify the sport by the sound.

____ ____ 1 ____

128

A SENSE OR NONSENSE?

Decide whether or not the following make sense.

	Sense	Nonsense
1. Our hockey team won because the other team's serve hit the backboard.	____	✓
2. It's important to have a good soccer hoop.	____	____
3. Our daughter plays on the school softball team, so we gave her a new mitt.	____	____
4. If you're going to play basketball, don't forget to bring your stick.	____	____
5. The coach told the football team not to forget their helmets.	____	____
6. Carlos is the catcher. This mask is for him.	____	____
7. Kevin lost several lacrosse pucks this season.	____	____
8. They had to stop the volleyball game because one of the players' shoulder pads fell off.	____	____

B WHO'S TALKING?

__d__ 1. "I couldn't play a game without my shinguards."

____ 2. "I wear this face guard to protect myself against a stick or ball."

____ 3. "I've got my helmet, and it's my turn to bat!"

____ 4. "There's the puck. Go after it!"

____ 5. "I'm only six feet tall, but I can touch the hoop with my hands."

____ 6. "We lost the point. The ball touched the net."

____ 7. "This helmet and these big shoulder pads protect me when I play this rough sport."

a. baseball player
b. volleyball player
c. basketball player
d. soccer player
e. football player
f. lacrosse player
g. hockey player

C LISTENING: *Which One?*

Listen and choose the best answer.

1. a. glove
   b. helmet

2. a. ball
   b. net

3. a. net
   b. mask

4. a. rim
   b. mitt

5. a. shoulder pads
   b. shin guards

6. a. ball
   b. stick

D WHICH WORD DOESN'T BELONG?

1. baseball	soccer ball	football	lacrosse ball
2. shoulder pads	skates	face guard	catcher's mask
3. bat	hockey stick	hockey puck	lacrosse stick
4. shinguards	catcher's mitt	hockey glove	softball glove
5. volleyball	softball	basketball	hockey puck

A WHAT'S THE WORD?

1. A _____snowboard_____ is a wide, flat ski that holds both feet.
2. A _____ is a round sled.
3. A _____ is a snow vehicle with a motor.
4. _____ help us keep our balance when we ski.
5. _____ protect the bottom of skates.
6. A _____ is the part of the skate that touches the ice.
7. _____ are used to attach ski boots to skis.

B WINTER SPORT MATCH

_c_ 1. on an ice rink or frozen pond   a. bobsledding

____ 2. going down a mountain, standing up with poles   b. cross-country skiing

____ 3. going through a field or woods, standing up with poles   c. skating

____ 4. going through a field or woods on a vehicle   d. sledding

____ 5. going down a hill very fast, wearing helmets   e. downhill skiing

____ 6. going down a hill very fast, sitting or lying down   f. snowmobiling

C WHICH WORD?

1. A. What kind of skiing do you like?
   B. I prefer (downhill   (cross-country)). I enjoy gliding through the woods.

2. A. Why are those people wearing helmets?
   B. That's the (sledding   bobsledding) team on their way to practice.

3. A. Do you want to go (skiing   sledding) this weekend?
   B. I can't. I lost my poles last weekend.

4. A. Look at my brand-new (snowmobile   saucer)!
   B. Wow! Does it require a lot of gasoline?

D WHAT'S YOUR OPINION?

1. In your opinion, which winter sport is the most dangerous? Why?

   ....

2. Which is the easiest? Why?

   ....

3. Which is the most difficult? Why?

   ....

4. Which is the most beautiful to watch? Why?

   ....

5. Which do you think is the most expensive? Why?

   ....

A ANALOGIES

1. sailboard : windsurfing as ___surfboard___ : surfing
2. goggles : eyes as _____ : feet
3. snorkel : snorkeling as _____ : scuba diving
4. waterskiing : lake as _____ : fast river
5. oars : rowboat as _____ : canoe
6. sailboat : wind as _____ : big waves
7. bathing suit : swimming as _____ : scuba diving
8. fishing pole : fishing as _____ : waterskiing

B WHAT DO YOU WEAR?

__d__ 1. You wear flippers
____ 2. You wear goggles
____ 3. You wear an air tank
____ 4. You wear a snorkel
____ 5. You wear a mask
____ 6. You wear a bathing cap

a. on your back.
b. over your eyes.
c. over your face.
d. on your feet.
e. on your head.
f. in your mouth.

C LISTENING: Which Sport?

Listen and choose the correct water sport.

1. a. snorkeling
   b. swimming
2. a. fishing
   b. scuba diving
3. a. surfing
   b. fishing
4. a. rowing
   b. surfing
5. a. kayaking
   b. sailing
6. a. sailing
   b. windsurfing

D WHICH WORD?

1. I caught a big fish, but it broke my (line   bait) and got away!
2. You must wear a (bathing cap   life jacket) when you use a raft.
3. You got a bite! Quick! Turn the (net   reel) to pull it in!
4. My eyes are stinging because I didn't wear (goggles   a wet suit) in the pool.
5. This is a perfect day for (surfing   sailing). The weather is clear and the waves are very big.
6. Timmy, remember to hold on to the (pole   towrope) very tightly when you go waterskiing.

A WHAT'S THE SPORT?

baseball	football	lift	swim
basketball	gymnastics	run	tennis

1. You serve when you play _____ tennis _____.
2. You dive when you _____.
3. When you use weights, you _____.
4. You stretch and bend before you _____.
5. You hit, pitch, and catch when you play _____.
6. You throw, pass, and kick when you play _____.
7. You dribble, shoot, and bounce the ball when you play _____.
8. You do somersaults, cartwheels, and handstands when you do _____.

B WHAT'S THE ACTION?

bend	dive	kick	run	stretch
bounce	hit	pitch	serve	swim
catch	hop	reach	shoot	walk

1. Tina really knows how to _____ hit _____ the ball. She got three home runs in our last game.
2. Hold the bat like this, Tommy. Now, when I _____ the ball, hit it as far as you can.
3. Make sure no one is nearby when you _____ arrows at the target with your bow.
4. It's important to _____ your muscles before doing any sports or exercise.
5. I love to _____ in the pool at the community center, but it's too shallow to _____.
6. Any volleyball player can hit the ball over the net, but very few really know how to _____ it well.
7. Please don't _____ the ball up and down! It makes too much noise.
8. In baseball, you have to use a glove when you _____ the ball.
9. In soccer, you aren't allowed to touch the ball, only _____ it.
10. In case of emergency, _____, don't run, to the nearest exit.
11. To enter a marathon, you really have to like to _____.
12. Since I had surgery on my knees, it hurts when I _____.
13. Raise your arms and _____ as high as you can.
14. Can you _____ up and down on one foot?

A ENTERTAINMENT REPORT

actors	comedians	conductor	music	singer
actresses	Comedy	movie	Orchestra	theater
bands	concert hall	movie theaters	screen	

There are a lot of entertainment activities happening this weekend in Riverside City. There are music concerts at the __concert hall__ 1, plays at the _____ 2, and new films at several _____ 3 around town.

The Riverside _____ 4 is performing Beethoven's famous *Fifth Symphony*, led by special guest _____ 5 Norman Randolph from the New York Philharmonic. There are also a number of smaller music events happening at _____ 6 clubs around town. A couple of local _____ 7 are playing at Johnny's, and Marla Renoit, the famous European _____ 8, will be doing a few shows at the Main Street Cafe.

Riverside City's very own Theater Group is doing Shakespeare's *As You Like It*. The performance should be spectacular as many of the performers, both the _____ 9 and _____ 10, have been doing Shakespeare for many years.

Several new films are being released on the big _____ 11 this week as well. So be sure to check your local _____ 12 listings for times and locations.

Finally, if you're looking for some laughs over the weekend, Saturday night is Improv Night at Lenny's _____ 13 Club downtown. Check it out to see your favorite _____ 14!

B LISTENING

Listen and choose the best answer.

1. a. opera singer
   b. musician
2. a. play
   b. ballet
3. a. actor
   b. actress
4. a. singer
   b. ballerina
5. a. musician
   b. actor
6. a. opera
   b. movies
7. a. concert
   b. conductor
8. a. screen
   b. actor

A WHAT'S ON TV?

Match the types of TV programs with their descriptions. Then fill in the name of a television program you know for each type.

cartoon	game show	news program	sitcom	sports program
drama	nature program	reality show	soap opera	talk show

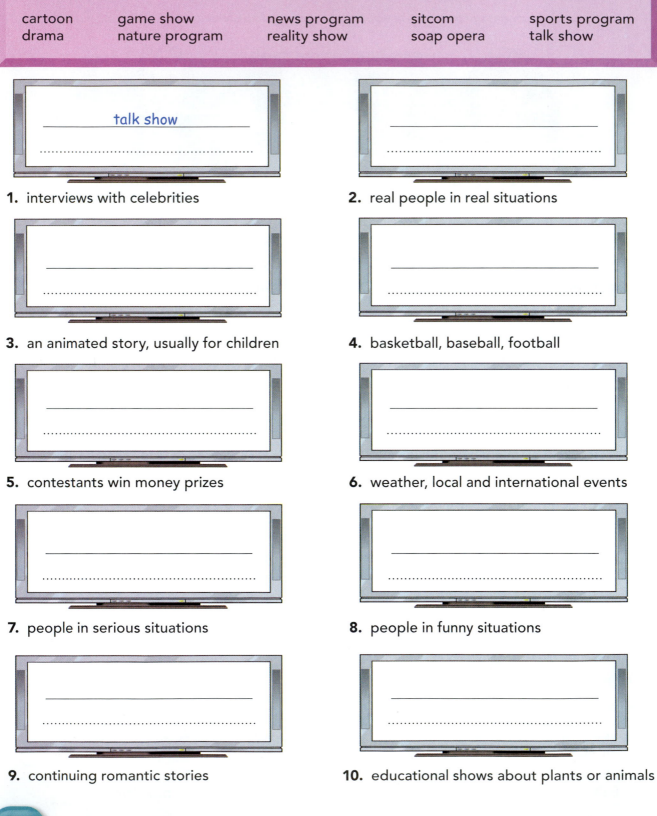

_____ talk show _____

....

1. interviews with celebrities

2. real people in real situations

3. an animated story, usually for children

4. basketball, baseball, football

5. contestants win money prizes

6. weather, local and international events

7. people in serious situations

8. people in funny situations

9. continuing romantic stories

10. educational shows about plants or animals

B WHAT'S PLAYING AT THE MOVIES?

| action movie | comedy | drama | horror film | war movie |
| cartoon | documentary | foreign film | science fiction | western |

1. A classic Jeff Carrey ___comedy___! You won't stop laughing!

2. A contemporary _____ about a cowboy who falls in love.

3. Astronauts fly their space station to a new galaxy! This is _____ at its best.

4. Director Jill Bond filmed life in Sub-Saharan Africa in her latest _____.

5. Children of all ages will love this new _____! It has beautiful animation and a magnificent story.

6. This French movie is the most popular _____ of the year. See it and you'll know why everybody is talking about it.

7. The most frightening movie of the year! You won't want to see this scary _____ alone!

8. Suspense, danger, and excitement in every minute of this amazing _____!

9. A beautiful and talented writer gets a rare disease. The most tearful _____ of the year!

10. World War II has never been so realistically depicted. A truly magnificent _____!

C LISTENING

Listen and put a number next to the type of music you hear.

| ☐ classical music | ☐ country music | ☐ jazz | ☐ gospel music |
| ☐ rock music | ☐ hip hop | 1 folk music | ☐ reggae |

135

MUSICAL INSTRUMENTS

A WHICH INSTRUMENT DOESN'T BELONG?

1. trumpet	tuba	trombone	banjo
2. cymbals	drum	accordion	tambourine
3. drum	bass	harp	electric guitar
4. electric keyboard	organ	bassoon	piano
5. cello	oboe	flute	piccolo
6. flute	violin	harp	trumpet

B LIKELY OR UNLIKELY?

Put a check in the best column.

	Likely	Unlikely
1. Our school band has several keyboard instruments.	____	✓
2. The electric guitar is a popular string instrument.	____	____
3. I plugged in my trumpet and I'm ready to play!	____	____
4. I wanted to learn a brass instrument, so I decided to take oboe lessons.	____	____
5. I couldn't play my harmonica because my foot was broken.	____	____
6. Our neighbors complain because I make a lot of noise when I practice the drums.	____	____
7. That string quartet had a viola, a bass, a bassoon, and a cello.	____	____
8. My sister plays the harp in her school band.	____	____
9. I love to hear the organ music in church.	____	____
10. I had no problem carrying the bass, but the violin was a little too heavy for me.	____	____

C ASSOCIATIONS

__e__	1. trombone	a.	church
____	2. violin	b.	country music
____	3. electric guitar	c.	classical music
____	4. banjo	d.	marching band
____	5. organ	e.	mouth
____	6. harmonica	f.	rock band

D LISTENING: *Which Instrument?*

Listen and decide which musical instrument you're listening to.

☐	trumpet	☐	organ	☐	harmonica
☐	drums	1	flute	☐	acoustic guitar
☐	piano	☐	violin	☐	electric guitar

A WHERE ARE THEY?

<u> f </u> 1. The scarecrow is in the _____.

_____ 2. The chickens are in the _____.

_____ 3. The pig is in the _____.

_____ 4. The cows are in the _____.

_____ 5. The horse is in the _____.

_____ 6. The fruit trees are in the _____.

_____ 7. The goat is in the _____.

_____ 8. The hens are in the _____.

a. barnyard

b. stable

c. pasture

d. hen house

e. chicken coop

f. garden

g. pig pen

h. orchard

B WHICH WORD?

1. The farmer and his family live in the (hen house (farmhouse)).

2. We grow (hay   alfalfa) on our farm.

3. We sell most of our (wheat   cotton) to the flour mill.

4. The (hired hand   rooster) is loading the hay into the barn.

5. The cows and the sheep are grazing in the (garden   pasture).

6. We have goats, turkeys, and lambs in our (barnyard   garden).

7. The (corn   fruit) is almost ready for harvest from the field.

8. The farm worker is using the (horse   tractor) to plant crops.

9. We keep a (scarecrow   farm worker) in our garden to keep the birds away.

10. Our (tractor   irrigation system) brings water to areas that would otherwise be dry.

C WHO'S MY MOTHER?

Below are baby animals. Can you guess what the corresponding adult animals are?

1. piglet _____pig_____

2. chick _____

3. lamb _____

4. calf _____

5. foal _____

6. kid _____

D ANIMAL SOUNDS!

See if you can match the following sounds with the animals below.

| a. moo! b. neigh! c. cock-a-doodle-do! d. baah! e. oink! |

<u> c </u> 1. rooster   _____ 3. horse   _____ 5. sheep

_____ 2. cow   _____ 4. pig

Do these animals make the same sounds in your language? What sounds do they make?

137

A WHO'S TALKING?

1. "I'm a large animal known for my big antlers." ___moose___
2. "I have sharp quills all over my body." _____
3. "I'm known as man's best friend." _____
4. "Look for me near a river. I'll be building a dam." _____
5. "I have spots and a long, thin neck." _____
6. "I make a sound that sounds like someone laughing." _____
7. "I'm a kind of bear with white fur, and I live in cold climates." _____
8. "I'm a large animal with a trunk and tusks made of ivory." _____
9. "If you come to Africa and see an animal with a hump—that's me!" _____
10. "I'm a common household pet whose babies are called *kittens*." _____
11. "I carry my young ones in a pouch." _____
12. "I'm a mammal, but I also lay eggs." _____
13. "I'm like a horse, but smaller even when I'm full grown." _____
14. "I'm a kind of bear with black and white fur." _____
15. "I'm small and also called a *bunny*." _____
16. "I'm a horse-like animal with alternating black and white stripes." _____
17. "I am a big, black cat that lives in the jungle and hunts for food." _____
18. "I'm a kind of monkey that has fur that looks orange." _____
19. "I'm black and white and produce a bad odor when I'm threatened." _____
20. "I look like a mouse with wings, and I hang upside down during the day." _____

B ANALOGIES

1. zebra : stripes *as* jaguar : ____spots____
2. mouse : mice *as* wolf : _____
3. camel : hump *as* lion : _____
4. bear : claw *as* tiger : _____
5. elephant : trunk *as* rhinoceros : _____

C ANIMAL EXPRESSIONS

Certain qualities are attributed to certain animals. See if you can guess which ones they are. Are they the same in your culture?

1. as busy as a ____beaver____
2. as sly as a _____
3. as strong as a _____
4. as quiet as a _____
5. as stubborn as a _____

6. as cute as a _____
7. as hungry as a _____

Add two of your own.

8. ....
9. ....

A COLORFUL BIRDS!

Without looking back at the Picture Dictionary, try to match the colors with the following birds.

_c_	**1.** Peacocks are _____.		**a.**	blue
____	**2.** Swans are _____.		**b.**	pink
____	**3.** Penguins are _____.		**c.**	multicolored
____	**4.** Flamingos are _____.		**d.**	black
____	**5.** Cardinals are _____.		**e.**	black and white
____	**6.** Crows are _____.		**f.**	white
____	**7.** Blue jays are _____.		**g.**	red

B WHAT'S THE BIRD?

1. This bird drills through bark and wood on trees.   _woodpecker_

2. This bird is colorful and can learn to say words.   _____

3. This bird is the symbol of the United States.   _____

4. This bird has pink feathers, long legs, and a long neck.   _____

5. This bird has white feathers and stands on one leg.   _____

6. This bird lives in cities and can sometimes be used
to carry messages.   _____

7. This bird is famous for being wise and is active at night.   _____

8. This bird keeps food in its large beak and lives near the sea.   _____

9. This bird likes the cold and lives in Antarctica.   _____

C WHAT'S THE INSECT?

1. This insect has eight legs and makes a web to live in.   _spider_

2. This insect can be seen at night.   _____

3. This insect is green and can jump very fast and far.   _____

4. This insect is red with black spots and is small and quiet.   _____

5. This insect eats wood and causes damage to houses.   _____

6. This insect makes honey and stings you if you get too close.   _____

7. This insect looks like a worm but turns into a butterfly.   _____

8. This insect's name means "one hundred legs."   _____

9. When this insect bites you, it takes some blood and makes you itch.   _____

A WHICH WORD?

1. I got stung by a ((jellyfish)   toad) while I was swimming at the beach last week.
2. (Crabs   Squids) release black ink and swim away when they feel danger.
3. (Otters   Cod) are playful animals that live near the sea.
4. A (shark   dolphin) looks like a fish but is a mammal.
5. A sea (horse   lion) is a very small undersea creature.

B WHICH WORD DOESN'T BELONG?

1. flounder   (squid)   bass   tuna
2. iguana   toad   porpoise   alligator
3. octopus   sea urchin   sea lion   sea horse
4. snail   walrus   sea lion   whale
5. scale   gill   shell   fin
6. cobra   crocodile   boa constrictor   rattlesnake

C WHAT'S THE WORD?

dolphin	eels	starfish	stingray

1. A. This is a great _____dolphin_____ show!
   B. I agree. I love to see them do their tricks.

2. A. Do you want to see the _____?
   B. No, Daddy. They look scary—like underwater snakes.

3. A. Have you ever seen a _____?
   B. No. They live at the bottom of the ocean.

4. A. Look at all the _____ on the beach!
   B. They must have washed up on the shore.

lizard	newt	rattlesnake	tortoise	turtle

5. A _____ is like a salamander and is usually red in color.

6. If you see a _____ shaking its tail and making a noise, be careful!

7. A _____ can live in dry environments, even in the desert.

8. Turtles and tortoises are similar. _____s have flippers and find it difficult to walk

   on land. _____s have legs and can walk very well on land.

A **CATEGORIES**

bark	cherry	limb	stem
birch	elm	oak	thorn
branch	geranium	orchid	trunk
bud	hibiscus	petal	violet

Types of Flowers

geranium
_____
_____
_____

Parts of a Flower

_____
_____
_____
_____

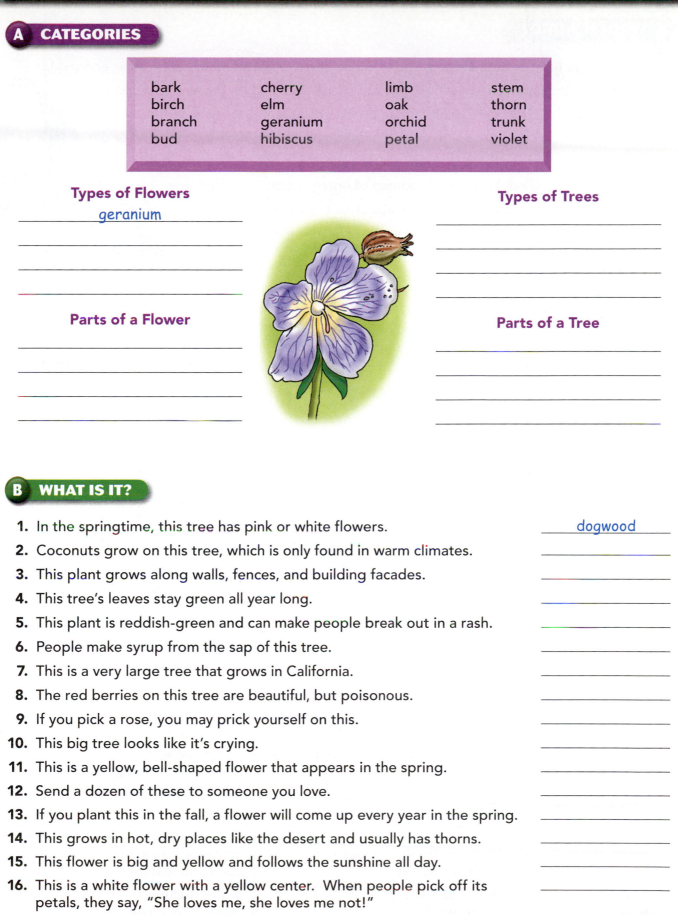

Types of Trees

_____
_____
_____
_____

Parts of a Tree

_____
_____
_____
_____

B **WHAT IS IT?**

1. In the springtime, this tree has pink or white flowers.   _dogwood_
2. Coconuts grow on this tree, which is only found in warm climates.   _____
3. This plant grows along walls, fences, and building facades.   _____
4. This tree's leaves stay green all year long.   _____
5. This plant is reddish-green and can make people break out in a rash.   _____
6. People make syrup from the sap of this tree.   _____
7. This is a very large tree that grows in California.   _____
8. The red berries on this tree are beautiful, but poisonous.   _____
9. If you pick a rose, you may prick yourself on this.   _____
10. This big tree looks like it's crying.   _____
11. This is a yellow, bell-shaped flower that appears in the spring.   _____
12. Send a dozen of these to someone you love.   _____
13. If you plant this in the fall, a flower will come up every year in the spring.   _____
14. This grows in hot, dry places like the desert and usually has thorns.   _____
15. This flower is big and yellow and follows the sunshine all day.   _____
16. This is a white flower with a yellow center. When people pick off its petals, they say, "She loves me, she loves me not!"   _____

A WHICH WORD?

1. The average temperature in the world may rise due to ((global warming) solar energy).
2. One way to conserve energy is to (carpool   save water) on the way to work.
3. (Geothermal   Nuclear) energy is clean and efficient, but there is dangerous waste.
4. It's important to conserve resources by (recycling   using hydroelectric power).
5. Many fish and animals living in rivers are poisoned by (gas   water pollution).
6. Burning (oil   wind) is the main source of energy in the U.S. right now.
7. My husband and I are very concerned about air (energy   pollution).
8. (Acid   Toxic) rain is very harmful to rivers, lakes, and wildlife.
9. We heat our home by (radiation   natural gas).

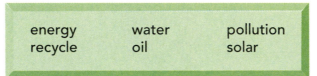

B CONSERVATION AT HOME

energy	water	pollution
recycle	oil	solar

Our family is very environmentally conscious. We do many things around the house to save _____energy_____ **1**. First, instead of using _____ **2** to heat our home in the winter, we use _____ **3** energy by collecting sunlight from panels on the roof. Also, we _____ **4** all of our plastic, metal, and paper trash instead of just throwing it away. Another thing we do is save _____ **5** by making sure our faucets aren't dripping. We also do things around the neighborhood to keep it clean and safe. Once a month, we go to the river to remove trash and try to reverse the effects of water _____ **6**.

C WHICH WORD DOESN'T BELONG?

1. oil   (rain)   gas   wind
2. carpool   recycle   save water   burn coal
3. geothermal   global warming   acid rain   toxic waste
4. hydroelectric solar   geothermal   radiation

D LISTENING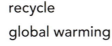

Listen and choose the best answer.

1. a. air pollution
   b. solar energy

2. a. oil
   b. water

3. a. hydroelectric power
   b. radiation

4. a. acid rain
   b. wind

5. a. global warming
   b. radiation materials

6. a. water pollution
   b. hazardous waste

A WHICH WORD?

1. A. My house was destroyed by a (landslide (tornado)).
   B. That's terrible! How fast was the wind?

2. A. The woods are very dry now because there hasn't been any rain in a while.
   B. It sounds like there's a possibility of a (forest fire mudslide).

3. A. All the heavy rain over the last few days caused the river to overflow.
   B. Was there a (typhoon flood)?

4. A. Did you hear about the (typhoon tsunami)?
   B. Yes. It was caused by an underwater earthquake a few miles off shore.

5. A. Many homes in the mountains were destroyed during the earthquake.
   B. Yes. The strong shock caused a (landslide wildfire).

6. A. Shh! Don't make loud noises on the hillside like that.
   B. Why? Will it cause an (earthquake avalanche)?

7. A. The mountain has been smoking for weeks!
   B. Scientists are warning that there might be (a volcanic eruption an avalanche).

8. A. What happened to your apartment building during the recent (mudslide earthquake)?
   B. The ground shook and our building moved back and forth, but luckily it wasn't damaged.

B WHAT IS IT?

1. This is a storm with heavy winds and rain that occurs in the Pacific Ocean.   _____typhoon_____

2. This sometimes occurs during a drought when bushes are too dry.   _____

3. This occurs in snowy mountains when a loud sound causes
   the snow to fall.   _____

4. This is a kind of storm that has very high winds that blow in a cyclone.   _____

5. This occurs when the water level rises many feet above the normal level.   _____

6. This occurs when there is a long period with very little rainfall.   _____

7. This is a violent snowstorm with very strong winds.   _____

8. This is a funnel-shaped cloud extending toward the ground
   with violent winds.   _____

C LISTENING

Listen and decide which natural disaster is happening.

___ hurricane	_1_ tsunami	___ blizzard	___ drought	___ earthquake

ANSWER KEY AND LISTENING SCRIPTS

A. WHAT'S THE QUESTION?

1. What's your name?
2. What's your first name?
3. What's your middle initial?
4. What's your last name?
5. What's your address?
6. What's your e-mail address?
7. What's your social security number?
8. What's your date of birth?

B. WHAT INFORMATION DO YOU NEED?

1. name, address
2. area code, telephone number
3. address
4. date of birth, telephone number, cell phone number
5. name/first name/first name and last name (depending on who you're introducing)
6. first name, middle initial, last name, address, city, state, zip code, area code, telephone number, social security number, date of birth

C. LISTENING

Listen and choose the correct answer.

A. Tell me your name again.
B. It's Patterson. My name is Robert V. Patterson.
A. And do you have a number where we can reach you, Mr. Patterson?
B. Yes. You can call me at two five nine–three six nine oh.
A. Is that area code seven one eight?
B. Yes, that's right. You can also call me on my cell phone. The number is seven six seven–three four oh–six five eight three.
A. And where do you live, Mr. Patterson?
B. At forty Harrison Road.
A. Is that here in Easton?
B. No. It's in Weston. And the zip code there is two two four nine oh.
A. Did you say two two nine four oh?
B. No. Two two four nine oh.
A. Well, I think that's all the information I need. Oh, one more thing. I forgot to ask you for your e-mail address.
B. It's r–v–p at worldlink dot com.

Answers

1. c   4. b   7. b
2. b   5. a   8. c
3. a   6. a   9. c

WORKBOOK PAGE 2

A. WHO ARE THEY?

1. grandmother
2. uncle
3. aunt
4. cousins
5. sister-in-law
6. niece
7. nephews
8. father-in-law
9. brother-in-law

B. TRUE OR FALSE?

1. True   4. True
2. False   5. False
3. False   6. True

C. WHAT'S THE RELATIONSHIP?

1. husband : wife
2. father : son
3. brother : brother
4. mother-in-law : daughter-in-law
5. aunt : niece
6. grandfather : granddaughter
7. father-in-law : son-in-law
8. grandmother : grandson
9. sister-in-law : sister-in-law
10. cousin : cousin

WORKBOOK PAGE 3

A. FINISH THE SENTENCE

1. c   5. d
2. e   6. b
3. g   7. a
4. f

B. 20 QUESTIONS: *What's the Object?*

1. pen
2. clock
3. marker
4. screen
5. map/globe
6. chalk
7. pencil sharpener
8. monitor
9. ruler
10. graph paper
11. binder/notebook
12. workbook
13. seat/chair
14. eraser
15. calculator
16. desk
17. eraser
18. bookcase/bookshelf
19. thumbtack
20. keyboard

WORKBOOK PAGE 4

A. OPPOSITES

1. b   5. g
2. d   6. c
3. e   7. f
4. a

B. MATCH THE ACTIONS

1. c   4. b
2. f   5. d
3. a   6. e

C. WHAT'S THE ACTION?

1. Listen to   4. Look at
2. Discuss   5. Go to
3. Look up   6. Correct

D. LISTENING

Listen and write the number of the sentence that has the same meaning.

1. Please pass out the tests.
2. Please take a seat.
3. Please use another piece of paper.
4. Please go over the mistakes.
5. Please hand in the homework.
6. Work alone.

Answers

2   5
1   3
4   6

WORKBOOK PAGE 5

A. OPPOSITES

1. under
2. above
3. left
4. in front of
5. between

B. WHERE IS IT?

1. on   5. in
2. above   6. right of
3. behind   7. in front of
4. between   8. below

C. WHAT'S WRONG WITH THIS CLASSROOM?

The wastebasket is on the desk.
The clock is below the chalkboard.
The keyboard is behind the computer.
The pencil sharpener is above the bulletin board.
The printer is under the table.
The globe is on the overhead projector.
The mouse is in the bookcase.
The map is in front of the screen.

WORKBOOK PAGE 6

A. WHICH WORD?

1. undressed   6. take a bath
2. makeup   7. dinner
3. teeth   8. comb
4. make   9. make
5. taking a shower 10. gets up

B. LISTENING

Listen and choose the best answer.

1. Elizabeth is very tired, and she has to get up early tomorrow. She really should . . . .
2. Millie went sailing this afternoon. It was very windy, and now her hair looks terrible. She really needs to . . . .
3. Frank is having an examination at

the doctor's office. The doctor is asking him to take off his clothes. "Frank, you need to . . . !"

4. Johnny's alarm clock is ringing. It's seven A.M., and he has to get to school by eight o'clock. "Johnny, it's time to . . . !"

5. My five-year-old nephew was eating chocolate and got it all over his face. He needs to . . . .

6. We were so busy at work today that we didn't have time to . . . .

7. Barbara is almost ready to go out to the party, but she still has to . . . .

8. My thirteen-year-old son is really growing up. Soon he'll be ready to . . . .

Answers

2	4
6	1
8	3
5	7

C. IT'S TIME TO GET UP!

1. up	5. shave
2. face	6. hair
3. teeth	7. bed
4. shower	8. breakfast

WORKBOOK PAGE 7

A. WHAT'S THE ACTIVITY?

1. cleaning
2. feed the baby
3. leave work
4. ironing
5. drives
6. studying
7. take the bus
8. go to the store
9. do the laundry
10. washes the dishes
11. walk
12. feed the cat

WORKBOOK PAGE 8

A. KEEPING BUSY

1. exercises	5. relaxes
2. listens	6. reads
3. writes	7. plants flowers
4. swim	8. plays cards

B. WHAT'S THE ACTIVITY?

1. relax
2. watch TV
3. exercises
4. practice the piano
5. use the computer
6. plays basketball
7. plant flowers
8. reads

WORKBOOK PAGE 9

A. WHAT'S THE RESPONSE?

1. e	3. f	5. g	7. c
2. d	4. a	6. b	

B. CAN YOU REMEMBER?

1. Thank you.
   Thanks.
2. Good-bye.
   Bye.
3. Can you please repeat that?
   Can you please say that again?
4. Hello.
   Hi.
5. I don't understand.
   Sorry. I don't understand.
6. Hello. My name is . . . .
   Hi. I'm . . . .

WORKBOOK PAGE 10

A. WEATHER TALK

1. drizzling
2. Celsius
3. sunny
4. cloudy
5. muggy
6. thunderstorm
7. smoggy
8. lightning
9. foggy
10. snowstorm

B. GOOD IDEA OR BAD IDEA?

1. a		7. b
2. a		8. b
3. b		9. a
4. a		10. b
5. b		11. a
6. a		12. b

WORKBOOK PAGE 11

A. ORDINALS

1. fourth
2. second
3. sixth
4. eighty-fifth
5. fortieth
6. first
7. thirtieth
8. third

B. WHAT'S THE NUMBER?

1. higher
2. twelfth
3. sixteen
4. billion
5. lower
6. tenth

C. LISTENING: *Same or Different?*

As you listen, read the sentences below. Write S if the sentences are the same or D if the sentences are different.

1. Amanda lives at nine seventy-five Central Avenue.
2. Our town has a population of five thousand five hundred.
3. My zip code is two nine two zero nine.
4. Bernardo's new computer costs five thousand one hundred ninety nine dollars.

5. Susan's phone number is three six five–zero seven nine one.
6. My social security number is oh five oh–three three–one oh two nine.

Answers

1. D
2. S
3. S
4. D
5. D
6. D

D. ROMAN NUMERALS

1. 8
2. 14
3. 25
4. 43
5. 54
6. 175
7. 1010
8. 66
9. 19
10. 77
11. 48
12. 101

WORKBOOK PAGE 12

A. WHAT TIME IS IT?

1. two fifteen/a quarter after two
2. one twenty/twenty after one
3. eight ten/ten after eight
4. twelve forty-five/a quarter to one
5. ten forty/twenty to eleven
6. six fifty/ten to seven
7. nine thirty-five/ twenty-five minutes to ten
8. noon/twelve noon
9. midnight/twelve midnight
10. three thirty/half past three
11. four fifty-five/five to five
12. four oh five/five after four

B. LISTENING: *True or False?*

Listen and decide whether the following statements are True (T) or False (F).

1. Anthony's plane will arrive in London at twenty after five in the morning.
2. I usually have lunch at twelve o'clock.
3. My mother had to wait until a quarter after five to see her doctor.
4. My daughter finally went to bed at a quarter after ten.
5. William's bus will arrive from Seattle at two thirty-eight in the afternoon.
6. I have an appointment to see my professor at ten minutes to three.
7. Roger works at the convenience store from ten in the morning until half past eleven at night.

Answers

1. T	3. F	5. T	7. T
2. T	4. F	6. F	

A. LISTENING

Listen and write the amount of money you hear.

1. I bought a new shirt for my husband for twenty-nine fifty.
2. Here you are. Your change comes to four dollars and sixty-three cents.
3. The subway is expensive. For one ride you have to pay two twenty-five.
4. I got a great deal on my air ticket. It was only a hundred and seventy-nine dollars.
5. I can't buy any candy. I only have fifteen cents.
6. The taxi ride to the airport cost me more than nineteen dollars.
7. With the tax, that comes to seven hundred and fourteen dollars and fifty-three cents.
8. Do you like my new jacket? I only paid eighty-nine ninety-nine!
9. I don't care if they say it's an antique! I wouldn't pay one cent for this old piece of junk!

Answers

1. $29.50
2. $4.63
3. $2.25
4. $179
5. 15¢
6. $19.00
7. $714.53
8. $89.99
9. 1¢

B. HOW MUCH DO THEY COST?

1. c   4. f
2. b   5. d
3. a   6. e

C. ANOTHER WAY OF SAYING IT

1. ten cents
2. five cents
3. one cent
4. a dollar
5. thousand dollars

D. GETTING CHANGE

1. $3.25
2. 25¢
3. 5¢
4. $10
5. 65¢
6. $7.50

A. U.S CALENDAR QUIZ

1. February
2. January
3. fourth, July
4. Monday
5. April, May
6. November
7. September
8. April
9. June
10. March

A. COMPLETE JULIE'S SCHEDULE

(See page 172.)

B. LISTENING: *True or False?*

Listen and decide whether the following statements are True (T) or False (F).

1. Bob's brother lives in Atlanta and his sister lives in Chicago. Bob called his brother yesterday morning and his sister yesterday evening.
2. Marie enjoys seeing movies and plays. She saw a movie last weekend, and she's going to see a play this weekend.
3. Thomas likes to exercise. He jogs twice a week, and he goes swimming once a week.
4. The Baxters are having a very busy weekend. They drove to the beach yesterday afternoon, and they're going to drive to the mountains tomorrow afternoon.
5. Mabel saw her doctor last Monday, and she's going to see her dentist next Monday.
6. Michael is taking Spanish this semester, and he's going to take French next semester.
7. The Garcias take a vacation every summer. Last summer they went to Alaska, and this summer they're going to Canada.
8. Kevin has a dog named Rusty and a cat named Friskie. Kevin bathed Rusty last night. Tonight he's going to bathe Friskie.

Answers

1. T   5. T
2. T   6. T
3. F   7. F
4. F   8. T

A. WHAT'S THE WORD?

1. town
2. house
3. condominium
4. dormitory
5. houseboat
6. shelter
7. mobile home
8. farm
9. nursing home
10. the city
11. ranch
12. the country

B. LISTENING: *What Are They Talking About?*

Listen and decide what kind of housing these people are talking about.

1. I live on the fourth floor. My neighbors on the third and fifth floors are very nice.
2. We like the Sanchez family very much. We're lucky. After all, their place is attached to ours.
3. We love living here on the farm. What a change from the city! Every morning before breakfast we milk the cows.
4. The Johnsons are so happy with their new house. It's close to the city, and it's also close to the country.
5. Mr. Tyler, I know your father will be happy living here. There are many other people his age, and we have a lot of activities I'm sure he'll enjoy.
6. I have a great room. My roommate is very friendly, and I'm right near the center of the campus.

Answers

1. a
2. a
3. b
4. a
5. b
6. a

A. CAN YOU FIND . . . ?

7 Things to Put Other Things On or In

bookcase	mantel
coffee table	wall
end table	wall unit
magazine holder	

5 Things that Are Decorative

drapes
picture/photograph
plant
rug
throw pillow

7 Things that Use Electricity

DVD player	stereo system
floor lamp	TV
lamp	VCR
speaker	

3 Things We Sit On

armchair
loveseat
sofa/couch

5 Things that Are Part of the Structure of the House

ceiling
fireplace
floor
wall
window

2 Things that Lower Light

drapes
lampshade

B. WHICH WORD?

1. lamp
2. mantel
3. unit

4. stereo
5. fireplace
6. loveseat
7. drapes
8. painting
9. stereo system
10. DVD player
11. photograph
12. wall
13. lamp
14. an end table
15. bookcase

WORKBOOK PAGE 18

A. CAN YOU FIND . . . ?

5 Things that Hold Hot Beverages and Foods

china
coffee pot
serving platter
serving bowl
teapot

6 Things that Hold Cold Beverages and Foods

china
creamer
pitcher
salad bowl
serving bowl
serving platter

5 Things Used to Decorate a Table

candle
candlestick
vase
china
tablecloth

2 Things that Hold Food Seasonings

pepper shaker
salt shaker

3 Pieces of Furniture

china cabinet
(dining room) chair
(dining room) table

2 Things that Give Light

candle
chandelier

B. WHICH WORD?

1. tablecloth
2. platter
3. cabinet
4. vase
5. dish
6. tray
7. knife
8. chair
9. napkin
10. candles
11. saucer
12. pitcher
13. sugar
14. dish
15. buffet

WORKBOOK PAGE 19

A. WHAT IS IT?

1. alarm clock
2. night table/nightstand
3. fitted sheet
4. electric blanket
5. jewelry box
6. pillow
7. mirror
8. lamp
9. blinds
10. bed frame

B. LISTENING: *Frannie's Furniture Store*

Listen to the following advertisement and write the prices you hear.

For three days, Frannie's Furniture Store is having its annual sale. We have fantastic buys on every bed in the store. You can buy a twin bed this week for the low, low price of just two hundred and nineteen dollars. That's right, just two nineteen. If you need something a little larger, all of our double beds are on sale this week, too, for only two ninety-nine. Can you believe it?! Two ninety-nine! That's the lowest price in the city for a double bed. And now for even bigger news! Frannie's famous king- and queen-size beds are also on sale this week—with huge savings. You can own a queen-size bed for just four forty-five. That's right. Just four forty-five. But if a king-size bed is what you had in mind, hold on to your hats because Frannie's king-size beds are at the lowest price they've ever been. Every king-size bed in the store is on sale this week for the unbelievably low price of six hundred and ninety-seven dollars. Can you believe it? Six ninety-seven for a king-size bed?! The price has never been lower! Perhaps you're looking for a sofa bed for your living room. A sofa bed is a comfortable sofa during the day. And like magic, it converts into a bed at night. Frannie's sofa beds are on sale this week, and this week only, for just nine hundred and nine dollars. Nine oh nine for a sofa bed?! That's unbelievable!! And they're available in your choice of colors and fabrics. And that's not all. Perhaps you're looking for a bunk bed or a trundle bed for your child's room. You came to the right place. Every bunk bed is on sale this week for just three hundred and twenty-three dollars. Can you believe it? Three twenty-three for a bunk bed?! And they're available in seven popular colors. Or perhaps you'd prefer a trundle bed. Look no further. Trundle beds are only three thirty-two this week. That's right. For just three hundred and thirty-two dollars, you can own one of Frannie's comfortable and convenient trundle beds—also available in seven beautiful colors. And finally, do you need a bed that you can keep in a closet, folded up, and take out if an unexpected guest arrives to stay for a while? In that case, you should come on over to Frannie's and take a look at Frannie's huge selection of cots. Every cot in the store is just seventy-nine dollars this week. At that price, you can afford to buy two or even three—to keep in your house or apartment, just in case. You'll never see a sale like this again . . . ever! So come on over to Frannie's Furniture Store. It's at one forty-five Central Avenue in Westville—across from the Midtown Mall. The sale is for three days only, and it starts today!

Answers

(See page 172.)

C. WHAT'S THE WORD?

1. clock radio
2. mattress
3. flat sheet
4. queen-size, king-size
5. bunk bed
6. sofa bed

WORKBOOK PAGES 20–21

A. CAN YOU FIND . . . ?

5 Things to Cook Food With

microwave/microwave oven
oven
stove/range
toaster
toaster oven

5 Things You Use When You Wash Dishes

dish rack/dish drainer
dish towel
dishwasher
dishwasher detergent
dishwashing liquid

12 Appliances

electric can opener/can opener
electric mixer/mixer
garbage disposal/disposal
blender
coffeemaker
dishwasher
food processor
microwave/microwave oven
oven
refrigerator
stove/range
toaster
toaster oven
trash compactor

B. ANALOGIES

1. tea kettle
2. paper towel holder
3. sink
4. cutting board

5. microwave (oven)
6. food processor
7. spice rack
8. dishwasher

C. WHAT'S THE OBJECT?

1. e	4. b	7. a
2. c	5. f	
3. g	6. d	

D. LISTENING

Listen and choose the best answer.

1. How long should I bake the pie in the . . . ?
2. This garbage is taking up too much room. We'd better use the . . . .
3. Ouch! That baking dish was hot! I should have used a . . . .
4. I found a great recipe in this . . . .
5. When I cut vegetables, I always use . . . .
6. Oh, no! What a waste of water! You forgot to turn off the . . . !
7. Let's sit and have a cup of coffee here at the . . . .
8. It burns everything! I think we need a new . . . .
9. How can we clean these dishes? We don't have any more . . . .

Answers

1. a	4. a	7. b
2. b	5. b	8. a
3. b	6. a	9. b

E. WHICH WORD DOESN'T BELONG?

1. freezer (The others are hot.)
2. oven (The others are associated with water.)
3. tea kettle (The others are appliances.)
4. kitchen table (The others are containers.)
5. placemat (The others are used when you wash dishes.)
6. toaster (The others are for mixing.)

F. WHAT'S WRONG WITH THIS KITCHEN?

The microwave is sideways.
The dishwasher is upside down.
The faucet is on the window.
The blender is in the freezer.
The spice rack is on the refrigerator.
The canisters are on the stove.
The burners are on the kitchen table.
The toaster is under the table.
The dishes are in the garbage pail.
The electric can opener is under the sink.
The trash compactor is on the counter.
The tea kettle is in the oven.

WORKBOOK PAGE 22

A. BABYTOWN

Baby Equipment

baby backpack
baby carriage

car seat
diaper pail
potty
walker

Toys

doll
rattle
stuffed animal
teddy bear

Electrical Items

intercom
night light

Furniture

changing table
chest of drawers
cradle
crib

Feeding

booster seat
food warmer

B. WHICH WORD?

1. mobile
2. chest
3. toy chest
4. stroller
5. high chair
6. stuffed animal
7. night light
8. stretch suit
9. safety seat
10. monitor

WORKBOOK PAGE 23

A. LIKELY OR UNLIKELY?

	Likely	Unlikely
1.	___	✓
2.	✓	___
3.	✓	___
4.	___	✓
5.	✓	___
6.	___	✓
7.	___	✓
8.	✓	___
9.	___	✓
10.	___	✓
11.	___	✓

B. COMPLETE THE SENTENCES

1. toothbrush
2. dispenser
3. curtain
4. towel
5. cabinet
6. rack
7. holder

C. WHAT'S THE ACTION?

1. f
2. e
3. d
4. b
5. h, k
6. i
7. c, h
8. h

9. g, k, l
10. d
11. a
12. j, l
13. d
14. g
15. k, l

WORKBOOK PAGES 24–25

A. WHAT'S THE OBJECT?

1. doorbell
2. front light
3. barbecue
4. lawnmower
5. tool shed
6. garage
7. gutter
8. chimney
9. shutter
10. satellite dish
11. storm door
12. deck, patio/patio, deck

B. HOME REPAIRS

1. screen
2. garage
3. porch
4. light
5. barbecue

C. WHICH WORD?

1. roof
2. deck
3. storm door
4. screen
5. drainpipe
6. side door

D. LISTENING: *What Are They Talking About?*

Listen and decide what's being talked about.

1. You should have yours cleaned. There's a danger your house might catch on fire!
2. I'm nervous every time someone walks on it. It really needs to be repaved.
3. Don't forget to turn it on when we leave tonight!
4. We love to just sit and relax there every evening after dinner.
5. I agree. It's the best place for the TV antenna.
6. You're right! They all need to be replaced. Bugs are getting into the house from every window!

Answers

1. a	4. a	
2. b	5. b	
3. b	6. a	

E. WHAT'S WRONG WITH THIS HOUSE?

The satellite dish is on the porch.
The mailbox is on the roof.
The chimney is on the garage.
The garage door is in front of the house.

The front door is in the garage.
The driveway is in front of the house.
The front walk is in front of the garage.
The doorbell is on the second floor.
There's only one shutter on each
  window.
The TV antenna is on the front walk.
The lamppost is on top of the garage.
The front light is on the garage.

WORKBOOK PAGE 26

A. OUR NEW PLACE

1. third
2. neighbors
3. moving truck/moving van
4. building manager
5. key
6. elevator
7. stairway
8. apartment ads/classified ads
9. vacancy signs
10. landlord
11. lease
12. security deposit
13. tenants
14. swimming pool
15. whirlpool
16. parking lot
17. parking space
18. doorman
19. buzzer
20. intercom
21. fire
22. emergency stairway
23. superintendent
24. smoke detectors
25. storage locker
26. laundry
27. balcony

WORKBOOK PAGE 27

A. WHO SHOULD THEY CALL?

1. appliance repairperson
2. chimneysweep
3. exterminator
4. carpenter
5. painter
6. electrician
7. locksmith
8. heating and air conditioning service
9. plumber
10. roofer
11. cable TV company
12. home repairperson/"handyman"

B. LISTENING: *Who to Call?*

*Listen and write the number under the
appropriate home repairperson to call.*

1. Oh, no! I think I locked my keys in
   the car!
2. We'd better call now, or we won't
   be able to watch all our favorite
   programs this weekend.
3. Let's call right away! There are
   cockroaches in the kitchen!
4. It's freezing in here!
5. Did you see? The wall is cracked in
   the living room!

6. Uh-oh! The bathtub is leaking!
7. Oh, no! The front light doesn't go
   on!
8. We need to have a few things fixed
   around the house.

Answers

7	4	1	6
2	5	8	3

WORKBOOK PAGE 28

A. WHAT DOES HE NEED?

1. e	4. c, l
2. b, g, n	5. c, d, j, k
3. h, m	6. a, i, o

B. WHICH WORD?

1. broom
2. recycling
3. wax
4. ammonia
5. sponge
6. scrub brush
7. take out
8. cleaner
9. bag

C. LISTENING

*Listen and choose the appropriate
cleaning item to complete the
conversation.*

1. A. Are you ready to mop the
      kitchen floor yet?
   B. No. First I have to sweep it with
      a . . . .
2. A. We haven't washed our windows
      in a long time.
   B. You're right. We haven't. Let's
      wash them now. I'll get some
      paper towels and . . . .
3. A. I'm very concerned about the
      environment.
   B. I am, too. That's why I put all my
      used bottles in a . . . .
4. A. Did you finish cleaning the
      bathroom?
   B. I couldn't. We ran out of . . . .
5. A. Let's dust and polish the
      furniture.
   B. Do we have enough . . . ?
6. A Your floors have been looking
      very clean and shiny!
   B. That's because I'm using a new
      brand of . . . .

Answers

1. b	4. b
2. a	5. b
3. a	6. a

WORKBOOK PAGE 29

A. ASSOCIATIONS

1. i
2. c
3. e
4. a
5. h
6. g

7. f
8. k
9. b
10. d
11. j

B. WHICH WORD?

1. an extension cord
2. fuses
3. masking tape
4. sandpaper
5. roller
6. paintbrush
7. oil
8. work gloves
9. a tape measure
10. fly swatter

C. WHAT'S THE OBJECT?

1. mousetrap
2. batteries
3. electrical tape
4. flashlight
5. plunger
6. step ladder
7. glue
8. fly swatter
9. tape measure, yardstick

WORKBOOK PAGE 30

A. CAN YOU FIND . . . ?

3 Tools for Making Holes

(drill) bit
electric drill
hand drill

3 Tools for Cutting

circular saw/power saw
hacksaw
saw/handsaw

**12 Tools and Supplies for Fastening
and Unfastening**

bolt
hammer
machine screw
monkey wrench/pipe wrench
nail
nut
Phillips screwdriver
pliers
screwdriver
vise
washer
wood screw
wrench

B. WHICH WORD?

1. an ax
2. saw
3. hammer
4. bolt, wrench
5. pipe wrench
6. scraper
7. hacksaw
8. plane
9. sander
10. vise

Listen to the sounds. Write the number next to the tool you hear.

1. [sound: power saw]
2. [sound: sandpaper]
3. [sound: saw]
4. [sound: electric drill]
5. [sound: hammer]
6. [sound: scraper]

Answers

4	3
2	5
6	1

WORKBOOK PAGE 31

A. WHICH WORD?

1. rake
2. watering can
3. sprinkler
4. shovel
5. hedge clippers
6. garden hose

B. WHAT'S THE OBJECT?

1. lawnmower
2. garden hose
3. yard waste bag
4. nozzle
5. shovel
6. fertilizer

C. PROBABLE OR IMPOBABLE?

	Probable	Improbable
1.		✓
2.	✓	
3.	✓	
4.		✓
5.		✓
6.		✓
7.	✓	
8.	✓	
9.		✓
10.		✓

D. LISTENING: *What Are They Talking About?*

Listen and write the number next to the correct gardening word.

1. We use it all the time to trim our hedges.
2. I cut the grass with it every week.
3. It certainly helps my plants grow.
4. Where can we put all these leaves?
5. It reaches every part of my yard.
6. There are leaves everywhere! This will help to clean them up quickly.

Answers

6	5
4	2
1	3

WORKBOOK PAGE 32

A. WHERE CAN I GET . . .?

1. clothing store/department store/discount store
2. convenience store/grocery store
3. drug store/pharmacy
4. barber shop
5. gas station/service station
6. delicatessen/deli/grocery store
7. bakery
8. flower shop/florist
9. car dealership
10. book store
11. clinic
12. eye-care center/optician
13. cleaners/dry cleaners
14. computer store
15. coffee shop/donut shop/fast-food restaurant
16. bank

B. WHICH WORD DOESN'T BELONG?

1. barber shop (The others are associated with food.)
2. donut shop (The others are associated with paper.)
3. florist (The others are associated with cars.)
4. delicatessen (The others are associated with medicine.)
5. service (The others are "stores.")
6. electronics (The others are "shops.")
7. child-care center (The others are associated with food.)

C. ANALOGIES

1. bakery
2. eye-care center
3. donut shop
4. electronics store
5. clinic
6. child-care center/day-care center

WORKBOOK PAGE 33

A. WHERE CAN I GET . . .?

1. hair salon
2. travel agency
3. hair salon/nail salon
4. shoe store/(shopping) mall
5. supermarket
6. hardware store
7. pet shop/pet store
8. health club
9. toy store
10. ice cream shop
11. library/school
12. hospital
13. restaurant
14. video store
15. post office
16. jewelry store/(shopping) mall

B. WHERE CAN I . . .?

1. laundromat
2. movie theater
3. park
4. ice cream shop/pizza shop
5. hotel/motel
6. photo shop
7. maternity shop/(shopping) mall
8. music store/(shopping) mall

C. ANALOGIES

1. pet shop/pet store
2. video store
3. library/school
4. restaurant
5. hotel
6. post office

WORKBOOK PAGE 34

A. WHAT'S THE WORD?

1. office building
2. drive-through window
3. pedestrian, intersection
4. parking garage
5. public telephone
6. jail
7. meter maid, parking meter
8. street light
9. courthouse
10. curb
11. newsstand
12. fire alarm box
13. street sign

B. GOOD IDEA OR BAD IDEA?

	Good Idea	Bad Idea
1.		✓
2.	✓	
3.		✓
4.	✓	
5.	✓	
6.		✓
7.	✓	
8.		✓
9.	✓	

WORKBOOK PAGE 35

A. WHICH WORD DOESN'T BELONG?

1. elderly
2. pregnant
3. middle-aged
4. shoulder-length
5. long
6. wavy
7. a teenager
8. slim

B. LISTENING: *Who Are They Talking About?*

Listen and decide who is being talked about.

1. A. Tell me about your daughter.
   B. Well, she just turned seventeen. She's thin because she exercises a lot, and she has short brown hair.

2. A. Can you describe your grandfather?
   B. Yes. He's tall and average weight. He wears glasses, and he's bald.

3. A. Tell me about your new boyfriend.
   B. He's really cute! He has short, red hair. And he's the perfect height for me—not too tall, and not too short.

4. A. How will I recognize you? What do you look like?
   B. Well, I'm relatively short and a bit heavy. My hair is curly and black, and I've got a beard.
5. A. Which one is your wife?
   B. She's the pregnant woman with shoulder-length black hair.
6. A. Which child is yours?
   B. She's that cute little toddler with curly blond hair.
7. A. What does your brother look like?
   B. He used to be heavy, but he recently lost a lot of weight, so now he's very slim. He has short straight brown hair.
8. A. What does your father look like?
   B. He's tall and heavy. He wears glasses, and he has a mustache.
9. A. Which one is your granddaughter?
   B. She's that tall teenager with long wavy black hair.
10. A. Can you describe the man who took your purse?
    B. I think so. He's was a tall heavy middle-aged man. No, wait a minute. Now that I think of it, he wasn't tall. I think he was average height.
    A. Anything else?
    B. He had a mustache. No, wait a minute. He didn't have a mustache. He had a beard. And I think his beard was black. Yes. He had a black beard. Or was it brown? Hmm. No. I'm pretty sure it was black.

Answers

6	9	4	1	8
10	2	7	5	3

C. WHICH WORD?

1. long
2. a mustache
3. Short
4. vision
5. black
6. bald
7. slim
8. physically

WORKBOOK PAGES 36–37

A. WHAT'S THE CATEGORY?

1. d
2. g
3. i
4. a
5. h
6. b
7. j
8. f
9. e
10. c

B. THE RIGHT WORD

1. soft
2. fast
3. hot
4. loud
5. bad
6. comfortable
7. thick
8. high
9. messy
10. difficult
11. honest
12. sharp
13. full
14. heavy
15. dry

C. SYNONYMS

1. d
2. f
3. j
4. b
5. h
6. e
7. c
8. k
9. l
10. i
11. h
12. g
13. a
14. g
15. k
16. e
17. l
18. g

D. "ICE COLD!"

1. ice
2. dirt
3. sky
4. bone
5. squeaky
6. skin
7. boiling
8. feather
9. soaking
10. brand
11. filthy
12. razor
13. chock
14. stick
15. pitch

E. LISTENING

Listen and choose the best answer.

1. This new floor wax is fantastic! Our kitchen floor has never looked so . . . .
2. I'm having a lot of trouble with the homework. These math problems are very . . . .
3. I think our dryer is broken. All the clothes are still . . . .
4. I can't possibly write with this pencil! It's too . . . .
5. We'll never get there on time because this traffic is so . . . .
6. That's strange. I thought I had locked the door, but when I returned home I found it . . . .
7. I really have to go on a diet. All my pants are too . . . .
8. My new car gets excellent mileage. After driving for just a few hours, the tank is almost . . . .
9. We can't possibly fit this sofa through the doorway. The sofa is too . . . .
10. The dentist has recommended braces for our son because his teeth are . . . .
11. I can't sleep on my mattress any more. It's really . . . .
12. Tommy, you should always tell the truth. You should never be . . . .

Answers

1. a	4. b	7. b	10. b
2. a	5. b	8. b	11. b
3. a	6. a	9. a	12. b

WORKBOOK PAGES 38–39

A. WHICH WORD DOESN'T BELONG?

1. excited (The others are sad words.)
2. bored (The others are angry words.)
3. confused (The others are tired words.)
4. surprised (The others are upset words.)
5. homesick (The others are eating or drinking words.)

B. ANALOGIES

1. ill
2. thirsty
3. exhausted
4. excited
5. frightened

C. THE NEXT WORD

1. b, c, e
2. b, d
3. b
4. a, b
5. b, c, d
6. b
7. b, c, e

D. SYNONYMS

1. h
2. d
3. c
4. g
5. f
6. b
7. e
8. a

E. WHICH WORD?

1. proud
2. embarrassed
3. homesick
4. annoyed
5. confused
6. frustrated
7. exhausted
8. full
9. shocked
10. sick

F. LISTENING: *How Are They Feeling?*

Listen and choose the best description of the person's feelings.

1. I can't believe it! I just got a parking ticket!
2. I've got a fever, my head is congested, and my nose is running.
3. I didn't get the promotion I was expecting.
4. I'm up way past my bedtime!
5. My girlfriend broke up with me last weekend, and I can't stop thinking about her.
6. I have an important math exam tomorrow, and I haven't studied.
7. Billy's parents bought him a dog. I wish I could get a dog, too!
8. I just found a dead mouse in my basement!

Answers

1. b	5. a
2. a	6. b
3. b	7. a
4. a	8. b

G. "RAGING MAD!"

1. c
2. e
3. b
4. a
5. d
6. i
7. g
8. f
9. h
10. j

A. WHAT'S THE FRUIT?

1. nuts
2. orange
3. lemon
4. banana
5. watermelon
6. peach
7. grapes
8. prunes
9. pineapple
10. coconut

B. WHICH FRUIT?

1. grapes
2. pears
3. an apricot
4. plantains
5. prunes
6. orange
7. tangerine
8. watermelon
9. blueberry
10. lime

C. "SOUR GRAPES!"

1. b
2. b
3. a
4. b
5. a
6. a

WORKBOOK PAGE 41

A. TOSSED SALAD

1. tomato
2. lettuce
3. green pepper
4. celery
5. cucumber
6. carrot
7. mushrooms
8. radish
9. artichoke
10. scallions

B. WHICH VEGETABLE DOESN'T BELONG?

1. tomato (The others are white vegetables.)
2. spinach (The others are yellow vegetables.)
3. brussels sprout (The others are long vegetables.)
4. kidney (The others are kinds of peppers.)
5. beet (The others are kinds of beans.)
6. bok choy (The others come in a head.)

C. TRUE OR FALSE?

1. F
2. T
3. F
4. F
5. T
6. F
7. F
8. F

D. CAN YOU REMEMBER?

3 Kinds of Squash

acorn
butternut
zucchini

4 Kinds of Beans

black
kidney
lima
string/green

3 Kinds of Peppers

green/sweet
jalapeño
red

WORKBOOK PAGE 42

A. CATEGORIES

	Category
1. chops	chicken
2. tripe	seafood
3. shrimp	meat
4. duck	fish
5. roast	poultry
6. salmon	meat
7. filet of sole	shellfish

B. WHICH WORD?

1. turkey
2. breasts
3. ground
4. beef
5. mussels
6. catfish
7. seafood
8. chops
9. lamb
10. poultry

C. LISTENING

Listen and choose the best response.

1. Let's make some stew for dinner!
2. What's your favorite fish?
3. Let's go to the new seafood restaurant downtown!
4. I'm trying to avoid eating meat. What do you recommend?
5. What's your favorite part of the chicken?
6. I'm going to the supermarket. Would you like lamb for dinner?
7. I'm hungry! What's for breakfast?
8. Do you have a seafood recommendation?
9. Do you sell chicken here?
10. I'm allergic to shellfish.

Answers

1. a		6. b	
2. b		7. b	
3. a		8. a	
4. a		9. a	
5. a		10. b	

WORKBOOK PAGE 43

A. LIKELY OR UNLIKELY?

	Likely	Unlikely
1.	___	✓
2.	✓	___
3.	✓	___
4.	___	✓
5.	✓	___
6.	___	✓
7.	✓	___
8.	___	✓
9.	___	✓

B. WHICH WORD?

1. milk
2. orange
3. drink
4. cottage
5. diet
6. cheese
7. tea
8. margarine
9. decaf
10. bottled

C. CATEGORIES

	Category
1. apple	milk
2. coffee	cold beverages
3. tea	dairy products
4. fruit punch	hot beverages
5. orange juice	dairy products
6. diet	juices
7. grape juice	low-calorie beverages

WORKBOOK PAGE 44

A. WHICH WORD?

1. dinners
2. provolone
3. seafood
4. Swiss
5. salad
6. beef
7. ice cream

B. WHICH FOOD DOESN'T BELONG?

1. nuts (The others are frozen foods.)
2. ham (The others are kinds of cheese.)
3. potato chips (The others are deli items.)
4. seafood salad (The others are snack foods.)
5. turkey (The other deli foods are meat.)

C. A PICNIC

1. potato
2. tortilla
3. lemonade
4. orange
5. corned/roast
6. roast/corned
7. turkey
8. Swiss/American/cheddar
9. American/cheddar/Swiss
10. cheddar/Swiss/American
11. potato salad
12. seafood

WORKBOOK PAGE 45

A. WHICH WORD DOESN'T BELONG?

1. mayonnaise (The others are jams and jellies.)
2. flour (The others are baked goods.)
3. rice (The others are types of pasta.)
4. soup (The others are condiments.)

5. pickles (The others are things you pour on food.)
6. relish (The others are liquid.)

B. WHAT'S THE WORD?

1. mustard	7. bread
2. ketchup	8. flour
3. cookies	9. salad dressing
4. oil	10. vegetables
5. tuna fish	11. salsa
6. crackers	12. soy sauce

C. LISTENING

Listen and choose the best answer.

1. A. What should we have for dessert tonight?
   B. Let's open some canned . . . .
2. A. I'm not feeling very well.
   B. You should rest in bed and have some . . . .
3. A. What's your favorite kind of sandwich?
   B. Peanut butter and . . . .
4. A. What do you usually have for breakfast?
   B. I usually have a bowl of . . . .
5. A. This salad tastes terrible!
   B. I think I used too much . . . .
6. A. What's your favorite snack food?
   B. I like salsa and . . . .
7. A. Let's make pancakes for breakfast.
   B. Great idea! Do we have any . . . ?
8. A. What are you looking for?
   B. I can't find the cooking . . . .
9. A. The hamburgers are ready.
   B. Okay. Here are the . . . .
10. A. Oh, no! We don't have any more bread.
    B. No problem. We can make sandwiches on . . . .
11. A. Let's start by frying some garlic.
    B. Okay. Here's the pan, and here's some . . . .
12. A. What would you like for dessert?
    B. I'd like a piece of . . . .

Answers

1. b		7. b	
2. b		8. a	
3. a		9. a	
4. a		10. b	
5. b		11. b	
6. a		12. a	

WORKBOOK PAGE 46

A. WHAT'S THE WORD?

1. trash bags
2. diaper
3. soap
4. dog food
5. tissues
6. paper plates
7. paper cups
8. straw
9. aluminum foil
10. paper towels

B. WHICH WORD DOESN'T BELONG?

1. sandwich bags (The others are types of food.)
2. plastic wrap (The others are made of paper.)
3. wipes (The others are used to wrap food.)
4. diapers (The others are used for cleaning.)
5. aluminum foil (The others are related to eating or drinking.)
6. cat food (The others are baby products.)

C. ANALOGIES

1. cat food	4. wrap
2. paper cups	5. trash bags
3. wipes	6. baby food

WORKBOOK PAGE 47

A. LIKELY OR UNLIKELY?

	Likely	Unlikely
1.	✓	___
2.	___	✓
3.	___	✓
4.	___	✓
5.	✓	___
6.	✓	___
7.	✓	___
8.	___	✓
9.	✓	___

B. WHICH WORD DOESN'T BELONG?

1. candy (The others are related to payment.)
2. scanner (The others are people.)
3. customer (The others are employees.)
4. aisle (The others hold supermarket products.)
5. scale (The others are items to buy in the checkout area.)

C. WHAT'S THE WORD?

1. cashier
2. scale
3. bagger/packer
4. candy
5. coupons
6. produce
7. clerk
8. shopping basket

D. ASSOCIATIONS

1. d	4. e
2. f	5. c
3. a	6. b

WORKBOOK PAGE 48

A. WHAT'S THE CONTAINER?

1. pound
2. bag
3. roll
4. box
5. can
6. bunch
7. carton
8. container

B. WHICH WORD IS CORRECT?

1. cans
2. stick
3. roll
4. bunch
5. six-pack
6. loaves
7. half-gallon
8. dozen
9. tube
10. container
11. jar, bottle
12. packages, rolls

C. LISTENING: *What Are They Talking About?*

Listen and decide what's being talked about.

1. I bought a can the other day.
2. Please pick up a quart when you go to the store.
3. We should get two pounds.
4. You can get four jars for two dollars.
5. We ate a whole dozen!
6. We really could use one or two heads.
7. Could you pick up a liter when you're at the store?
8. We only need one box.
9. I think there's an extra tube in the bathroom.

Answers

1. a		4. b		7. b	
2. b		5. a		8. b	
3. a		6. a		9. a	

WORKBOOK PAGE 49

A. TRUE OR FALSE?

1. T
2. T
3. F
4. F
5. T
6. F
7. F
8. F
9. T
10. T
11. F
12. F

B. WHICH WORD?

1. pounds
2. teaspoons
3. half pound
4. a quart
5. pint

C. RECIPES

1. 2 cups
2. 2 teaspoons
3. tsp.
4. Tbsps.
5. cups
6. 1/2 cup
7. 1/4, 1/2

A. WHAT SHOULD I DO?

1. e	5. h
2. f	6. b
3. a	7. c
4. g	8. d

B. LISTENING: *What Are They Talking About?*

Listen and decide what's being talked about.

1. You need to beat them now.
2. It tastes very good when you barbecue it on the grill.
3. Have you peeled it yet?
4. Let's steam some for dinner tonight.
5. Should I slice it now?
6. I like to stir-fry them.
7. Bake it for one hour.
8. Roast it in the oven for an hour and fifteen minutes.
9. The last time we had them, we baked them. Let's broil them tonight.

Answers

1. a	4. a	7. a
2. b	5. a	8. b
3. b	6. b	9. b

C. LISTENING: *What's the Category?*

Listen and choose the appropriate category.

1. lettuce	cabbage	celery
2. bread	rolls	cake
3. carrots	cheese	onions
4. lemonade	orange juice	milk
5. hot dogs	hamburgers	steak
6. chicken	potatoes	eggs

Answers

5	1	3
4	2	6

A. WHICH KITCHENWARE WORD IS CORRECT?

1. colander	6. rolling pin
2. ladle	7. carving knife
3. skillet	8. timer
4. sheet	9. wooden spoon
5. spatula	

B. WHAT'S THE OBJECT?

1. d	5. c	9. g
2. f	6. a	10. l
3. b	7. i	11. j
4. e	8. k	12. h

C. WHICH WORD DOESN'T BELONG?

1. double boiler (The others are used for mixing.)
2. saucepan (The others are used for baking.)
3. grater (The others are used for cooking.)
4. can opener (The others are used to hold food.)
5. garlic press (The others are used for cooking.)

D. LISTENING

Listen and choose the best answer.

1. I use this when I stir-fry vegetables.
2. I use this whenever I make an omelet.
3. You'll need this if you're going to serve pancakes.
4. If you're going to make an apple pie, you'll need this to peel the apples.
5. You'll need this to cut the turkey.
6. Here. Use this to cover the pot.

Answers

1. b	4. a
2. a	5. b
3. b	6. a

A. WHAT'S THE FOOD?

1. e	4. b	7. i
2. h	5. g	8. a
3. f	6. d	9. c

B. WHICH WORD DOESN'T BELONG?

1. taco (The others are condiments.)
2. soda (The others are desserts.)
3. pizza (The others are Mexican foods.)
4. napkins (The others are typically made of plastic.)
5. fish sandwich (The others are made with meat.)

C. WHICH WORD?

1. pizza
2. frozen yogurt
3. ketchup
4. soda
5. plastic utensils

D. LISTENING: *What Food Are They Talking About?*

Listen and decide what food is being talked about.

1. I'd like Italian dressing to go with my order.
2. I'd like a bowl with two scoops, please.
3. I'd like six pieces, please.
4. Do you want to put some on your hot dog?
5. I'd like two slices, please.
6. This sandwich is delicious. Is it salmon or tuna?

Answers

1. a	4. a
2. b	5. b
3. a	6. b

A. WHAT'S THE FOOD?

1. f	4. i	7. b
2. d	5. h	8. g
3. e	6. a	9. c

B. WHICH WORD?

1. white bread
2. tuna fish sandwich
3. sausages
4. sandwich
5. roast beef
6. decaf coffee
7. tea
8. danish
9. pancakes
10. bacon

C. LISTENING: *What Food Are They Talking About?*

Listen and decide what food is being talked about.

1. A. Do you have the ingredients?
   B. I think so. I've got the eggs, flour, sugar, and milk.
2. A. How many slices should I put in the sandwich?
   B. Three or four.
3. A. Do you like it with cream and sugar?
   B. Just sugar, please.
4. A. It's so hot today! I need to cool off.
   B. Then I know what you should have to drink.
5. A. Would you like some?
   B. No, thank you. If I have caffeine this late, I'll never be able to fall asleep!
6. A. This sandwich is delicious!
   B. Thanks. I mix it with a special homemade mayonnaise.

Answers

1. a	4. b
2. b	5. b
3. a	6. a

A. WHAT'S THE VERB?

1. pays	4. clear
2. serve	5. seat
3. take	6. leave

B. WHICH WORD?

1. dessert cart	5. table
2. booster	6. salad bar
3. waiter	7. chef
4. busperson	8. booth

C. LISTENING

Listen and circle the best answer.

1. May I take your . . . ?
2. Hello. My name is Nancy, and I'll be your . . . .
3. There are some excellent desserts on the . . . .

4. Henry, please clear the . . . .
5. Johnny, remember to cut your food with your . . . .
6. May I please have the . . . ?

Answers

1. order
2. server
3. menu
4. table
5. knife
6. check

D. WHAT'S WRONG WITH THIS PLACE SETTING?

The cup is on the salad plate.
The water glass is on the saucer.
The knife is between the teaspoon and the soup spoon.
The salad fork is to the right of the dinner fork.
The napkin is under the soup spoon.
The bread-and-butter knife is in the soup bowl.

WORKBOOK PAGE 55

A. ORDERING DINNER

3
10
4
8
1
9
6
5
2
7

B. YOUR SERVER HAS A FEW QUESTIONS

1. c
2. d
3. e
4. b
5. f
6. a

C. LISTENING

Listen and decide what food is being talked about.

1. These carrots haven't been cooked long enough.
2. My dessert was wonderful. The chocolate was very rich.
3. Can I have some more ketchup, please?
4. These were overcooked, and now they're soggy!
5. We need some more salsa, please.
6. I'm glad I ordered this. It's very tender.

Answers

1. a
2. a
3. b
4. b
5. a
6. b

WORKBOOK PAGE 56

A. COLOR ASSOCIATIONS

1. orange
2. green
3. white, gray
4. red
5. yellow
6. green
7. blue
8. green
9. purple
10. black

B. MIXING COLORS

1. purple
2. gray
3. green
4. pink
5. brown
6. light green
7. orange

C. COLORFUL EXPRESSIONS

1. green
2. black
3. blue
4. red
5. black
6. Blue
7. gray
8. white
9. yellow
10. gold
11. white
12. silver

WORKBOOK PAGE 57

A. WHO WEARS WHAT?

1. B
2. W
3. M
4. W
5. W
6. B
7. B
8. W
9. W
10. W
11. B
12. B
13. W
14. B
15. B
16. B
17. M
18. B

B. WHICH WORD?

1. shirt
2. tuxedo
3. shorts
4. suit
5. jumper
6. leggings
7. skirt
8. overalls
9. pants
10. uniform

C. LISTENING

Listen and choose the best answer.

1. My wife is a security officer. She wears a blue and white . . . .
2. My grandfather is a farmer. When he works on his farm, he usually wears . . . .
3. I really like my new three-piece suit. To go with it, I should get a very nice . . . .
4. If you're going to wear that skirt, I think you should wear this white . . . .
5. Jack's party is going to be very informal. I think I'll wear . . . .
6. If you're going to wear a tunic, I think you should wear these . . . .
7. It's going to be a very formal party. I think I'll wear my black . . . .
8. The weather is going to be cool this evening. You should probably wear a . . . .
9. Carol is going to have a baby. She needs to buy some . . . .
10. When the weather is hot, I usually wear a . . . .

Answers

1. a
2. a
3. b
4. b
5. a
6. a
7. b
8. a
9. a
10. b

WORKBOOK PAGE 58

A. WHICH WORD DOESN'T BELONG?

1. gloves (The others are worn on the head.)
2. sweater jacket (The others are used when it's raining.)
3. windbreaker (The others are worn in cold weather.)
4. coat (The others are accessories.)
5. rain boots (The others are worn on the head.)

B. SHOPPING FOR WINTER CLOTHES

1. jacket
2. down jacket/parka
3. parka/down jacket
4. raincoat
5. rain boots
6. ski hat
7. scarf
8. gloves
9. ear muffs

C. WHICH WORD?

1. sunglasses
2. sweater
3. glove
4. muffler
5. umbrella
6. mittens

WORKBOOK PAGE 59

A. WHICH WORD DOESN'T BELONG?

1. boxers (The other are worn by women.)
2. knee-highs (The others are sleepwear.)
3. bra (The others are worn by men.)
4. panties (The others are worn on the legs.)
5. jockey shorts (The others are worn by women.)

B. WHICH WORD?

1. socks
2. blanket sleeper
3. panties
4. pajamas
5. T-shirt
6. shorts
7. half slip
8. jockstrap
9. long johns
10. slippers

C. FINISH THE SENTENCE

1. d
2. f
3. a
4. e
5. c
6. b

D. LISTENING: *What's Being Described?*

Listen and decide what's being described.

1. You put it on after a shower or before you get dressed in the morning. It's often thick and made of a soft fabric.
2. This is worn by babies and small children. It's one piece and covers the whole body and feet.
3. This is often worn by men and boys under their shirts. It's usually white and made of soft cotton.
4. These are thick socks that cover the shins completely.
5. Many men wear these underneath their pants. They usually come in many colors and patterns.
6. This is worn by men when they exercise or play sports.

Answers

6	2
4	1
3	5

WORKBOOK PAGE 60

A. WHAT KIND OF SHOES DO THEY NEED?

1. d, j
2. a, l
3. b, f, i
4. h
5. j, k
6. e
7. c, g

B. WHICH WORD DOESN'T BELONG?

1. cover-up (The others are for swimming.)
2. tank (The others are types of shorts.)
3. moccasins (The others are types of boots.)
4. pumps (The others are for the beach.)
5. high heels (The others are casual types of shoes.)

C. A DAY AT THE LAKE

1. hiking
2. work
3. flip-flops/sandals
4. sandals/flip-flops
5. trunks
6. shirt
7. sweatpants
8. running
9. bathing

WORKBOOK PAGE 61

A. LIKELY OR UNLIKELY?

	Likely	Unlikely
1.	✓	
2.		✓
3.	✓	

4.		✓
5.	✓	
6.		✓
7.	✓	
8.		✓
9.	✓	
10.		✓
11.	✓	
12.		✓

B. WHAT IS IT?

1. locket
2. barrette
3. wallet
4. book bag
5. makeup bag
6. suspenders
7. cuff links
8. key ring/key chain
9. change purse

C. LISTENING: *What Is It?*

Listen and decide what's being described.

1. This is for carrying coins.
2. You wear this on your wrist for decoration.
3. You take this with you when you go camping.
4. This is a necklace made from colorful stones or plastic.
5. They come in many varieties, and people wear them on their ears.
6. They're white and beautiful. They're a popular gift for women.
7. It's for carrying school textbooks.
8. It's what the future groom gives to the future bride.
9. This tells the time.
10. People keep important papers in this.
11. This holds up your pants or skirt.
12. It's usually plain gold, and people in the United States wear it on their left hand.

Answers

2	4	12	3
6	1	9	11
5	10	8	7

WORKBOOK PAGE 62

A. NEW CLOTHES

1. denim
2. leather
3. cotton
4. corduroy
5. crew
6. silk
7. short-sleeved
8. sweaters

B. LISTENING: *Shopping for Clothes*

Listen and choose the best answer.

1. I want something with just one color. So I think I'll buy . . . .
2. If this jersey is too small, you should try . . . .
3. I don't like the one with the small circles. I prefer . . . .
4. This one won't be warm enough. I think I'll buy. . . .
5. These socks are too high. I think I'll buy . . . .
6. I haven't gotten my ears pierced yet, so I'll have to buy . . . .

Answers

1. a	4. b
2. a	5. a
3. b	6. b

C. SUMMER OR WINTER?

1. S	6. S
2. W	7. B
3. B	8. S
4. W	9. B
5. S	

D. LISTENING: *The Fashion Show*

Match the description you hear with the appropriate design.

1. Greta looks fantastic in this yellow and blue plaid suit.
2. This season, stripes are very popular. Look at Stephanie in this beautiful striped blouse and matching skirt.
3. Checks are also very popular. Dave is ready for a party in this exciting green and white checked shirt.
4. Flowers are always fashionable. Tiffany is all set for spring in this lovely multicolored flowered dress.
5. And paisley is back in style this year—especially for men's ties and handkerchiefs.
6. Everybody loves polka dots! Look at Erica! She's ready for the beach in this exciting red and white polka-dotted bathing suit.
7. Prints are always in style, as you can see from this print jersey that Beth is wearing.
8. And solid black is always a good choice. Julie looks like a million dollars in this solid black evening gown!

Answers

6	5	2	3
7	1	8	4

WORKBOOK PAGE 63

A. CLOTHING REPAIRS

1. long
2. broken
3. shorten
4. take
5. stained

B. SHOPPING

1. plain
2. low
3. short
4. heavy
5. dark
6. narrow

C. LISTENING: *Gossip at a Family Picnic*

Listen and complete each nasty sentence of this couple gossiping at a family picnic.

A. Just look at Kelly! Her skirt is much too short. She needs to . . . .
B. And will you look at Tim's pants! I can't believe he would wear pants with a pocket that's . . . .
A. My! My! Look at Aunt Maxine! She's put on a few pounds and her dress is VERY . . . !
B. And Uncle Frank! It's absolutely disgraceful! He's wearing a shirt with two buttons that are . . . .
A. Don't you think that for such a hot summer day Thelma's dress is awfully . . . ?
B. Yes, I do. And look at Cousin Janice! She can hardly walk! She has such wide feet, and she insists on wearing shoes that are much too . . . !
A. And Cousin Bob! You'd think he was going to a funeral instead of a picnic. His outfit is so . . . !
B. I'm having a marvelous time. It's so nice being with family members, isn't it.
A. It certainly is.

Answers

1. b	5. a
2. a	6. b
3. b	7. a
4. b	

A. DOING THE LAUNDRY

1. sort
2. dark/light
3. light/dark
4. load
5. laundry detergent
6. fabric softener
7. bleach
8. unload
9. lint trap
10. static cling remover
11. put

B. ANALOGIES

1. shelves
2. closet
3. ironing board
4. drawer
5. ironed clothing

C. LISTENING

Listen and choose the best answer.

1. You can hang up these shirts outside on the . . . .
2. Before you load the washer, make sure you . . . .
3. Oh, no! The electricity went out when the clothes were in the . . . .
4. After you iron the shirts, put them on . . . .

5. When you take the clothes out of the dryer, put them in the . . . .
6. When I iron my shirts, I always use . . . .

Answers

1. b
2. a
3. a
4. b
5. a
6. a

A. GOING SHOPPING

1. Electronics
2. Women's Clothing
3. Household Appliances
4. Men's Clothing
5. Housewares
6. Jewelry
7. Perfume Counter
8. Furniture
9. Children's Clothing

B. LISTENING: *Attention, Shoppers!*

Match the following announcements to the appropriate department.

1. Are you looking for something special for a birthday or anniversary? Diamond earrings are on sale this week at low, low prices!
2. Children's outfits are half-price this week! Get them while they last!
3. Need a new stove or refrigerator? Every stove and refrigerator in the store is on sale now!
4. Do you need a toaster, blender, or food processor? They're all twenty percent off this week only!
5. Thinking about that big screen TV? How about a new stereo system? They're all at affordable prices now!
6. Colognes, perfumes, and lotions from all the well-known manufacturers available here!
7. Dresses and coats for work and play from leading designers! For the best selection, hurry over now!
8. New designer shirts at low, low prices! Today only!
9. Matching beds, dressers, and night tables! Prices dramatically reduced!

Answers

6	8	9
1	7	3
4	2	5

C. DEPARTMENT STORE MATCH

1. d	4. c
2. f	5. b
3. e	6. a

D. LISTENING: *Where Are They?*

Listen and decide in which departments or areas of a department store you would most likely hear the following conversations.

1. A. Excuse me. Where can I try on these pants?
   B. There's a dressing room over there.
2. A. This one is very comfortable, and I know it'll look great in our living room.
   B. I agree. I think we should buy it.
3. A. Would you push "nine," please?
   B. Certainly.
4. A. May I help you?
   B. Yes. I'd like a cup of tea.
5. A. Do you have holiday wrapping paper?
   B. Yes, we do.
6. A. Excuse me. Where can I find electric mixers?
   B. I'm sorry, but we're all out.
7. A. This is moving so slowly!
   B. I know. We should have taken the elevator.
8. A. Would you like to return this?
   B. Yes, I would.
   A. Do you have the receipt?
   B. Yes. Here it is.
9. A. Will this microwave oven fit in the trunk?
   B. Yes. I'm sure it will.

Answers

3	7	5
6	8	9
2	1	4

A. LIKELY OR UNLIKELY?

	Likely	Unlikely
1.	✓	
2.	✓	
3.		✓
4.		✓
5.	✓	
6.	✓	
7.	✓	
8.		✓

B. SHOPPING FOR CLOTHES

1. buy
2. tried on
3. size
4. sale sign
5. price tag
6. regular
7. sale
8. sales tax
9. pay for

C. WHAT SHOULD THEY DO?

1. exchange	4. label
2. price tag	5. return
3. try it on	

157

A. WHAT IS IT?

1. remote control
2. TV
3. clock radio
4. VCR
5. camcorder
6. DVD player
7. battery charger
8. speaker
9. hand-held video game
10. turntable
11. headphones
12. shortwave radio

B. LISTENING: *A Sale at Ace Electronics*

Listen to the commercial and fill in the correct information.

Celebrate the New Year with the annual January Sale at Ace Electronics! Come take advantage of unbelievable savings before it's too late. Suny forty-eight-inch plasma TVs with remote control—twenty-five percent off. To go with that TV, Sandstone DVD players are on sale for up to fifty percent off! That's right. Fifty percent!! And for those of you on the go, check out our portable digital audio players—starting as low as $60. Listen to your favorite tunes on quality equipment. Prices on portable CD players have also been slashed from ten to seventy percent. And don't forget to pick up the latest video games and save up to 30% percent on the hottest titles. We have high-powered stereo systems starting at $199. Hurry! Come to Ace Electronics while supplies last!

Answers

1. 25%
2. 50%
3. $60
4. 10, 70%
5. 30%
6. $199

C. WHICH WORD DOESN'T BELONG?

1. shortwave (The others are video equipment.)
2. portable TV (The others are audio equipment.)
3. DVD (The others are types of TVs.)
4. VCR (The others are components of a stereo system.)
5. stereo system (The others come in "personal/portable" models.)

A. CROSSWORD

(See page 172.)

B. WHICH WORD?

1. 35 millimeter
2. cell phone
3. battery
4. calculator
5. camera case
6. personal organizer
7. memory disk
8. adding

C. LISTENING

Listen and choose the best answer.

1. I'd like to get a close-up of that flower. Where's my . . . ?
2. If you want to take pictures at the party, don't forget to use the . . . .
3. Can you send it to me on my fax . . . ?
4. I never do complicated math by hand any more. I use a . . . .
5. I need to buy a new memory disk for my . . . .
6. "Please leave a message after the beep" is the recording often heard on . . . .
7. Put the camera on top of the . . . .
8. If you like to walk around while talking, you should really get a . . . .
9. If you want to charge your cell phone overseas, you'll need . . . .
10. I knew we were in for a long boring evening when our neighbors took out their . . . .

Answers

1. b	6. a
2. a	7. b
3. b	8. a
4. b	9. b
5. a	10. a

A. WHICH WORD DOESN'T BELONG?

1. computer game (The others are computer hardware.)
2. printer (The others are inserted into the computer.)
3. cable (The others are hand-controlled devices.)
4. disk drive (The others are external devices.)
5. flat panel (The others are types of software.)

B. AT THE COMPUTER STORE

1. desktop
2. monitor
3. flat panel screens
4. modem
5. floppy disk
6. CD-ROMs
7. CD-ROM drives
8. software
9. spreadsheet
10. computer game
11. joystick

C. LISTENING

Listen and choose the best answer.

1. If you want to do some work while you're on the plane, you should take your . . . .
2. Something's wrong! I can't see anything on my . . . .
3. We need to plug the new computer into that . . . .
4. My computer is so old it can't even run . . . .
5. You can transfer photos to your computer with a . . . .
6. I need to connect the printer to the computer. Could you please hand me the . . . ?

Answers

1. b	4. b
2. a	5. b
3. a	6. a

A. WHICH TOY DOESN'T BELONG?

1. kiddie pool (The others have wheels.)
2. coloring book (The others are implements used for drawing or painting.)
3. puzzle (The others are round.)
4. doll house (The others are used outdoors.)
5. toy truck (The others are replicas of people or animals.)

B. BIRTHDAY PRESENTS

1. construction
2. model
3. clay
4. play
5. jigsaw puzzles, board game

C. A LETTER TO SANTA

1. doll house
2. doll furniture
3. hula hoop
4. bubble bath
5. walkie-talkie (set)
6. science kit
7. pail/shovel
8. shovel/pail
9. beach ball
10. markers
11. crayons
12. paint

A. BANKING ACTIONS

1. c	4. b
2. a	5. d
3. e	

B. BANK SERVICES

1. withdrawal slip
2. deposit slip
3. vault
4. passbook
5. credit card
6. check

C. LIKELY OR UNLIKELY?

	Likely	Unlikely
1.	✓	__
2.	✓	__
3.	__	✓
4.	✓	__
5.	✓	__
6.	__	✓
7.	__	✓

D. LISTENING: *A Bank Robbery*

Listen and decide whether the following statements are True (T) or False (F).

Yesterday afternoon a robbery took place at the Main Street Bank. Three robbers gave a note to one of the tellers and demanded ten thousand dollars. The teller called the bank officer who had the combination to the vault and she opened it. The robbers ordered the teller and the bank officer to put the money in a bag as well as the contents of the safe deposit boxes. The security guard, who had been in the lobby where the ATM machines are located, set off the silent alarm, but before the police arrived to intercept the robbers, they got away!

Answers
1. F
2. T
3. F
4. F
5. T

WORKBOOK PAGE 72

A. WHICH WORD?
1. monthly
2. mortgage
3. select
4. check
5. ATM
6. traveler's
7. bill
8. balance

B. SAVING MONEY
1. electric
2. oil
3. water
4. telephone
5. cable TV
6. credit card
7. rent
8. car

C. LISTENING: *Household Bills*

Listen and decide which household bill these people are talking about.

1. It's high because we made a lot of calls to our family in Brazil.
2. I can't believe how much it is! I think it's because I take too many long showers.
3. It's high this month because we've been using our air conditioner a lot.
4. Look! It went up, and the landlord didn't tell us.
5. The monthly payment to the bank is high, but I'm still glad we bought this house.
6. Do you think we should change to gas heat? Our bill is unbelievably high this month!

Answers
1. b
2. a
3. a
4. b
5. b
6. b

WORKBOOK PAGE 73

A. WHICH WORD IS CORRECT?
1. sheet
2. letter
3. stamp machine
4. envelope
5. zip code
6. postal clerk
7. certified
8. slot
9. roll of stamps
10. scale
11. passport application
12. return address
13. address
14. letter
15. stamp
16. express
17. postcard
18. selective service
19. change-of-address

B. LISTENING

Listen and choose the best answer.

1. My name is Angela. I'm your new . . . .
2. When you write the address, remember to include the . . . .
3. I'm going to the post office to mail a . . . .
4. I don't want a sheet of stamps. I prefer a . . . .
5. Please put these letters in the . . . .
6. I'd like to buy a . . . .
7. Our cousins in Australia just sent us an . . . .
8. I'd like to send this first . . . .

Answers
1. b
2. a
3. a
4. b
5. a
6. b
7. a
8. b

WORKBOOK PAGES 74–75

A. OUR TOWN LIBRARY
1. card
2. online
3. author
4. title
5. shelves
6. checkout
7. clerk
8. reference
9. dictionary
10. encyclopedias
11. atlas
12. periodical
13. newspapers
14. magazines
15. microfilm
16. photocopier
17. media
18. CDs
19. tape
20. videotapes/DVDs
21. DVDs/videotapes
22. children's
23. foreign language
24. librarian

B. LIKELY OR UNLIKELY?

	Likely	Unlikely
1.	✓	__
2.	__	✓
3.	✓	__
4.	__	✓
5.	__	✓
6.	✓	__
7.	✓	__
8.	__	✓
9.	✓	__
10.	__	✓
11.	__	✓
12.	__	✓

C. LISTENING: *What Are They Talking About?*

Listen and decide what's being talked about.

1. If you don't have one, you won't be able to take books out of the library.
2. This is where I go when I take my little granddaughter to the library.
3. This is the area of the library where I can find books in French, Spanish, and Italian.
4. You can find newspapers, journals, and magazines here.
5. You'll find CDs, DVDs, and computer software here.
6. This is where I go when I need to look for information in an encyclopedia.
7. You go here when you want to check out a book.
8. This has a computerized listing of all the books in the library.
9. This is the person I ask whenever I have any questions about where to find something in the library.
10. I can listen to an author reading his or her novel while I go jogging in the park.
11. I'd like to find a good bilingual one, with definitions I can understand.
12. I enjoy looking at maps of the world. That's why I love to look at one whenever I have the time.

Answers

12	11	8
10	3	4
7	1	9
2	5	6

WORKBOOK PAGE 76

A. WHICH WORD DOESN'T BELONG?

1. church (The others are public buildings.)

159

2. emergency room (The others are vehicles.)
3. recycling center (The others are people.)
4. child-care center (The others are places of worship.)
5. police car (The others are places.)

B. LISTENING

Listen and choose the best answer.

1. A. What do you usually do on the weekend?
   B. I try to get some exercise at the . . . .
2. A. Is Jerry still a sanitation worker?
   B. Yes. He handles waste at the city . . . .
3. A. Do you have a few minutes to talk?
   B. Sorry. I don't. I'm on my way to pick up my two-year old at the . . . .
4. A. We need to continue our discussion about the problems we've been having in our city.
   B. I know. Let's get together this afternoon in the . . . .
5. A. I hear your wife just got a job at the town recreation center.
   B. She's very excited about it. She's going be their new . . . .
6. A. Do you hear that siren?
   B. Yes. An ambulance is taking a patient to the . . . .

Answers

1. b
2. b
3. a
4. a
5. b
6. b

C. WHICH WORD?

1. an ambulance
2. activities director
3. dump
4. swimming pool
5. fire engines
6. mayor
7. playroom
8. emergency operator

WORKBOOK PAGE 77

A. THE EVENING NEWS

1. blackout
2. gang violence
3. vandalism
4. assault
5. burglary
6. car accidents
7. chemical spill
8. train derailment
9. water main break
10. downed power lines

B. LISTENING: *Help!*

Listen and choose the best answer.

1. Someone help! My house is burning!
2. Help! Police! Someone took my child!
3. Don't come any closer! You might get electrocuted! Call the fire department!
4. Oh, no! That man is dead! He's been killed!
5. I can't believe it! They took my money and all my jewelry!
6. Stop that man! He just took my wallet!

Answers

1. a	4. b
2. a	5. a
3. b	6. b

C. ANALOGIES

1. kidnapping
2. drunk driving
3. blackout
4. mugging
5. assault

WORKBOOK PAGES 78–79

A. WHICH WORD DOESN'T BELONG?

1. nerve (The others are part of the eye.)
2. nose (The others are internal parts of the body.)
3. chin (The others are below the waist.)
4. knuckle (The others are part of the foot.)
5. heel (The others are part of the hand.)
6. veins (The others are organs.)
7. hip (The others are part of the mouth.)

B. WHICH WORD?

1. elbow	8. waist
2. neck	9. jaw
3. shin	10. ribcage
4. fingers	11. abdomen
5. nose	12. shoulder
6. ankle	13. gallbladder
7. cornea	14. heart

C. WHAT'S THE ACTION?

1. m	9. c
2. d	10. o
3. l	11. g
4. i	12. f
5. b	13. p
6. n	14. k
7. h	15. a
8. j	16. e

D. GUESS THE WORD!

1. neck, neck
2. chin
3. tongue
4. back

5. foot
6. elbow
7. heart
8. cheek, check
9. face, face
10. thumb
11. shoulder
12. nose
13. skin, bone
14. chest
15. stomach
16. leg

WORKBOOK PAGES 80–81

A. WHAT'S THE DIAGNOSIS?

1. b	8. b
2. b	9. b
3. a	10. a
4. a	11. b
5. b	12. a
6. a	13. b
7. a	14. b

B. ABSOLUTELY MISERABLE!

1. hurt	7. chills
2. ankle	8. blisters
3. wrist	9. congested
4. knee	10. bloated
5. cornea	11. neck
6. hip	

C. LISTENING: *What's the Problem?*

Listen and choose the best answer.

1. I don't feel well. I ate too much spicy food at dinner last night.
2. I got an insect bite, and now I can't stop scratching my arm.
3. I felt it after I walked up several flights of stairs.
4. It happened while I was playing soccer. I fell and I couldn't get up.
5. I've been having trouble chewing for the past several days.
6. I'm really uncomfortable. I can't turn to the right, and I can't turn to the left.
7. I can't talk!
8. "Achoo! Excuse me."

Answers

1. a
2. b
3. a
4. b
5. b
6. a
7. b
8. a

D. OH, MY ACHING BACK!

1. upset
2. hacking
3. itchy
4. pounding
5. high
6. scratchy
7. aching

A. GOOD IDEA OR BAD IDEA?

	Good Idea	Bad Idea
1.		✓
2.	✓	
3.	✓	
4.		✓
5.	✓	
6.		✓
7.		✓
8.	✓	
9.		✓
10.		✓

B. A DAY AT THE BEACH

1. CPR
2. tourniquet
3. kit
4. antihistamine
5. tweezers

C. LISTENING

Listen and choose the best answer.

1. A. Help! My husband is choking!
   B. I can help. I know . . . .
2. A. I fell off my bicycle and scraped my knee!
   B. I'll sterilize it with this . . . .
3. A. Ooh! I have a terrible headache.
   B. Here. Take a few . . . .
4. A. Are you in pain? Did you break something?
   B. I think I broke my finger. Do you know how to make . . . ?
5. A. Someone help! My uncle fell. He doesn't have a pulse!
   B. Let me try . . . .
6. A. Do you have a first-aid kit? My sister sprained her ankle.
   B. No. But I have . . . .

Answers

1.	b	4.	b
2.	a	5.	a
3.	a	6.	a

A. ASK A DOCTOR!

1. asthma
2. the flu/influenza
3. ear infection
4. measles
5. strep throat
6. depressed
7. allergic reaction
8. heart attack

B. HOW DID IT HAPPEN?

1. injured
2. frostbite
3. fell
4. shock
5. unconscious
6. heatstroke
7. electric shock
8. overdosed on drugs

C. WHICH WORD DOESN'T BELONG?

1. poison (The others are diseases.)
2. unconscious (The others are injuries.)
3. heatstroke (The others are diseases.)
4. heart attack (The others are medical conditions.)

A. MY MEDICAL EXAM

1.	height	4.	eye chart
2.	weight	5.	stethoscope
3.	blood pressure	6.	health

B. LIKELY OR UNLIKELY?

	Likely	Unlikely
1.		✓
2.		✓
3.	✓	
4.		✓
5.	✓	
6.		✓
7.		✓

C. CROSSWORD

(See page 172.)

A. WHICH WORD?

1. shot
2. cotton balls
3. clean
4. stitches
5. cast
6. brace
7. ice pack
8. medical history
9. anesthetic

B. WHAT DID THE DOCTOR DO?

1. ice pack
2. cast, crutches
3. examined, cleaned
4. drilled, filled
5. alcohol, gauze, tape
6. medical history, examination

C. LISTENING

Listen and choose the best answer.

1. Before I drill your tooth, I'm going to give you a shot of . . . .
2. I need to dress the wound with tape and . . . .
3. I gave my insurance card to the . . . .
4. I've examined your injury, and for your pain I'm going to give you . . . .
5. I was a dental assistant for a few years. Then I went to school and studied to become . . . .
6. In order to prevent germs from spreading, doctors and nurses wear . . . .

Answers

1.	a	4.	a
2.	b	5.	b
3.	b	6.	a

A. GOOD ADVICE OR BAD ADVICE?

	Good Advice	Bad Advice
1.	✓	
2.		✓
3.	✓	
4.	✓	
5.		✓
6.	✓	
7.		✓
8.	✓	
9.		✓
10.		✓
11.		✓
12.		✓

B. ASSOCIATIONS

1.	c	5.	d
2.	g	6.	a
3.	b	7.	h
4.	e	8.	f

C. GIVING ADVICE

1. an air purifier
2. take vitamins
3. have surgery
4. a heating pad
5. going on a diet

A. AILMENTS AND REMEDIES

1. cough syrup, cough drops
2. lotion, cream/creme
3. eye drops
4. aspirin, non-aspirin pain reliever
5. throat lozenges
6. decongestant spray/nasal spray
7. ointment, cream/creme, lotion
8. vitamins
9. antacid tablets
10. aspirin, non-aspirin pain reliever, ointment, cream/creme
11. aspirin, non-aspirin pain reliever, cold tablets, throat lozenges, decongestant spray/nasal spray
12. throat lozenges

B. INTERNAL OR EXTERNAL?

1.	I	4.	I	7.	I
2.	E	5.	E	8.	I
3.	I	6.	I	9.	I

C. TAKE OR USE?

1.	take	4.	use
2.	take	5.	use
3.	use	6.	take

A. WHICH SPECIALIST?

1. an allergist
2. pediatrician
3. ENT specialist

4. orthopedist
5. physical therapist
6. gynecologist

B. LISTENING: *What Kind of Doctor?*

Listen and write the number next to the correct medical specialist.

1. Can you hear this in your right ear?
2. What sort of problems have you been having with your stomach and digestion?
3. It looks like you'll need a new pair of glasses.
4. I need to do some tests on your heart.
5. It looks like you're going to need braces.
6. I'm going to put this on your skin to see if it reacts.
7. What can you tell me about your mother?
8. Don't move. I'm going to straighten your spinal column.

Answers

2	1	3	8
7	5	6	4

C. A FAMILY OF DOCTORS

1. gerontologist
2. pediatrician
3. psychiatrist
4. chiropractor
5. ophthalmologist
6. gastroenterologist
7. cardiologist

WORKBOOK PAGE 89

A. WHICH WORD?

1. I.V.
2. control
3. hospital gown
4. call
5. dietitian
6. waiting
7. vital signs
8. lab

B. LISTENING: *Where in the Hospital Are They?*

Listen and decide where these people are in the hospital.

1. I'm going to take a few X-rays of your chest. Please stand over there.
2. Hurry! We need to get this man off the gurney! There's another ambulance on the way!
3. I'll be starting the operation now. Nurse, hand me the scalpel.
4. I feel like we've been here for hours. When will we be able to see a doctor?
5. It looks like we'll be very busy all week. We have a lot of samples to analyze.
6. Based on your medical chart, you seem to be doing much better. I

think you'll be able to go home in two or three days.
7. Pay close attention to this screen to see if any patients on the floor need us.
8. Push! Push! It's a boy!

Answers

3	4	6	8
7	2	5	1

C. WHO ARE THEY?

1. c	5. f
2. g	6. b
3. a	7. d
4. h	8. e

WORKBOOK PAGE 90

A. WHAT'S USED WHERE?

1. g
2. j
3. k
4. b, c, e, f, o
5. i, n
6. h
7. l
8. a, d, m, p

B. WHICH WORD?

1. gargle	7. polish
2. gel	8. clipper
3. razors	9. polish remover
4. body	10. mascara
5. brush	11. whiten
6. blade	

C. WHICH WORD DOESN'T BELONG?

1. bubble bath (The others are types of makeup.)
2. soap (The others are used to cut nails.)
3. aftershave (The others are used while shaving.)
4. deodorant (The others are used in the mouth.)
5. foundation (The others are used on the hair.)

D. ANALOGIES

1. shoe polish
2. cologne
3. toothpaste
4. nail file
5. hot comb/curling iron

WORKBOOK PAGE 91

A. WHICH WORD?

1. bib	5. formula
2. pins	6. cloth diapers
3. pacifier	7. cotton swabs
4. powder	8. vitamins

B. OUR NEW BABY

1. change
2. disposable
3. feed
4. nipple
5. rock
6. rocking

7. bathe
8. baby shampoo
9. cotton swabs
10. child-care center
11. hold
12. play with
13. pacifier

C. LISTENING: *What Are They Talking About?*

Listen and decide which baby item these people are talking about.

1. They're much more convenient than the cloth ones.
2. I always put one on my baby whenever she eats.
3. It's very gentle and doesn't hurt their eyes.
4. I give them to my child every day. My doctor says they're very important for her health.
5. They're sharp, so be careful when you change the baby!
6. I wish my mother didn't make me eat this horrible stuff!

Answers

1. a	4. a
2. b	5. b
3. a	6. a

WORKBOOK PAGE 92

A. CAREER GUIDANCE

1. law
2. vocational
3. medical
4. adult
5. graduate

B. ANALOGIES

1. medical school
2. middle school/junior high school
3. community college
4. high school
5. vocational school

C. AN "EDUCATED" FAMILY

1. nursery school
2. Elementary
3. Middle
4. high
5. University
6. vocational
7. community college
8. graduate

WORKBOOK PAGE 93

A. WHICH WORD?

1. library
2. lockers
3. coach
4. office
5. nurse's
6. auditorium
7. custodian
8. track
9. security
10. science
11. guidance counselor

12. vice-principal
13. locker room, field

B. ASSOCIATIONS

1. f   5. c
2. e   6. b
3. a   7. d
4. h   8. g

C. LISTENING: *Who's Talking?*

Listen and decide who is talking.

1. Is it okay to clean in here?
2. I want you to report for practice right after classes end.
3. As head of the school, I am pleased to welcome you all to Midville High.
4. Next! What would you like to have?
5. When you finish the test, you can have lunch.
6. As we discussed at our last meeting, I think you should take college writing next semester.

Answers

1. a   4. b
2. b   5. a
3. a   6. a

WORKBOOK PAGE 94

A. WHICH COURSE?

1. d   7. e
2. c   8. b
3. l   9. g
4. a   10. k
5. j   11. f
6. i   12. h

B. LIKELY OR UNLIKELY?

	Likely	Unlikely
1.		✓
2.		✓
3.	✓	
4.	✓	
5.		✓
6.	✓	

C. LISTENING: *Which Subject?*

Listen and choose the best answer.

1. We're going to have a test tomorrow on multiplication and division.
2. Can you name all the countries in South America?
3. This week we're going to analyze Beethoven's symphonies.
4. You'll need to mix the water and flour evenly to make good dough.
5. We'll be dissecting frogs tomorrow.
6. Let's get warmed up! Put your hands above your heads and stretch.

Answers

1. a   4. a
2. b   5. a
3. b   6. a

WORKBOOK PAGE 95

A. THEY CAN'T DECIDE

1. football
2. chess
3. debate
4. band
5. chorus
6. orchestra
7. cheerleading
8. government
9. drama
10. AV crew
11. newspaper
12. literary magazine

WORKBOOK PAGE 96

A. ARITHMETIC PROBLEMS

1. $6 + 9 = 15$
2. $41 - 11 = 30$
3. $14 \times 5 = 70$
4. $200 \div 4 = 50$
5. $9 \times 7 = 63$
6. $99 - 19 = 80$
7. $11 \div 11 = 1$
8. $15 + 37 = 52$

B. LISTENING: *Fractions*

Listen and decide whether the following statements are True (T) or false (F).

1. We should get gas. The tank is about one-third full.
2. Do you think we need more milk? The container is half empty.
3. I didn't do well on the test. I got two thirds of the answers wrong!
4. Did you know that twenty-five percent of the people in our high school are left-handed?
5. I'm almost finished reading the book. I've already read about three quarters of it.

Answers

1. T   4. F
2. F   5. T
3. T

C. PERCENTS

1. $45
2. $90
3. $18
4. $1200
5. $14
6. $150
7. $145
8. $15

D. TYPES OF MATH

1. algebra
2. geometry
3. statistics
4. Trigonometry
5. calculus

WORKBOOK PAGE 97

A. SOLID SHAPES

1. pyramid
2. cylinder
3. cube
4. cone
5. sphere

B. WHAT'S THE WORD?

1. centimeters
2. yard
3. curved
4. kilometers
5. inches
6. apex
7. rectangle
8. isosceles
9. hypotenuse
10. ellipse/oval
11. circumference
12. perpendicular
13. distance, miles
14. parallel

C. ANALOGIES

1. isosceles triangle
2. curved line
3. ellipse/oval
4. mile
5. cube
6. width
7. depth

WORKBOOK PAGE 98

A. A TEACHER'S COMMENTS

1. feedback
2. first
3. revised
4. corrections
5. organizing
6. paragraph
7. periods
8. question
9. interrogative
10. commas
11. exclamation
12. declarative
13. quotation
14. brainstorming
15. title

B. PARTS OF SPEECH

1. adverb
2. preposition
3. article
4. noun
5. verb
6. adjective
7. pronoun

WORKBOOK PAGE 99

A. WHAT TYPE OF WRITING?

1. f, h, n   7. a, i, m
2. c, g, l   8. c, f, h, k
3. c, e, h   9. i, m
4. h   10. b
5. d   11. c, k
6. f, h, j   12. l

B. WHICH WORD?

1. newspaper article
2. postcard

3. report
4. article
5. thank-you note
6. invitations
7. autobiography

A. GEOGRAPHY MATCH

1. d
2. j
3. h
4. e
5. i
6. k
7. c
8. g
9. f
10. a
11. l
12. b

B. WHICH WORD?

1. waterfall
2. desert
3. forest
4. cliffs
5. jungle
6. stream
7. lakes
8. an island
9. plains
10. seashore

C. LISTENING: *Sounds*

Listen to the sounds and identify the type of geography.

1. [sound: waterfall]
2. [sound: brook]
3. [sound: jungle]
4. [sound: seashore]
5. [sound: desert]

Answers

2	1	5	4	3

WORKBOOK PAGE 101

A. WHICH WORD?

1. Petri dish, microscope
2. computer, slides
3. Bunsen burner, forceps
4. chemical, dropper
5. planning, observations
6. flask, funnel
7. magnet, scale
8. flask, graduated cylinder

B. ASSOCIATIONS

1. g
2. e
3. a
4. f
5. b
6. d
7. c

C. LIKELY OR UNLIKELY?

	Likely	Unlikely
1.		✓
2.	✓	
3.		✓

4. _____ ✓
5. _____ ✓

WORKBOOK PAGE 102

A. CELESTIAL BODIES

1. comet
2. galaxy
3. Mercury
4. the moon
5. The Big Dipper
6. telescope
7. meteor
8. Saturn
9. Uranus
10. satellite
11. Mars
12. lunar eclipse
13. Jupiter
14. quarter moon
15. the sun
16. Venus

B. WHICH WORD?

1. solar eclipse
2. asteroids
3. an observatory
4. constellation
5. astronaut
6. space station
7. new
8. stars
9. satellites

WORKBOOK PAGE 103

A. WHAT'S THE OCCUPATION?

1. firefighter
2. food-service worker
3. factory worker
4. homemaker
5. carpenter
6. chef/cook
7. accountant
8. barber
9. gardener/landscaper

B. ANALOGIES

1. hairdresser
2. actor/actress
3. babysitter
4. butcher
5. artist

C. LISTENING: *Who's Talking?*

Listen and decide who is talking.

1. I can't remember my lines!
2. I'll be there with your order in twenty or thirty minutes.
3. I just bought seven new horses.
4. Here's your change—thirty-nine cents. Thank you, and have a nice day!
5. Hello. This is RealTech. What seems to be the problem?
6. Whoa! Look at this big one I've just caught!
7. I read a book to Samantha, she played with her toys, and then she went to bed.
8. How are you feeling today, Mr. Johnson? Are you ready for your sponge bath?

Answers

3	7	4	5
2	1	6	8

D. LIKELY OR UNLIKELY?

	Likely	Unlikely
1.	✓	
2.		✓
3.	✓	
4.		✓
5.		✓
6.		✓
7.	✓	
8.	✓	
9.		✓
10.		✓
11.		✓
12.	✓	

WORKBOOK PAGE 104

A. WHAT'S THE OCCUPATION?

1. mechanic
2. translator
3. secretary
4. security guard
5. journalist/reporter
6. pharmacist
7. lawyer
8. pilot
9. repairperson

B. ANALOGIES

1. pharmacist
2. messenger/courier
3. painter
4. lawyer
5. telemarketer
6. manicurist

C. LISTENING: *Who's Talking?*

Listen and decide who is talking.

1. All right, class. Please turn to page fifty-three.
2. Good morning. Dr. Brown's office. May I help you?
3. What would you like for dessert?
4. We'll be landing in just a few minutes.
5. Doctor, this patient is complaining about chest pain.
6. This package will cost $3.50 to send first class.
7. I've been serving in the army for three years.
8. What about Hawaii? That would be a nice place for a vacation.
9. I need to take in the waist on this dress.
10. Sit still and say, "Cheese!"
11. Let me look at your paw, Rover.
12. You're under arrest!

Answers

5	4	12	6
3	7	1	8
2	11	9	10

D. LIKELY OR UNLIKELY?

	Likely	Unlikely
1.	✓	
2.	✓	
3.		✓
4.		✓
5.		✓

6. ✓ ___
7. ___ ✓
8. ✓ ___
9. ___ ✓

A. WHAT'S THE ACTION?

1. drive
2. serve
3. wash
4. fly
5. operate
6. repair
7. grow
8. play
9. sing
10. draw
11. paint
12. clean
13. design
14. prepare
15. mow
16. type
17. act
18. deliver
19. sew
20. sell
21. translate
22. manage
23. speak
24. assemble
25. take care of

B. WHAT DO THEY HAVE IN COMMON?

1. b
2. h
3. f
4. e
5. d
6. a
7. c
8. g

C. WHAT'S THE CATEGORY?

1. grow
2. drive
3. write
4. fly
5. design/build
6. cook/eat
7. play
8. assist
9. deliver
10. serve
11. wash
12. study
13. fix/repair
14. operate

WORKBOOK PAGE 107

A. LOOKING FOR A JOB

1. interviews
2. responded
3. prepare
4. dress
5. skills and qualifications
6. thank-you
7. hired

B. LISTENING

Listen and choose the best answer.

1. The job ad says it's full-time, Monday through Friday.
2. We're in immediate need of waitstaff for a new restaurant, no experience required.
3. The position is part-time on the weekends.

4. In addition to very good working conditions, we offer an excellent benefits package.
5. We have a full-time position starting June 1st.
6. We're looking for someone part-time in the evenings, Monday through Wednesday.

Answers

1. a
2. b
3. b
4. a
5. b
6. b

C. GOOD IDEA OR BAD IDEA?

	Good Idea	Bad Idea
1.	___	✓
2.	___	✓
3.	✓	___
4.	___	✓
5.	___	✓
6.	✓	___
7.	✓	___
8.	___	✓
9.	✓	___
10.	___	✓

WORKBOOK PAGE 108

A. WHICH WORD?

1. receptionist
2. storage room
3. manager
4. coat rack
5. shredder
6. vending
7. cubicle
8. coffee machine
9. copier
10. reception area
11. make some copies
12. computer
13. conference room
14. swivel chair

B. LISTENING: *Where Are They?*

Listen and decide where the conversation is taking place.

1. A. It's one o'clock. Lunchtime is over.
   B. We'd better get back to work.
2. A. Good morning. I'm here for a meeting with Mr. Gomez.
   B. Have a seat and I'll call him now.
3. A. Can you tell me how much this will cost to send?
   B. Certainly. Just put it on the postal scale.
4. A. Let's see. Glue. Where do you think it might be?
   B. Look over there on the third shelf.
5. A. It's six thirty, and everyone is still in their cubicles!
   B. We have to finish a big report by the end of the week.

Answers

2 1 3
4 5

C. WHAT ARE THEY DOING?

1. c
2. b
3. e
4. d
5. a
6. f

WORKBOOK PAGE 109

A. WHAT'S THE WORD?

1. pushpin
2. glue stick
3. mailing label
4. ink cartridge
5. packing tape
6. letterhead
7. index card
8. mailer

B. MAXINE'S NEW JOB

1. appointment book
2. letter tray/stacking tray
3. organizer/personal planner
4. Post-It note pad
5. paper clip
6. electric pencil sharpener
7. correction fluid
8. thumbtack
9. rotary card file

C. GOOD IDEA OR BAD IDEA?

	Good Idea	Bad Idea
1.	✓	___
2.	___	✓
3.	___	✓
4.	✓	___
5.	✓	___
6.	___	✓

WORKBOOK PAGE 110

A. WHAT'S THE WORD?

1. forklift
2. time clock
3. warehouse
4. union notice
5. loading dock
6. personnel office
7. suggestion box
8. payroll office
9. line supervisor, assembly line

B. WHICH WORD DOESN'T BELONG?

1. dolly (The others are people.)
2. worker (The others are pieces of machinery.)
3. locker room (The others are related to payment.)
4. warehouse (The others are related to movement of products.)
5. suggestion box (The others are areas of a factory.)

C. WHICH WORD?

1. hand truck
2. conveyor
3. payroll office
4. workers
5. quality control supervisor

WORKBOOK PAGE 111

A. WHAT'S THE OBJECT?

1. cherry picker

2. tape measure
3. wheelbarrow
4. dump truck
5. pneumatic drill
6. bulldozer
7. backhoe
8. crane
9. ladder
10. scaffolding

B. WHAT'S THE WORD?

1. wire
2. insulation
3. lumber
4. plywood
5. concrete
6. pipe
7. drywall
8. blueprints
9. girder
10. toolbelt
11. shingle
12. brick

WORKBOOK PAGE 112

A. A SAFETY MEMO

1. Hard hats
2. earplugs, earmuffs
3. back support
4. vests
5. boots, toe guards
6. masks
7. respirators
8. latex gloves
9. goggles, glasses
10. flammable
11. emergency exits, fire extinguishers
12. defibrillators

WORKBOOK PAGE 113

A. DIRECTIONS TO GRANDMA'S HOUSE

1. train
2. ticket
3. window
4. board
5. track
6. compartment
7. conductor
8. bus
9. stop
10. taxi
11. driver

B. WHICH WORD DOESN'T BELONG?

1. platform (The others are types of transportation.)
2. ferry (The others are places.)
3. meter (The others are people.)
4. station (The others are places in a bus or train station.)
5. rider (The others are types of fares.)

C. ANALOGIES

1. taxi stand
2. track
3. timetable

4. taxi/cab/taxicab
5. subway station

WORKBOOK PAGE 114

A. WHICH VEHICLE?

1. convertible
2. a tow truck
3. jeep
4. minivan
5. motorcycle
6. moving

B. LISTENING: *Which Type of Vehicle?*

Listen and decide which type of vehicle these people are talking about.

1. I love this car. It's small, but there's extra storage space behind the rear seat.
2. Ours has a kitchen, a sleeping area, and a bathroom!
3. This one is big enough to hold all the furniture in our apartment!
4. My husband and I are very concerned about the environment, so this is the only kind of car we would consider buying.
5. Remember. You always have to wear a helmet when you ride this.
6. We rented one for my sister's wedding. Our whole family was able to fit in it!

Answers

3	4	6
5	1	2

C. VEHICLE MATCH

1. b
2. a
3. e
4. c
5. f
6. d

WORKBOOK PAGE 115

A. WHICH WORD?

1. jumper cables
2. ignition
3. navigation system
4. transmission
5. windshield wipers, rear defroster
6. brake
7. speedometer
8. nozzle, gas
9. emergency brake
10. stick shift, clutch
11. dipstick
12. visor
13. turn signal
14. roof rack
15. taillight
16. tire
17. trunk
18. hood

B. LISTENING: *Calling About a Car*

Listen to the following telephone conversation and circle the answers as you listen.

A. Hi. I'm calling about the ad for the nineteen-hundred-dollar car. Is it still for sale?
B. Yes, it is.
A. What kind of car is it?
B. It's a Hondu sedan in almost perfect condition.
A. Almost perfect?
B. Well, it has a few minor problems.
A. A few minor problems?
B. Yes. One of the headlights is broken.
A. Oh, that's not a problem at all.
B. Well, uh . . . I've also been having a little trouble with the transmission. The fact of the matter is, it may need a new clutch.
A. I see. Tell me, is there anything else wrong with the car?
B. Well, as a matter of fact, the fan belt is a bit old.
A. I see.
B. And it probably wouldn't hurt to get a new radiator hose while you're at it.
A. A new radiator hose?
B. Yes. And I suppose it also wouldn't hurt to have the accelerator checked.
A. The accelerator?
B. Yes. Oh. And incidentally, the brakes have been squeaking . . . just a little. But those are minor things. And aside from the little problem with the heater and the horn, everything is really in tip-top shape!
A. What's wrong with the heater and the horn?
B. They don't work.
A. I see. Tell me, does ANYTHING in the car work?
B. Oh, yes. The radio and the muffler work fine!

Answers

1. b
2. a
3. b
4. a
5. a
6. a
7. b
8. a
9. b
10. a

WORKBOOK PAGE 116

A. GOOD IDEA OR BAD IDEA?

	Good Idea	Bad Idea
1.	✓	
2.		✓
3.		✓
4.	✓	

5. ___   ✓
6. ___   ✓
7. ✓   ___
8. ___   ✓
9. ___   ✓
10. ___   ✓
11. ✓   ___
12. ___   ✓

B. LISTENING TO DIRECTIONS

Listen and put a check next to the correct directions.

A. Good morning. Blake Insurance Company.
B. Hello. I'd like directions to your office from South Richmond, please.
A. Certainly. Take the interstate north and get off at Exit 6.
B. Exit 6?
A. Yes, that's right. When you get off the exit, stay in the left lane and turn onto Third Avenue.
B. Okay. I'm with you so far.
A. Go through the intersection. After that, go past two traffic lights.
B. Did you say two traffic lights?
A. Yes. At the third traffic light, turn right onto Elm Street. Go straight for three blocks, and you'll see Blake Insurance on the left, at the corner of Elm Street and Cherry Street.
B. Thanks very much.

Answers

✓   ✓
✓   ✓
___   ___
✓   ✓

C. WHICH WORD?

1. crosswalk
2. broken
3. on
4. one-way
5. tollbooth
6. bridge

WORKBOOK PAGE 117

A. WHICH PREPOSITION?

1. up
2. past
3. out of
4. off
5. onto
6. down
7. through
8. off
9. around
10. through
11. on
12. around
13. off
14. out of
15. over
16. in
17. across
18. on
19. onto
20. down
21. past

B. WHAT'S THE PREPOSITION?

1. over
2. up, down
3. on, off

4. across
5. into, out of
6. around
7. through

WORKBOOK PAGE 118

A. WHICH WORD?

1. no
2. hand signal
3. outlet
4. slippery when wet
5. compass
6. detour
7. pedestrian

B. ROAD TEST

1. go straight
2. one-way
3. turn left
4. hand
5. turn right
6. detour
7. railroad crossing
8. 3-point turn
9. parallel
10. handicapped

WORKBOOK PAGE 119

A. A FRUSTRATING DAY!

1. suitcases
2. ticket counter
3. baggage cart
4. ticket agent
5. baggage
6. security checkpoint
7. metal detector
8. security officer
9. X-ray
10. carry-on bag
11. boarding area
12. boarding pass
13. immigration
14. passport
15. customs
16. customs declaration

B. WHICH WORD?

1. baggage claim check
2. arrival and departure monitor
3. gate
4. garment bag
5. a passport
6. luggage cart

WORKBOOK PAGE 120

A. PROBABLE OR IMPROBABLE?

	Probable	Improbable
1.	✓	___
2.	___	✓
3.	___	✓
4.	✓	___
5.	___	✓
6.	___	✓
7.	___	✓
8.	✓	___
9.	___	✓
10.	___	✓
11.	___	✓

12. ✓   ___
13. ___   ✓

B. WHICH WORD?

1. seat
2. runway
3. flight
4. gate
5. instruction card
6. air sickness

C. LISTENING

Listen and choose the best answer.

1. Excuse me, sir. Security regulations require that you empty your pockets before you . . . .
2. Passengers, Flight 203 to Vancouver will be taking off shortly. Please . . . .
3. Excuse me, ma'am. We're experiencing turbulence. Please . . . .
4. Sir, because the ticket counter is very busy, we're going to ask you to . . . .
5. Passengers, in preparation for takeoff, please fasten your seat belts and . . . .
6. After you put your bag on the conveyor belt, ...
7. You'll need a boarding pass in order to . . . .
8. Do you have a watch or any loose change? Alright, then please . . . .

Answers

1. a
2. b
3. b
4. a
5. a
6. b
7. b
8. a

WORKBOOK PAGE 121

A. WHICH WORD?

1. valet parking, parking attendant
2. room, elevator
3. captain, bellhop
4. gift shop, desk clerk
5. concierge, restaurant
6. ice machine, front desk

B. LIKELY OR UNLIKELY?

	Likely	Unlikely
1.	✓	___
2.	___	✓
3.	___	✓
4.	✓	___
5.	✓	___
6.	___	✓
7.	✓	___
8.	___	✓
9.	___	✓

C. WHAT'S THE WORD?

1. Room service
2. housekeeper
3. lobby

4. Valet parking
5. room key

WORKBOOK PAGE 122

A. WHAT'S THE WORD?

1. bird-watching
2. knitting
3. photography
4. cards
5. sewing
6. stamps
7. chess
8. building
9. pottery
10. coins

B. WHICH WORD?

1. telescope, Astronomy
2. dice, Monopoly
3. painting, drawing
4. backgammon, online
5. an origami, pattern
6. safety pin, magnifying glass

WORKBOOK PAGE 123

A. WHICH PLACE DOESN'T BELONG?

1. museum (The others are outdoor places.)
2. amusement park (The others are indoor places.)
3. play (The others are places where people buy things.)
4. craft fair (The others have amusement rides.)
5. flea market (The others are places where people go to observe nature.)
6. amusement park (The others are "nature" places.)

B. WHERE SHOULD THEY GO?

1. aquarium
2. planetarium
3. concert
4. beach
5. botanical gardens
6. movies
7. yard sale
8. historic site
9. zoo
10. play

WORKBOOK PAGE 124

A. WHAT'S THE WORD?

1. duck pond
2. bench
3. trash can
4. sandbox
5. water fountain
6. picnic
7. jogging
8. tennis court
9. playground
10. bicycle
11. carousel
12. climbing wall

B. LISTENING: *Where Are They?*

Listen and decide where these people are.

1. A. Let's go on the seesaw!
   B. Great idea!
2. A. How long have we been running?
   B. For over twenty minutes.
3. A. What did you bring?
   B. Some sandwiches, some drinks, and some fruit.
4. A. Which horse do you want to sit on?
   B. The green and red one over there.
5. A. I'll play first base. You play third base.
   B. Alright. And Jerry is the pitcher.
6. A. Wow! That was an incredible jump!
   B. I'm glad I was wearing elbow pads.

Answers

1. a
2. b
3. a
4. b
5. a
6. b

C. WHICH WORD?

1. bench
2. sand
3. rack
4. climber
5. grill
6. ballfield
7. slide

WORKBOOK PAGE 125

A. WHICH WORD?

1. kite
2. boogie board
3. stand
4. snack bar
5. umbrella
6. seashells
7. ball
8. towel
9. sunglasses
10. cooler
11. surfboard
12. waves
13. lifeguard

B. LIKELY OR UNLIKELY?

	Likely	Unlikely
1.		✓
2.	✓	
3.	✓	
4.		✓
5.	✓	
6.		✓
7.	✓	
8.		✓

C. WHAT'S THE ACTION?

1. e
2. g
3. b
4. h
5. i
6. a
7. f
8. d
9. c

WORKBOOK PAGE 126

A. PLANNING A CAMPING TRIP

1. hiking
2. boots
3. compass
4. trail
5. GPS
6. rock climbing
7. rope
8. backpack
9. camping stove
10. tent
11. matches
12. Swiss army knife

B. WHICH WORD?

1. GPS
2. hatchet
3. bike
4. hiking boots
5. stakes
6. lantern

C. LISTENING

Listen and choose the best answer.

1. I'm thirsty! Where's the . . . ?
2. If you're going mountain biking, don't forget to wear a . . . .
3. This is the first time I've ever slept in a . . . .
4. There are so many bugs around here! We should have brought . . . .
5. Are you hungry? There's a lot of delicious food in this . . . .
6. I'm going camping next week. Can I borrow your . . . ?

Answers

1. a
2. a
3. b
4. a
5. a
6. b

WORKBOOK PAGE 127

A. WHICH SPORT DOESN'T BELONG?

1. running (The other sports all use balls.)
2. bowling (The others involve physical contact.)
3. Frisbee (The others use nets.)
4. wrestling (The others are outdoor sports.)
5. horseback riding (The others are done indoors.)
6. archery (The others involve riding.)

B. ANALOGIES

1. bow and arrow
2. pool stick
3. boxing trunks
4. paddle
5. birdie/shuttlecock
6. helmet
7. rollerblades/inline skates

C. NAME THE SPORT!

1. bowling
2. billiards/pool
3. martial arts
4. gymnastics
5. golf
6. cycling/biking
7. archery
8. boxing
9. wrestling

D. WHICH WORD?

1. rowing
2. treadmill
3. belt
4. racket
5. horse
6. reins

WORKBOOK PAGE 128

A. TRUE OR FALSE?

1. F
2. F
3. T
4. F
5. F
6. T

B. CORRECT OR INCORRECT?

1. I
2. C
3. I
4. C
5. C
6. I
7. I
8. C

C. WHAT'S THE SPORT?

1. Hockey, rink
2. Baseball
3. softball, ballfield
4. soccer, football
5. Basketball, court
6. Volleyball

D. LISTENING: *Team Sports Sounds*

Listen and identify the sport by the sound.

1. [sound: football]
2. [sound: hockey]
3. [sound: basketball]
4. [sound: baseball]

Answers

4 3 1 2

WORKBOOK PAGE 129

A. SENSE OR NONSENSE?

	Sense	Nonsense
1.		✓
2.		✓
3.	✓	
4.		✓
5.	✓	
6.	✓	
7.		✓
8.		✓

B. WHO'S TALKING?

1. d
2. f
3. a
4. g
5. c
6. b
7. e

C. LISTENING: *Which One?*

Listen and choose the best answer.

1. You shouldn't catch a baseball without a . . . .
2. I almost broke my nose when I got hit in the face by the . . . .
3. The goalkeeper in hockey always wears a . . . .
4. The catcher in baseball has a special glove called a . . . .
5. Football players need to wear. . . .
6. You can't play lacrosse without a lacrosse . . . .

Answers

1. a
2. a
3. b
4. b
5. a
6. b

D. WHICH WORD DOESN'T BELONG?

1. football (The others are round.)
2. skates (The others are worn for protection.)
3. hockey puck (The others are made of wood.)
4. shinguards (The others are worn on the hands.)
5. hockey puck (The others are balls.)

WORKBOOK PAGE 130

A. WHAT'S THE WORD?

1. snowboard
2. sledding dish/saucer
3. snowmobile
4. Ski poles/Poles
5. Skate guards
6. blade
7. Bindings

B. WINTER SPORT MATCH

1. c
2. e
3. b
4. f

5. a
6. d

C. WHICH WORD?

1. cross-country
2. bobsledding
3. skiing
4. snowmobile

WORKBOOK PAGE 131

A. ANALOGIES

1. surfboard
2. fins
3. (air) tank
4. (white-water) rafting
5. paddles
6. surfboard
7. wet suit
8. towrope

B. WHAT DO YOU WEAR?

1. d
2. b
3. a
4. f
5. c
6. e

C. LISTENING: *Which Sport?*

Listen and choose the correct water sport.

1. Where did you get that mask and fins?
2. I'm a little concerned about my air tank. It's almost empty!
3. Did you bring enough bait?
4. We need to use both oars.
5. Hold on to your paddle!
6. I just love it here on this sailboard!

Answers

1. a
2. b
3. b
4. a
5. a
6. b

D. WHICH WORD?

1. line
2. life jacket
3. reel
4. goggles
5. surfing
6. towrope

WORKBOOK PAGE 132

A. WHAT'S THE SPORT?

1. tennis
2. swim
3. lift
4. run
5. baseball
6. football
7. basketball
8. gymnastics

B. WHAT'S THE ACTION?

1. hit
2. pitch

3. shoot
4. stretch
5. swim, dive
6. serve
7. bounce
8. catch
9. kick
10. walk
11. run
12. bend
13. reach
14. hop

WORKBOOK PAGE 133

A. ENTERTAINMENT REPORT

1. concert hall
2. theater
3. movie theaters
4. Orchestra
5. conductor
6. music
7. bands
8. singer
9. actors/actresses
10. actresses/actors
11. screen
12. movie
13. Comedy
14. comedians

B. LISTENING

Listen and choose the best answer.

1. Listen to that voice! What a wonderful . . . !
2. I'd love to see a dance performance. Let's go to the . . . .
3. You've never heard of her? She's a very famous . . . .
4. Our niece loves to dance. When she grows up, she wants to be a . . . .
5. Have you heard him play the guitar? He's a very talented . . . .
6. I love music, but I've never been to the . . . .
7. Have you ever seen Charles Miller? He's a very famous . . . .
8. This is my favorite movie theater. It has a very large . . . .

Answers

1. a
2. b
3. b
4. b
5. a
6. a
7. b
8. a

WORKBOOK PAGES 134–135

A. WHAT'S ON TV?

1. talk show
2. reality show
3. cartoon
4. sports program
5. game show
6. news program
7. drama
8. sitcom
9. soap opera
10. nature program

B. WHAT'S PLAYING AT THE MOVIES?

1. comedy
2. western
3. science fiction
4. documentary
5. cartoon
6. foreign film
7. horror film
8. action movie
9. drama
10. war movie

C. LISTENING

Listen and put a number next to the type of music you hear.

1. [sound: folk music]
2. [sound: classical music]
3. [sound: jazz]
4. [sound: gospel music]
5. [sound: country music]
6. [sound: rock music]
7. [sound: reggae]
8. [sound: hip hop]

Answers

2	5	3	4
6	8	1	7

WORKBOOK PAGE 136

A. WHICH INSTRUMENT DOESN'T BELONG?

1. banjo (The others are brass instruments.)
2. accordion (The others are percussion instruments.)
3. drum (The others are string instruments.)
4. bassoon (The others are keyboard instruments.)
5. cello (The others are woodwind instruments.)
6. harp (The other instruments are held in the hand.)

B. LIKELY OR UNLIKELY?

	Likely	Unlikely
1.		✓
2.	✓	
3.		✓
4.		✓
5.		✓
6.	✓	
7.		✓
8.		✓
9.	✓	
10.		✓

C. ASSOCIATIONS

1. d
2. c
3. f
4. b
5. a
6. e

D. LISTENING: *Which Instrument?*

Listen and decide which musical instrument you're listening to.

1. [sound: flute]
2. [sound: drums]
3. [sound: harmonica]
4. [sound: organ]
5. [sound: violin]
6. [sound: trumpet]
7. [sound: piano]
8. [sound: acoustic guitar]
9. [sound: electric guitar]

Answers

6	4	3
2	1	8
7	5	9

WORKBOOK PAGE 137

A. WHERE ARE THEY?

1. f		5. b
2. e		6. h
3. g		7. a
4. c		8. d

B. WHICH WORD?

1. farmhouse
2. alfalfa
3. wheat
4. hired hand
5. pasture
6. barnyard
7. corn
8. tractor
9. scarecrow
10. irrigation system

C. WHO'S MY MOTHER?

1. pig
2. chicken
3. sheep
4. cow
5. horse
6. goat

D. ANIMAL SOUNDS!

1. c
2. a
3. b
4. e
5. d

WORKBOOK PAGE 138

A. WHO'S TALKING?

1. moose
2. porcupine
3. dog
4. beaver
5. giraffe
6. hyena
7. polar
8. elephant
9. camel
10. cat
11. kangaroo
12. platypus
13. donkey
14. panda
15. rabbit
16. zebra

17. panther
18. orangutan
19. skunk
20. bat

B. ANALOGIES

1. spots
2. wolves
3. mane
4. paw
5. horn

C. ANIMAL EXPRESSIONS

1. beaver
2. fox
3. horse
4. mouse
5. donkey
6. kitten
7. bear

WORKBOOK PAGE 139

A. COLORFUL BIRDS!

1. c
2. f
3. e
4. b
5. g
6. d
7. a

B. WHAT'S THE BIRD?

1. woodpecker
2. parrot
3. eagle
4. flamingo
5. crane
6. pigeon
7. owl
8. pelican
9. penguin

C. WHAT'S THE INSECT?

1. spider
2. firefly
3. grasshopper
4. ladybug
5. termite
6. bee
7. caterpillar
8. centipede
9. mosquito

WORKBOOK PAGE 140

A. WHICH WORD?

1. jellyfish
2. Squids
3. Otters
4. dolphin
5. horse

B. WHICH WORD DOESN'T BELONG?

1. squid (The others are fish.)
2. porpoise (The others are amphibians.)
3. sea horse (The others are sea animals.)
4. snail (The others are large.)

5. shell (The others are parts of a fish.)
6. crocodile (The others are reptiles.)

C. WHAT'S THE WORD?

1. dolphin
2. eels
3. stingray
4. starfish
5. newt
6. rattlesnake
7. lizard
8. Turtle, Tortoise

WORKBOOK PAGE 141

A. CATEGORIES

Types of Flowers

geranium
hibiscus
orchid
violet

Types of Trees

birch
cherry
elm
oak

Parts of a Flower

bud
petal
stem
thorn

Parts of a Tree

bark
branch
limb
trunk

B. WHAT IS IT?

1. dogwood
2. palm
3. ivy
4. pine
5. poison ivy
6. maple
7. redwood
8. holly
9. thorn
10. weeping willow
11. daffodil
12. rose
13. bulb
14. cactus
15. sunflower
16. daisy

WORKBOOK PAGE 142

A. WHICH WORD?

1. global warming
2. carpool
3. Nuclear
4. recycling
5. water pollution
6. oil
7. pollution
8. Acid
9. natural gas

B. CONSERVATION AT HOME

1. energy
2. oil
3. solar
4. recycle
5. water
6. pollution

C. WHICH WORD DOESN'T BELONG?

1. rain (The others are sources of energy.)
2. burn coal (The others are types of conservation.)
3. geothermal (The others are environmental problems.)
4. radiation (The others are sources of energy.)

D. LISTENING

Listen and choose the best answer.

1. It's so hard to breathe in the city with all this . . . .
2. I'm very concerned about the environment. That's why I try to conserve . . . .
3. All the energy in this town is provided by . . . .
4. One of the effects of air pollution is . . . .
5. Nuclear power is very promising if a way can be found to dispose of the . . . .
6. One of our local factories was fined for dumping . . . .

Answers

1. a		4. a	
2. b		5. b	
3. a		6. b	

WORKBOOK PAGE 143

A. WHICH WORD?

1. tornado
2. forest fire
3. flood
4. tsunami
5. landslide
6. avalanche
7. a volcanic eruption
8. earthquake

B. WHAT IS IT?

1. typhoon
2. wildfire
3. avalanche
4. hurricane
5. flood
6. drought
7. blizzard
8. tornado

C. LISTENING

Listen and decide which natural disaster is happening.

1. Get away from the shore! The water is coming very fast!
2. The whole town was destroyed. Buildings crumbled and roads broke apart.

3. Most of our crops are dying! We need water very badly!
4. It snowed more than thirty-five inches last weekend!
5. The winds are very strong!   Get inside!

Answers

5   1   4   3   2

WORKBOOK PAGE 15

Sun 4	Mon 5	Tue 6	Wed 7	Thu 8	Fri 9	Sat 10
			doctor			
		singing lesson				play
	piano lesson			exercise class		

Sun 11	Mon 12	Tue 13	Wed 14	Thu 15	Fri 16	Sat 17
					dancing lesson	
	Spanish class	dentist	guitar lesson			
					concert	party

WORKBOOK PAGE 19

Twin Bed $219
Double Bed $299
Queen Bed $445
King Bed $697
Sofa Bed $909
Bunk Bed $323
Trundle Bed $332
Cot $79

WORKBOOK PAGE 68

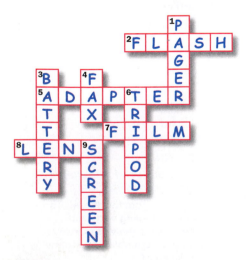

WORKBOOK PAGE 84

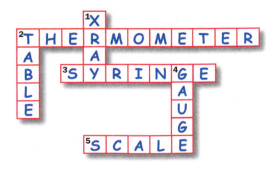

172